Pentecostalism and Globalization

 McMaster Divinity College Press
Theological Study Series

VOL. 1 Steven M. Studebaker, ed.
Defining Issues in Pentecostalism: Classical and Emergent

VOL. 2 Steven M. Studebaker, ed.
Pentecostalism and Globalization: The Impact of Globalization on Pentecostal Theology and Ministry

VOL. 3 David A. Croteau
You Mean I Don't Have to Tithe?: A Deconstruction of Tithing and a Reconstruction of Post-Tithe Giving

Pentecostalism and Globalization
The Impact of Globalization on Pentecostal Theology and Ministry

edited by
STEVEN M. STUDEBAKER

☞PICKWICK *Publications* • Eugene, Oregon

PENTECOSTALISM AND GLOBALIZATION
The Impact of Globalization on Pentecostal Theology and Ministry

McMaster Theological Studies Series 2

Copyright © 2010 Wipf and Stock Publishers. All rights reserved. Except for brief quotations in critical publications or reviews, no part of this book may be reproduced in any manner without prior written permission from the publisher. Write: Permissions, Wipf and Stock Publishers, 199 W. 8th Ave., Suite 3, Eugene, OR 97401.

Revised Standard Version of the Bible, copyright 1952 (2nd edition, 1971) by the Division of Christian Education of the National Council of the Churches of Christ in the United States of America. Used by permission. All rights reserved.

McMaster Divinity College Press
1280 Main Street West
Hamilton, Ontario, Canada
L8S 4K1

Pickwick Publications
A Division of Wipf and Stock Publishers
199 W. 8th Av.e, Suite 3
Eugene, OR 97401

www.wipfandstock.com

ISBN 13: 978-1-60608-404-5

Cataloging-in-Publication data:

Pentecostalism and globalization : the impact of globalization on pentecostal theology and ministry / edited by Steven M. Studebaker.

xiv + 244 p. ; 23 cm. — Includes Bibliographical references and index.

McMaster Theological Studies Series 2

ISBN 13: 978-1-60608-404-5

1. Pentecostalism. 2. Globalization. I. Studebaker, Steven M., 1968– . II. Title. III. Series.

BR1644 P41 2010

Manufactured in the U.S.A.

To Chris Ness and his family,
Pentecostal missionaries in the thick of global Pentecostal ministry

Contents

List of Contributors / ix

Acknowledgments / xiii

Introduction: Globalization, Global Christianity, and Global Pentecostalism—*Nikola T. Caric and Steven M. Studebaker* / 1

PART ONE: Pentecostalism and Globalization

1. The Roots of Pentecostal Globalization: Early Pentecostal Missions—*Allan Anderson* / 29

2. The Fruits of Pentecostal Globalization: Current Trends and Challenges—*Allan Anderson* / 50

3. The Impact of Globalization on Pentecostals in Canada—*Michael Wilkinson* / 70

PART TWO: Implications of Global Pentecostalism for Pentecostal Theology

4. Globalization and Spirit Baptism—*Steven M. Studebaker* / 87

5. Tongues and a Postmodern Generation of Pentecostals—*Randall Holm* / 109

PART THREE: Globalization and Pentecostal Ministry and Mission

6. Implications of Globalization for Pentecostal Leadership and Mission—*Byron D. Klaus* / 127

Contents

7   J. Philip Hogan's Spirit-Led Vision and the Globalization of Pentecostal Missions in the Twenty-First Century
    —*Ivan Satyavrata* / 151

8   Mission "Made to Travel" in a World without Borders
    —*Ivan Satyavrata* / 174

9   Friends in Mission: Following the Wind and Riding the Wave—*Ivan Satyavrata* / 198

10 Assessment and Interaction—*David Reed* / 221

Index of Names / 237

Index of Subjects / 241

Contributors

ALLAN ANDERSON, DTh (University of South Africa) is Head of the School of Philosophy, Theology and Religion and Professor of Global Pentecostal Studies at the University of Birmingham, England, where he has been since 1995. Allan was born in England, raised in Zimbabwe to Salvation Army missionary parents, and was a Pentecostal and Charismatic minister in Southern Africa for twenty-four years, nineteen of which were in theological education. He is the author of seven books, the most recent of which are *Zion and Pentecost* (University of South Africa Press, 2000), *African Reformation* (Africa World Press, 2001), *An Introduction to Pentecostalism* (Cambridge University Press, 2004) and *Spreading Fires: The Missionary Nature of Early Pentecostalism* (Orbis, 2007).

NIKOLA T. CARIC, MDiv (McMaster University) is a doctoral student in Christian Theology at McMaster Divinity College, Hamilton, Ontario. His research interest lies at the intersection of Christian Ethics and Globalization, particularly in how aspects of contemporary globalization might affect the ethical responsibilities of individuals. His interest in the global was piqued through directing several student mission programs in Ecuador and Mexico City, and he currently is involved with the Global Urban Trek, a ministry of InterVarsity Christian Fellowship USA.

RANDALL HOLM, PhD (Laval University) is Associate Professor of Biblical Studies at Providence College, Otterburne, MB. He has over twelve years of pastoral ministry experience. He is an active member in the Society for Pentecostal Studies and the author of several important articles and essays on Pentecostalism and the intersection of Christianity and contemporary culture.

BYRON D. KLAUS, DMin (Fuller Theological Seminary) is the President of the Assemblies of God Theological Seminary (AGTS) in Springfield, Missouri. He has over thirty-six years of global experience in pastoral ministry and higher education teaching and administration. He co-edited *The Globalization of Pentecostalism: A Religion Made to Travel*, which *International Bulletin of Missionary Research* recognized as one of the top 15 mission publications. He is also the author of numerous books, articles, and essays that treat various dimensions of Christian leadership and ministry and is a frequent speaker at scholarly and professional meetings. He is ordained with the Assemblies of God.

DAVID REED, PhD (Boston University) is Professor Emeritus of Pastoral Theology and Research Professor at Wycliffe College (Toronto School of Theology, University of Toronto). David has eighteen years of pastoral ministry experience and over twenty of experience in theological education. A long-time interest is the study of spirituality, congregational life, cultural trends, and the Pentecostal/charismatic movement, Oneness Pentecostalism in particular. This has resulted in publications and invitations to lecture in Mexico, New Zealand, and the Philippines. His book, *"In Jesus' Name": The History and Beliefs of Oneness Pentecostals* (2008), is a definitive historical and theological study of the third stream of modern Pentecostalism. He was ordained in the Episcopal Church.

IVAN SATYAVRATA, PhD (Oxford Centre for Mission Studies, UK) leads the Assemblies of God church and its network of ministries, founded by the late Mark Buntain, in Kolkata, India. These ministries include a hospital, medical services, and a school system for thousands of students. Nearly 20,000 children a day receive meals and basic care through the auspices of this mission. Previous to assuming his current role in 2006, he was President of Southern Asia Bible College in Bangalore, India, during which time he played an active role in evangelical theological education in India as Chairperson of the Asia Theological Association and the Langham Partnership Regional Council (South Asia). He now serves as Chairperson of the Board of The Center for Global Leadership Development (formerly Southern Asia Bible College). He also chairs the AG Association for Theological Education in South Asia, the Board of Bombay Teen Challenge, and serves on the Board of World Vision, India. He is the author of *The Holy Spirit: Lord and Life-Giver* (IVP Academic, 2009) and several scholarly articles on missions and inter-religious relations.

STEVEN M. STUDEBAKER, PhD (Marquette University) is Assistant Pro-fessor of Systematic and Historical Theology, holds the Howard and Shirley Bentall Chair in Evangelical Thought at McMaster Divinity College, Hamilton, Ontario. He is an active member in the Society for Pentecostal Studies, the editor of *Defining Issues in Pentecostalism: Classical and Emergent*, and author of *Jonathan Edwards' Social Augustinian Trinitarianism in Historical and Contemporary Perspectives* and several articles on Pentecostal theology. He is ordained with the Assemblies of God.

MICHAEL WILKINSON, PhD (University of Ottawa) is Associate Professor of Sociology, director of the Religion in Canada Institute, and coordinator of the Canadian Pentecostal Research Network at Trinity Western University, Langley, British Columbia. He is the author of *The Spirit Said Go: Pentecostal Immigrants in Canada* and editor of *Canadian Pentecostalism: Transition and Transformation* as well as scholarly articles on globalization and Pentecostalism in *Pneuma, Journal of Pentecostal Theology, Transformation,* and *Asian Journal of Pentecostal Studies*. Professor Wilkinson served on the "Globalization" committee at the Lausanne World Evangelization meetings in Thailand and was a contributor to the paper "Globalization and the Gospel: Rethinking Mission in the Contemporary World." Wilkinson is ordained with the Pentecostal Assemblies of Canada and served in PAOC congregations for ten years.

Acknowledgments

SEVERAL PEOPLE NEED TO be recognized in the organization of the Pentecostal Forum held at McMaster Divinity College October 25, 2008 and the subsequent transformation of the papers presented at it into the present book.

Stanley E. Porter (President) and Phil Zylla (Academic Dean) of McMaster Divinity College continue to support the conference by making McMaster Divinity College and its resources available to host the conference. Particular thanks go to Pat Webb, Director of Advancement at McMaster Divinity College, who underwrote the conference through her development budget.

Jeff Clarke, the then recruitment and admissions officer at McMaster Divinity College, especially deserves recognition for his exceptional coordination of the myriad of details involved in planning and executing the conference. Under his leadership, several Divinity College student volunteers were indispensable in providing on-site hospitality for the Forum attendees.

We appreciate all those who attended and participated in the discussions at the conference and trust that the presentations on different areas of Pentecostal thought enriched and stimulated them.

We are thankful for the presenters who took time to write papers (and subsequently revise them for publication), travel, spend time away from families, and disrupt their schedules to be a part of making the Pentecostal Forum and book possible.

We merit McMaster Divinity College Press and Wipf & Stock for recognizing the value of publishing the essays presented in this volume. In this respect, Lois Dow provided necessary editorial assistance in the final stages of the preparation of the manuscript and Nikola Caric co-wrote the introductory essay and helped to edit the overall volume.

I also want to thank Byron Klaus, President of Assemblies of God Theological Seminary, for enthusiastically supporting the inclusion of

Ivan Satyavrata's essays, which were originally delivered as the three-part lecture series "Following the Wind and Riding the Wave: Pursuing the Hogan Legacy into the Second Pentecostal Century," while Ivan was serving as the 2009–2010 J. Philip Hogan Professor of World Missions at Assemblies of God Theological Seminary. Many thanks also to Ivan for accepting the invitation to revise the lectures and include them as essays in this volume.

Introduction

Globalization, Global Christianity, and Global Pentecostalism

Nikola T. Caric and Steven M. Studebaker

Several years ago a friend involved with theological education in Africa asked me if I would donate some good evangelical theological books to the Pentecostal Bible training center he served in as a leader and teacher. I asked him, "Why don't you use African theological resources?" It seemed odd to import evangelical texts from North America and think that they would serve the interests of theological education in Africa. He responded with suspicion toward African theology and suggested that traditional evangelical theology was better suited than indigenous sources. I do not doubt the motivations of my friend, which were to provide a doctrinally sound education for his students in Africa. However, the approach does reflect a uni-directional flow of influence from the West to the Rest and inevitably assumes the superiority of "our" theology vis-à-vis that of others.

Two phenomena frame the discussions in this book. The first is that Pentecostalism emerged as and remains a global religious movement. The second is that globalization has increasingly become part of the fabric of human life and experience in the twenty-first century. How do these two movements relate to one another? Many have undertaken projects to explore the ramifications of globalization for the various spheres of human existence, such as global politics, economics, trade, and entertainment. Furthermore, scholars have increasingly devoted more attention to the nature of religious movements in diverse global settings. As part of this broader trend, many Pentecostals have pursued the study of the varied forms of worldwide Pentecostalism.[1] The purpose of this volume is to outline the nature of the global Pentecostal movement and explore ways it can speak to North American Pentecostalism. As Pentecostals in North America, we need to comprehend not only the *fact* of global Pentecostalism, but also its *impact* on the nature of Pentecostal theology and ministry within our more local or North American setting.

The essays in this volume, as a whole, examine Pentecostalism as a global phenomenon, how globalization (broadly understood) might affect Pentecostalism, and the implications for Pentecostals in North America. Christian writing on globalization has greatly increased within the last decade, as believers seek to understand the repercussions for the church and the theological disciplines in the context of globalization and global Christianity.[2] This introduction seeks to provide the larger context for the Pentecostal discussion about globalization by describing the various understandings of globalization and providing a few examples of how globalization affects theological disciplines in the church as a whole. The challenges faced by the church universal are informative for Pentecostalism and Charismatic Christianity because these too are global movements. The central argument of this introduction is that both Pentecostalism and Christianity as a whole face unique challenges in a global world as they have become phenomena that are "supraterritorial."[3] Essentially, they are not restricted to one or a few geographical or political territories—Christian/Pentecostal worship, theological reflection, and mission can be thought of as happening on the globe as a whole. However, the various local expressions of the faith that constitute global Christianity/Pentecostalism do not have a homogenous understanding or experience of Christianity and the processes of globalization (economic/political/cultural), and these diverse understandings and experi-

---

1. For examples that include a range of scholarly genres, see Anderson, *An Introduction to Pentecostalism*; Bergunder, *The South Indian Pentecostal Movement in the Twentieth Century*; Cox, *Fire from Heaven*; Dempster, Klaus, and Petersen, *The Globalization of Pentecostalism*; Hollenweger, *Pentecostalism*; Martin, *Pentecostalism*; Miller and Yamamori, *Global Pentecostalism*; Sánchez Walsh, *Latino Pentecostal Identity*; and Shaull and Cesar, *Pentecostalism and the Future of the Christian Churches*.

2. For example, the Library of Congress online catalog lists 151 sources that contain either "Christianity" or "church" in the subject category and "globalization" as a keyword, of which only sixteen were published prior to the year 2000 (the earliest being 1988). The LOC online catalog was accessed in October 2008 to obtain this data.

3. See below for further explanation of this term.

ences, through their belonging to global Christianity/Pentecostalism, can challenge each local expression of the faith to examine its own thought and practice.

The first section of the introduction briefly describes different concepts of "globalization." It overviews contemporary globalization (primarily as understood in the social sciences), the globalization of Christianity, and theological understandings of globalization. The second section provides a few examples of how contemporary globalization and the globalization of Christianity affect Christian thought and practice and how these challenges are instructive for Pentecostals, as they face similar challenges by virtue of being a global movement. The introduction concludes by highlighting the contribution of the essays in this volume to the discussion of global Pentecostalism and globalization.

DESCRIBING CONTEMPORARY GLOBALIZATION

The purpose of qualifying globalization as "contemporary" is to acknowledge that some scholars believe our context of globalization is not a brand new phenomenon, but the extension of a process (primarily economic and political) that began in the middle of the nineteenth century, or even in the sixteenth with the emerging European colonial powers.[4] However, there is also evidence that the second half of the twentieth century saw a new development unlike preceding globalizing movements. Jan Aart Scholte documents that certain areas of global human activity had massive increases in this time period, "incomparably higher" than earlier global activity. These areas include communications, travel, financial transactions, formation of global associations, global regulations, and a "global awareness" among people.[5] "Contemporary globalization," then, refers to this new phase of globalizing activity. Essentially, this is the creating of a world where new infrastructure (air travel, telecommunications, computers/internet) enables a significant increase in the movement of people, goods, finance, and ideas around the globe and the formation of global institutions and associations—coupled with a global

---

4. For a mid-nineteenth-century view see Hobsbawn, "The World Unified." For a sixteenth-century view, based on Marxist analysis of global capitalism, see Wallerstein, "Rise and Future Demise."

5. Scholte, *Globalization*, 117–20.

awareness.⁶ It is this contemporary globalization to which many recent publications on globalization and Christianity are responding.

The Spheres of Globalization, Broadly Speaking

Having provided a preliminary description of globalization above, this section explains some of the significant features of the process. Academic discussion on the main areas of globalization can be classified into four broad spheres, all of which are intimately connected. These are political globalization, economic globalization, cultural globalization, and the globalization of environmental and social problems.⁷

Political globalization consists of the triumph of the nation state as the dominant method of political organization in the world, the similarity of the basic function of government from state to state, and the global spread of the democratic political system. At the same time it also encompasses how the states organize together through intergovernmental organizations (e.g., the United Nations and the World Trade Organization) and the emergence of global political non-governmental organizations (e.g., Amnesty International and the International Olympic Committee). Within this there is a debate on whether the nation state, having become a global phenomenon, will recede in power in the face of further global economic and political integration.⁸ Under the sphere of political globalization could be added military globalization, consisting of the "expanding network of worldwide military ties" (e.g., NATO) and the worldwide arms trade and spread of military technology.⁹

Economic globalization is often the sphere of globalization writers are referring to when they neglect to qualify the term. It is one of the popular conceptions of globalization: the trader sitting at her computer in Tokyo selling Mexican Pesos or the factory worker in Indonesia making Nike shoes that will be sold to children in England. There are three major groupings within economic globalization. The first is the

---

6. Lechner and Boli, *Globalization Reader*, 1. However, one must be careful not to overstate the reach of globalization. Although it has probably affected every human being on earth to some extent, there is unevenness in the extent to which different populations are involved in the processes of globalization (Scholte, *Globalization*, 119).

7. This organizational structure can roughly be found in Held et al., *Global Transformations*, and Lechner and Boli, *Globalization Reader*.

8. Lechner and Boli, *Globalization Reader*, 211–13.

9. Held et al., *Global Transformations*, 88–89.

movement of goods and services through global trade and international markets and the mechanisms that support the process. The second is the emergence of international banks and the global financial market that orchestrate the daily worldwide trading of trillions of dollars of financial assets and currencies.[10] The third is the globalization of production and distribution networks that are most commonly represented by the multinational corporations engaged in manufacturing or resource extraction around the world. However, many smaller enterprises are also integrated into this network.[11]

Cultural globalization is probably the "most directly perceived and experienced" form of globalization.[12] The extensive increase in transportation, telecommunication, and broadcasting technologies have allowed cultural symbols and ideas to move around the globe at a greater rate. Western consumer images and products such as McDonalds, Coca-Cola, and Adidas are ubiquitous, but at the same time North Americans can easily watch Bollywood movies, listen to African music, and learn about Buddhism. One view posits a cultural homogenization of the world where dominant cultures (particularly Western ones) engage in "cultural imperialism" through media and economic superiority and subsume the distinctiveness of other cultures.[13] The rebuttal is that fears of cultural homogenization are exaggerated and that both cultural hybridization and persistent national/traditional cultures are an important part of the process.[14] The core issue is one of identity and how people are shaped by their own culture in the midst of its interaction with other world cultures.[15]

Concerning the globalization of environmental and social problems, Frank Lechner and John Boli write that conceiving of problems such as pollution, deforestation, human rights violations, or the oppression of women as global problems is new to the last three decades.[16] Previously, social and environmental problems (when they were admit-

---

10. Ibid., 189. The 2008 global financial crisis demonstrated the interconnectedness of the world's financial and banking systems.

11. Ibid., 236.

12. Ibid., 327.

13. Lechner and Boli, *Globalization Reader*, 287–89.

14. Held et al., *Global Transformations*, 327.

15. Lechner and Boli, *Globalization Reader*, 323–25.

16. Ibid., 363–64.

ted to be problems) were seen as local or national issues and were to be dealt with by the community or nation state—without outside interference. However, the greater connectedness of societies has given rise to the recasting of many social and environmental issues as global in scope (e.g., global poverty and global species extinction). This recasting is primarily carried out by the many international organizations and social movements that have proliferated in recent decades (e.g., Greenpeace and International Justice Mission). These organizations that function "between states and markets" have been termed "civil society." Often churches and Christian organizations are put into this category, and it is no surprise that one of the main areas of writing in the intersection between globalization and Christianity is in the area of global social/environmental problems.

Conceptual Language for Describing Contemporary Globalization

The above sections have described globalization through a detailing of the human activities by which it is constituted. This final section on contemporary globalization provides conceptual language for describing what globalization is. Two approaches will be presented, John Tomlinson's description of globalization as complex connectivity and Jan Aart Scholte's as respatialization. These concepts will prove useful below in describing the Christian responses to globalization.

Tomlinson chooses the term "complex connectivity" as the appropriate label for the empirical condition of globalization.[17] Essentially, this is the increasing interconnectedness of global movements of goods, information, people, finance, governmental and non-governmental organizations, and the transportation, communication, and other infrastructure that supports the entire process. Tomlinson goes on to elaborate connectivity with the term "proximity," a term often used in globalization literature to imply the idea of social relations spanning great distance, or a "shrinking world."[18] However, Tomlinson desires to be cautious of the term proximity and resists allowing connectivity to automatically imply proximity. To be sure, there is a "common conscious *appearance* of the world as more intimate" due to air travel and the ability to bring images from distant places into our own space, and the term proxim-

---

17. Tomlinson, *Globalization and Culture*, 1–2.
18. Ibid., 3. Another example is the oft-used concept "global village."

ity can be used metaphorically to communicate the perceived closeness between many people who share a common effect on their lives (e.g., the global financial market or the threat of global warming). But concretely, there are still vast physical distances between people and great cultural distances as well, the reality being that most of life for the vast majority of people is lived in the local context in their own local culture and not with the mindset of being intimately connected with distant people.[19] The idea of proximity Tomlinson argues for is one focused on the local, to describe how global processes cause "distant events and powers" to affect the local.[20] Complex connectivity is about the "changing nature" of the localities that constitute the global community.

Jan Aart Scholte develops the approach that characterizes globalization as "respatialization."[21] He suggests:

> A global (in the sense of transplanetary) social relation is one that can link persons situated at any inhabitable points on the earth. Globalization involves reductions of barriers to such transworld social contacts. With globalization people become more able—physically, legally, linguistically, culturally and psychologically—to engage with each other wherever on planet Earth they might be ... globalization refers to a shift in the nature of social space.[22]

Along with the idea of transplanetary social relations, a crucial concept in Scholte's description of globalization is supraterritoriality. Supraterritorial social interactions and phenomena are those that can operate on a global scale, unimpeded by territorial features (e.g., political or natural "spatial domains" on the earth), and often have the "qualities of transworld simultaneity ... and transworld instantaneity."[23]

An example will perhaps clarify. The news of the December 26, 2004 tsunami that devastated coastal communities in Indonesia, Sri Lanka, Thailand, India, and Myanmar was instantaneously and simultaneously transmitted throughout the world via the mass communication of television, radio, and the internet—an example of a supraterritorial social

19. Ibid., 4, 7–8.
20. Ibid., 9.
21. Scholte, *Globalization*, 15–17. This is in contrast to other approaches he deems inadequate (including globalization as internationalization, liberalization, universalization, and Westernization/modernization).
22. Ibid., 59.
23. Ibid., 60–64.

relation. The massive psychological impact on the world's population and subsequent outpouring of financial aid by millions of people was likewise supraterritorial. However, if we take the case of one individual located in Ontario, who called a charity with a presence in Indonesia to make a donation, and went to her local bank to transfer the funds, we have a transplanetary interaction taking place within territorial locations.

According to the above block quotation from Scholte then, we see globalization occurring in this example through the reduction of barriers enabling transplanetary and supraterritorial social relations (barrier reducing structures in this case include the internet/mass communication, the ability to wire money, and the existence of charities with global reach). Finally, it is important to note that the increase in supraterritoriality does not end the importance of territorial mechanisms (e.g., communication links such as airports and undersea cables are territorially fixed). Thus, he remarks that "territorial relations are no longer purely territorial, and supraterritorial relations are not wholly non-territorial."[24]

One can anticipate how the concepts of Tomlinson and Scholte can apply to Christian interactions with globalization. The cases below will provide examples of global connectivity changing the nature of the local, and a respatialization of the theological disciplines—i.e., Christian theology is something done on a global scale, in all places. However, the first task is to briefly describe the other "globalization" with which many Christian writers are interacting.

THE GLOBALIZATION OF CHRISTIANITY

Kenneth Hylson-Smith begins his recent book on global Christianity recounting the popular story in Western culture of the decline and future death of the Christian faith.[25] The story traces Christianity's diminishing power in Western culture from the Renaissance through the Enlightenment and into the twentieth century when even some Christians were proposing a "death of God" theology, and is filled with such characters as Bacon, Feuerbach, Darwin, Nietzsche, and Freud.[26]

24. Ibid., 77.
25. Hylson-Smith, *To the Ends of the Earth*, xi–xxi.
26. The exception to this decline in Western culture is found in the United States, which the proponents of this story (the secularization thesis) see as the exception that proves the rule.

However, Hylson-Smith's argument is that this story, the secularization thesis, of Christianity's dying is myopic in a global context. In fact, since 1700 Christianity has undergone "its greatest period of expansion ever," and despite a real concern for the faith in Western Europe, it is "currently more vigorous, healthy and widely embraced than at any previous time."[27] According to Hylson-Smith, in 1492 approximately 20 percent of the world's population could be considered Christian and only 2 percent of the non-Christians in the world had encountered Christianity in some form.[28] Presently, one third of the world's population is identified as Christian and in 1992 estimates put at 77 percent the amount of the world's population that had exposure to Christianity.

However, the story of the globalization of Christianity is larger than a growth in absolute and relative population and an increase in worldwide presence. It includes the changing geographical demographics of the church. Philip Jenkins uses the statistical data of population growth/decline, religious affiliation, and church attendance to predict that the global church will undergo (and is already undergoing) a massive geographical shift by 2050.[29] Given declining or low growth populations and declining numbers of Christians in the West and increasing populations and numbers of Christians in Latin America, Sub-Saharan Africa, and parts of Asia, the center of the Christian faith (at least numerically) has shifted to the global South.[30] Already more Catholic baptisms occur each year in the Philippines than in France, Spain, Italy, and Poland together, and by the middle of the twenty-first century, one African country, Uganda, could have "more active church members than the four or five largest European nations combined."[31]

This global Christianity is occurring within the context of contemporary globalization. The church has been present over vast geographic areas in the past, but in the present context there exists the greater

27. Hylson-Smith, *To the Ends of the Earth*, xxv.

28. Ibid., 165–66.

29. Jenkins, *Next Christendom*, 79–105. Jenkins is acutely aware of the difficulties associated with statistics and extrapolation (especially in the area of determining religious affiliation), but is convinced that the major trends should hold (see ibid., 85–89).

30. In the United States, however, population is expected to grow steadily and Christian adherence to remain stable (buoyed in part by the massive immigration of people from Latin America) (ibid., 99–105).

31. Ibid., 91–92. The latter claim obviously assumes continuing trends and the absence of a Christian revival in Europe.

awareness and ability of many Christians to see the evidence of a global Christianity, communicate with distant believers, and encounter myriad Christian expressions of faith.[32] In his exploration of Pentecostalism and globalization, André Droogers reminds us that part of the success of Christianity in general has been the combination of the universal and the particular as "Christian converts have shown how people can adopt a global view and at the same time remain faithful to their traditional identities."[33] The examples of responses to global Christianity below are a product of an encounter with the diversity of the local in Christianity, of a struggle with determining Christian thought and practice amidst so many Christian thoughts and practices. And with the shift in Christian population to the South, increasingly the expressions of Christian thought and practice are being developed in non-Western localities. Additionally, results of political and economic globalization influence the relationships within global Christianity. What is the response of Western Christians if brothers and sisters in Nigeria or Brazil voice discontent with the course of economic globalization, constructed primarily by Western countries? How does a faith that boasts global reach and influence respond to global social problems? These questions and others emerge at the confluence of global Christianity and contemporary globalization.

Theological Definitions of Globalization in the Context of Global Christianity

In the context of global Christianity, before the explosion of literature on globalization in the social sciences in the 1990s, Don Browning tried to determine what globalization meant to practitioners of various areas of theological education.[34] He determined that four major definitions or understandings existed. He details them in the following way:

> For some, globalization means the church's universal mission to evangelize the world, i.e., to take the message of the gospel to all people, all nations, all cultures and all religious faiths. Second,

---

32. One must be careful not to overstate the ability of much of the world's population to engage in global communication. Internet access and travel are not available to many people. However, leaders within the church certainly have greater access to global communication.

33. Droogers, "Globalisation and Pentecostal Success," 53.

34. Browning, "Globalization and the Task of Theological Education," 43.

there is the idea of globalization as ecumenical cooperation between the various manifestations of the Christian church throughout the world. . . . Third, globalization sometimes refers to dialogue between Christianity and other religions. Finally, globalization refers to the mission of the church to the world, not only to convert and to evangelize, but to improve and develop the lives of the millions of poor, starving and politically disadvantaged people.[35]

One can see how these concepts of globalization are related to an expanding global Christianity, and are included in this discussion because many of the responses to global Christianity in the context of contemporary globalization are influenced by them. This is especially so in the case of globalization as ecumenical cooperation, which includes "a new openness to and respect for the great variety of local concrete situations."[36] Additionally, the influence of the fourth understanding of globalization is present in the many Christian responses to the globalization of social problems. Furthermore, it must be pointed out that all of the understandings of "globalization" put forward by Browning have been a part of Christian life for centuries. Christians have long engaged in debate and dialogue both within the diversity of Christianity and with other religions, and the mission/s of evangelism and social transformation have always been integral to the faith. However, these aspects of Christianity take on a global character in the current context of contemporary globalization and global Christianity.

The examples below, then, approach contemporary globalization and the existence of global Christianity with varying understandings of what a globalizing Christianity entails, and from different theological and cultural viewpoints. However, they are all seeking to understand the implications of contemporary globalization and/or global Christianity for Christian thought and practice.

CHRISTIAN RESPONSES TO GLOBALIZATION

The Christian literature on globalization is vast and growing, and the following examples are a taste of some of the ways Christians are responding to contemporary globalization and being affected by a global Christianity. The first section explains the divergent views of the merits

35. Ibid., 43–44.
36. Ibid., 44.

of contemporary globalization from a Christian perspective, and how the local church is being called to respond in this context. The second section explores how the emergence of strong Christian centers outside of the West and the existence of a global Christianity are challenging Christian thought—through examples in the areas of biblical interpretation and church history.

Assessing Contemporary Globalization

There is no "one" ethical evaluation of globalization from a Christian perspective. Instead one must speak of Christian evaluations of globalizations—for there are varying understandings of globalization used in the evaluation as well. Assessments of the ethical merits of "globalization" range from exuberantly positive to strongly condemning, and everything in between. An example from each end of the spectrum will illustrate the wideness of opinion.

Patrick Nachtigall's *Faith in the Future* is a work written for a general Christian audience and is highly supportive of globalization and the opportunities it presents for Christianity, while it also addresses some of the current global challenges (e.g., poverty, terrorism, and sex trafficking). His opening chapter extols the virtues of globalization, especially how economic globalization creates wealth and puts pressure on nations to remain at peace due to the integration of economies.[37] The increasing "openness" of countries such as China is another major theme, and the opportunity this presents for Christian witness is emphasized. Nachtigall's enthusiasm for globalization is evident in statements such as "[globalization] is fantastic for Christianity" and "I believe Christ would tell us not to be afraid of these changes but rather to embrace them."[38]

On the other end of the spectrum is a work such as Sharon Delgado's *Shaking the Gates of Hell*. This book sees globalization as dominated by the interests of corporations and the inter-governmental organizations that are characterized as serving them (e.g., the World Trade Organization). It is not necessarily the case that the human institution of the corporation is inherently bad, but corporations have become "dominators of life" instead of servants.[39] Corporate globalization is linked to the concept

---

37. Nachtigall, *Faith in the Future*, 9–25.
38. Ibid., 20.
39. Delgado, *Shaking the Gates of Hell*, 4.

of "institutional evil" and the worship of Mammon. It is a system that is "overseeing the destruction of the earth" and is likened to the Beast in Revelation—a new Rome serving idols instead of God.[40] However, God is triumphant over the powers of the world, and Jesus, through his life and death, demonstrates a resistance to idolatry, injustice, and institutional evil. Followers of Jesus need to likewise resist the evil of corporate globalization as they hope to join in God's work against the powers of the world.[41]

Important to note is that most of the negative assessments of globalization, as with Delgado's above, are specifically addressing economic globalization as it has been expressed in its dominant form of neoliberalism (sometimes called corporate globalization). Delgado and those who think likewise are not opposed to globalization in its entirety. Instead, they are seeking a globalization that prioritizes other values over profit or sheer economic growth (justice or ecology for example). The reason Nachtigall and Delgado can both approach economic globalization from a Christian perspective and yet arrive at radically different conclusions is what they see as the outcomes of economic globalization. Globalization has increased wealth and brought people out of poverty, and has created more openings for the spread of the gospel. So, if one focuses on these areas, as Nachtigall does, it is possible to see the grace and movement of God in the process. However, an economic globalization framework that has been crafted largely by Western governments and corporations has privileged their interests and resulted in social and environmental injustice. To focus on the underside of globalization, as Delgado does, is to see the sin and corruption to which all human institutions are susceptible. This view will naturally see Christianity in opposition to economic globalization, and as providing resources for imagining a different way of interconnecting the world economically.

Local church communities in North America must discern how to respond to the opportunities and difficulties of contemporary globalization. The increased ability to send mission teams around the world for both evangelism and service requires deliberation about the costs and benefits of such endeavors. Could resources be spent differently in order to help churches in the two-thirds world, or empower them to evangelize within their own countries? Missiological models for a globalized

40. Ibid., 83–99.
41. Ibid., 191–214.

world must be developed with the input of both the sending and receiving parties. Churches will also need to discern their stance on economic globalization. Is it primarily a good system that needs to be encouraged by Christian support, while fixing the "rough" edges? Or should local churches be engaged in prayer and political action in hope of transforming economic globalization? Either way, the arena for response for the majority of a North American congregation is the local—be it engaging in environmental practices, changing consumption habits, or influencing politicians. Decisions in this area could be aided by listening to the voices of Christians in the two-thirds world. How is globalization affecting their lives, what about it can they consider the grace of God, and what must be called an injustice? Finally, many communities in North America are becoming more "globalized" themselves, as immigration brings a plurality of cultures and religions to the cities of Canada and the United States. Local churches face the challenge of sharing the gospel in a pluralistic society as they navigate multiple cultures and religions in, quite literally, a global neighborhood.

Globalization or Global Village? Interacting with "Third World" Hermeneutics

The interaction between biblical studies in Europe and North America and the discipline in the South (Sub-Saharan Africa in particular) in regards to methodology and interpretation is the subject of an essay by Justin Ukpong.[42] He begins by observing the current situation in Africa in biblical studies. Currently, exegetical methodologies developed in an African context are being used alongside (and in competition with) traditional Western methodologies that dominated in African theological education until relatively recently.[43] Additionally, it is the African background and context that creates the agenda for the reading of Scripture. Given this context, methodological practices and interpretations of Scripture quite different from traditional Western ones emerge. Specifically, he describes the practice of the "ordinary people's approach," which seems to be a methodology rooted in the perspective of the African reader as opposed to methodologies that attempt to be primarily rooted in the text or its historical context.

---

42. Ukpong, "Reading the Bible in the Global Village."
43. Ibid., 9–10.

The problem, according to Ukpong, is the relationship in the global academic community between Western methodologies and (most) Western scholars and the newer "Third World" methodologies and their scholars.[44] Interestingly, Ukpong uses an analogy from contemporary globalization to make his point. He first takes a negative view of the results and implementation of economic globalization. The structures and processes of economic globalization (trade, production, finance, and organizational structures such as the IMF or World Bank) are seen as a Western imposition on the rest of the world. In Ukpong's view, the way economic globalization has been constructed benefits Western countries to the detriment of "Third World" nations and peoples. These nations had little say in the construction of economic globalization and must abide by the rules of this economic system. Ukpong then draws a parallel to academic practices in biblical studies. As Western economic needs have priority in economic globalization, so "epistemological privilege" is given to the "Western mode of intellectual production." Ukpong continues:

> To be accepted within the academy, scholars from other cultures must do things the way they are done in the West. Accepted rules and techniques of scholarly production, now regarded as normative and universal, follow Western patterns of thought and practices with little or no consideration for cultural differences.[45]

The dominance of Western biblical studies is mirrored in the marginalization of African interpretations and methodologies. Ukpong protests that developments in biblical studies in Africa are largely ignored by many academic journals and African exegetical methodologies are rarely, if ever, discussed in textbooks.[46]

Ukpong advocates a move in biblical studies away from an imitation of economic globalization and towards an embrace of the concept of a true global village.[47] In a village the "concern of one person is the concern of all"; a global village would be a place where all voices could be heard and diverse contributions to the whole are welcomed, a "democratization of power." In biblical studies, the interpretations and methodolo-

---

44. Ibid., 25–35.
45. Ibid., 28.
46. Ibid., 35.
47. Ibid., 33–35.

gies developed in the "Third World" would have an equal hearing in the global academy with those developed in Europe and North America.

A Global Church History

In the introduction to the collection of essays in *Enlarging the Story: Perspectives on Writing World Christian History*, editor Wilbert Shenk posits that we must "rethink how the history and development of the church is to be conceptualized and interpreted."[48] One of the major shifts precipitating this call for change is the emergence of a truly global church, a move from a "Eurocentric" to a "polycentric" church.[49] In the discipline of church history this results in an end to the dichotomy between "church history" (the development of the church in the West) and "mission history" (the work of Christians outside the West).[50] The task of church history is to relate the interaction of the gospel with all of the cultures it encountered; otherwise church history is only a history of the church in the West and obscures many ecclesiastical and theological expressions of Christianity throughout the development of the church.[51]

Andrew Walls echoes Shenk's sentiment and states that in presenting church history the traditional approach treats the Mediterranean world in the early life of the church and the West thereafter, "and that anything else is an optional extra."[52] In opposition to this approach, Walls argues that the student of Christian history must see the process as something that "covers all six continents." However, he is not advocating one universal presentation, as each geographical or cultural part of the church will emphasize its own historical development.[53]

---

48. Shenk, "Introduction," vi.

49. Ibid., vi.

50. Ibid., xvi. Justo González makes this point clear: "the conversion of the Roman Empire and the conversion of the Germanic tribes were part of church history, but the conversion of Ethiopia and the planting of Christianity in Japan were part of the history of missions." (González, *Changing Shape of Church History*, 15).

51. Shenk, "Introduction," xvi–xvii.

52. Walls, "Eusebius Tries Again," 14. Of course, Walls is speaking of the traditional approach of Western church historians.

53. Presumably then, Walls would still encourage Christians in Western countries to concentrate on the history of the church in the West as this is their cultural/historical context. However, this takes place in the context of a knowledge about the global history of the church. Walls provides an example of practicing Christian history from a specific viewpoint as he outlines an African Christian history that focuses on African "initia-

The new paradigm for the discipline of church history advocated by Shenk and Walls is best summarized by Justo González's use of the phrase "the changing cartography" of church history.[54] For González, the "old map" that emphasized the North Atlantic is outdated and must be replaced by a polycentric map. The old map presented the Western expression of Christianity as the goal of church history, while the new map presents a Christianity that finds myriad expressions throughout the history of the church.[55]

The calls of Shenk, Walls, and González for a new way of writing church history are concretely realized in the textbook edited by Adrian Hastings, *A World History of Christianity*. This text was born out of an idea to create a church history survey that avoided Eurocentrism and "related more organically to the diversity of the world's cultures and regions."[56] The driving concept of the text is a "territorially-based history" that reveals the changing nature of Christianity as it encountered different cultures and peoples on all continents.[57] This history of Christianity is envisioned as a plural history, encompassing the views of different ages and places, as opposed to a "single dominant line."[58]

The unique structure of this text is immediately apparent. The usual structuring of chapters by time period or by event/person (moving chronologically) is replaced by a geographical structure. After the first two chapters describe the history of the church to AD 550, chapter 3 focuses on the Orthodox Church until the fall of Constantinople in 1453. Only after reading the story in the East does the reader return to the West and follow the history there until the eve of the Reformation. Then, in an obvious departure from the typical church history text, the entire history of Christianity in India is presented in chapter 5. The geographical pattern continues as the Christian story in Africa, Latin America, North America, Far East Asia, Australasia, and the conclusions

---

tives, responses, resistance, and appropriation" throughout the history of the church's presence in Africa (and extending to the Americas through slavery). This creates a narrative that flows through 2,000 years of African Christianity, instead of treating African Christianity as an offshoot of the Roman Empire, European colonialism, and twentieth-century Western mission work in Africa (ibid., 14–16).

54. González, *Changing Shape of Church History*, 7–18.

55. Ibid., 15–17.

56. Hastings, *World History of Christianity*, xi.

57. Hastings, "Introduction," 4–5.

58. Ibid., 4.

to Eastern (Orthodox) and Western Europe are presented. However, there is a chronology to the structure—the geographical regions are introduced in the order in which the gospel was presented and an enduring Christian community was established.[59]

The Global and Local Church and Pentecostalism

Returning to the language of Jan Aart Scholte, the global nature of the Christian faith can be described as supraterritorial. Christian mission, worship, and theological reflection occur all over the world, at all times, and are unrestricted to specific geographical or political territories. In other words, the arena for Christian thought and practice is the globe. Furthermore, since the Christian faith has gone global, it is no longer helpful to conceive of Christian practices as originating in only one geographical territory to be exported to others. Rather, Christian practices are now originating in myriad locations around the world. The above examples demonstrate some of the implications of this global view of Christianity. An understanding of church history that categorizes Christian activity in the West as "church" history and Christian activity in southern Africa or east Asia (for example) as the history of "missions" is challenged by the vibrancy of Christian churches in the two-thirds world, a vibrancy that is not just an extension of Western Christianity (if it could once be described that way), but a vibrancy that is originating its own theologies, worship practices, and mission strategies. These communities cannot be considered only "missions," they are, and have been, equally a part of the church's history.

While the challenge to traditional church history is perhaps uncontroversial, voices such as Justin Ukpong's in the areas of biblical studies or systematic theology may prove more difficult to accept. If Christian thought originating in the two-thirds world challenges Western paradigms, or even at times seems unlike any accepted scriptural interpretation or theological concept, is it the duty of Western Christians to somehow accept and weave all these strands into their own theology, or to create some kind of global Christian theological synthesis?[60] Here

---

59. The important phrase is "enduring Christian community." This is my (Nikola's) assumption as to why China follows Latin America even though the church was present in China prior to European colonization of the Americas—the earlier Christian communities in China were wiped out.

60. The same question could be asked of Christians in the two-thirds world, but they have already done their fair share of being shaped by Western theology. However,

we must balance the supraterritorial nature of global Christianity with John Tomlinson's insistence that even in a globalized world the local still dominates. Christianity may not be restricted to a few territorial places, but it still takes place within specific territories. Each local expression of the faith adapts thought and practice to local realities—cultural, economic, and political traditions. Despite the knowledge of different expressions of Christianity, the need to contextualize the gospel in the local takes precedence.

If the focus is on the local, is global Christianity destined to be a relativistic phenomenon? Not if the balance between global and local is kept, and if churches actualize the opportunity that global Christianity in the context of contemporary globalization brings. Each local church (or denominational organization) has the opportunity to examine its theology, biblical interpretation, worship, and missiology, against the diverse expressions of Christianity around the world.[61] Some of these encounters may simply result in the use of new worship music or mission strategies. Some may deeply challenge theological assumptions, such as biblical interpretation by slum dwellers or theology adapted to the context of China. Others may be obviously applicable, such as seeking wisdom from Indian churches on how to explain the gospel to immigrant Indian communities in North America. The result is a local church that is focused on ministering to its own context, but able to be corrected by global voices that have different theologies, scriptural interpretations, missiological methods, and assessments of contemporary globalization.

So, what does all this have to do with Pentecostalism? Simply, Pentecostalism (understood to include a variety of charismatic forms of Christianity) is a movement that mirrors the church universal in its supraterritorial nature. Pentecostalism has spread around the globe, and the same opportunities extolled above for any local church are available for Pentecostals within their denomination. North American Pentecostals (the assumed audience for this book) have the opportunity to be challenged by diverse Pentecostal theologies from other cultures around the globe. They have the opportunity to hear how Pentecostals

---

it could be asked of how two-thirds world churches handle the theologies and practices of other two-thirds world Christians.

61. The ability of churches to take advantage of this opportunity is unequal however. Communities with greater access to the infrastructure of globalization (e.g., internet connections) or to certain information mediums (e.g., academic journals) will have a wider sample of global Christian practices from which to draw.

have approached ministry in religiously pluralistic settings in other parts of the world, even as they struggle with pluralism in the cities of North America. And they have the opportunity to listen to the voices of Pentecostals living in poverty in the two-thirds world to help them assess the in/justice and effectiveness of contemporary globalization. This is a challenge then, to North American Pentecostals, to be open to the Pentecostal voices of the world even as they rightly concentrate on ministry in their local context.

THE MANY TONGUES OF PENTECOSTALISM

The theological principle that undergirds the project of this volume is that the Pentecostal movements are a work of the Spirit; they are a continuation of the outpouring of the Spirit of Pentecost (Acts 2:1–21). Although collapsing the Spirit's voice into the clamor of human religious experience is undesirable, at the same time, the Spirit is at work in the many tongues of the worldwide Pentecostal movement. John Tomlinson's notion of "complex connectivity" can help Pentecostals consider the theological basis for global Pentecostal theology. Although Tomlinson develops the concept of complex connectivity in sociological terms, Pentecostals can affirm it in respect to pneumatology. The Spirit at work among Pentecostal believers in suburban, urban, and rural churches in North America is the same Spirit at work in their counterparts around the world (and all Christian groups for that matter). Thus, Pentecostals are united through a complex connectivity of the Spirit. As a result, North American Pentecostals can discern the voice of the Spirit in their midst by listening to the tongues of Pentecost from around the world. Though we may not share a proximate space with Pentecostals around the world, we can allow their local theologies and practices to inform our local theologies and practices and thus participate in the globalization of theology, a globalization of theology that embraces reciprocal flows of influence. With that in view, this volume is an effort to "respatialize" theology on the basis of our common connection through the Spirit of Pentecost. For example, Pentecostal theology can become "supraterritorial" when North American Classical Pentecostals re-consider their understanding of Spirit baptism in light of global charismatic experiences that may not fit into the Classical Pentecostal paradigm.

The effort to allow global-local theologies to speak to local North American Pentecostalism should not make us forget the contextual nature of theology and ministry practice. As Ukpong maintains, the African context(s) provides the agenda(s) for the African reading(s) of Scripture. Similarly, North American Pentecostals read Scripture in light of their varied experiences and cultures. Consequently, North Americans should not merely adopt non-Western approaches any more than non-Western Pentecostal churches and movements should uncritically embrace Western theologies and practices. Without denying transcendental doctrinal truths, Christian churches, groups, and individuals need to contextualize the gospel in light of their cultural circumstances. Yet at the same time, Pentecostals everywhere can learn from their brothers and sisters from around the world. The Spirit of Pentecost speaks in many tongues, but speaks in terms of the one gospel of Jesus Christ.

In light of globalization and the global Pentecostal movements, Pentecostal theology should avoid two problematic alternatives. On the one hand, we should resist theological colonialism, which is but the religious expression of Western cultural imposition and hegemony. On the other hand, we should not succumb to the posture of Western guilt, which seeks to redress Western cultural colonialism by endless self-criticism and insipid valorization of all things non-Western. Both responses are inappropriate. The first is crass conceit. The second is no more than a reverse of the first. Moreover, both are out of step with the Holy Spirit (Gal 5:25). Pentecostals believe that the Holy Spirit is at work in the *global* Pentecostal movements. This theological conviction means that Pentecostal leaders in ministry and theology both here and there should listen to the diverse tongues of the Spirit to discern what the Spirit is saying to the churches (Rev 2:7), both around the world and in their local setting.

The effort to recognize and to take account of global Pentecostal movements is not new, but is, as is Pentecostal theology more generally, still nascent. Walter J. Hollenweger is probably the first to give the global Pentecostal movement theological and historical significance in respect to forming Pentecostal identity. On the basis of exhaustive consideration of worldwide Pentecostal movements, he developed an understanding of Pentecostalism that transcended the Classical Pentecostal and Charismatic paradigms that had been the primary lenses for Western Pentecostals.[62] Allan Anderson, following in the tradition of Hollenweger, has articulated the history of Pentecostalism in a way that

---

62. E.g., Hollenweger, *Pentecostalism*.

recognizes the multiple origins and diverse expressions of worldwide Pentecostalism.[63] Amos Yong's *The Spirit Poured Out on All Flesh* is an example of a constructive Pentecostal theological project that endeavors to develop a global Pentecostal pneumatology that recognizes and integrates the global Pentecostal movements. The present volume joins with these and many other efforts to think about the implications of the global Pentecostal movement for Pentecostal theology and ministry in North America.

The essays in this book appear in three sections. The first section focuses on the global history and nature of Pentecostalism. It contains two essays by Allan Anderson and one by Michael Wilkinson. Anderson's essays introduce Pentecostalism as a "polynucleated" phenomenon that arose among various groups around the world that share common emphases on the experience of the Holy Spirit and the exercise of spiritual gifts. His first essay traces the historical development of the global Pentecostal movement and attributes its growth to its missionary ethos. The second essay surveys the current state of global Pentecostalism and explores the significance and trends of the unprecedented and meteoric rise of Pentecostalism from mere handfuls of scattered revival seekers to over 600 million in the span of a century.

Wilkinson's contribution highlights the way concepts of globalization can help North American Pentecostals in general and Canadian ones in particular to understand their internecine doctrinal struggles, and shows the way globalization has influenced, implicitly and explicitly, contemporary Pentecostal theology and history. He concludes by discussing ways the experience of globalization in Canada influences Pentecostal perceptions and responses to (1) the challenges to traditional doctrines such as Spirit baptism, (2) multiculturalism, and (3) denominational identity and status.

The second section of the book explores ways North American Pentecostals can learn from the global Pentecostal movement. Steve Studebaker's and Randall Holm's pieces tackle traditional theological topics in North American Pentecostalism and seek to re-envision them in light of the global and pluriform nature of Pentecostalism. Studebaker's essay addresses the doctrine of baptism in the Holy Spirit that was the chief theological and historical distinctive doctrine of North American Classical Pentecostalism. However, beginning with

---

63. E.g., Anderson, *An Introduction to Pentecostalism*.

the Charismatic movement, the Classical Pentecostal understanding of Spirit baptism has been subjected to revision and even rejection. Given the increasing global nature of Pentecostalism, and particularly in light of the shift of its center of gravity from the global North to the global South or "Majority World," what is the status and the theological understanding of this historic doctrine in the future of Pentecostalism? This essay suggests that the diversity of the global Pentecostal movement can help North American Pentecostals to not only recognize, but also give theological significance to the varied features of Pentecostalism in their context. The essay also maintains that both the global diversity and local diversity of the experience of the Spirit has theological implications for the doctrine of Spirit baptism.

Holm's essay maintains that although tongues-speech, and in particular the signature doctrine of "initial evidence," has been the brand distinction of thoroughly modern Classical Pentecostals, today many point to a growing restlessness with this traditional construct within the Pentecostal church. Ironically, this foment is not occurring because of a lack of interest or belief in tongues, rather its impetus is largely the fusion of a growing Pentecostal indifference to the traditional tongues-speech construct (we speak in tongues, now what? or, in more cynical moments, so what?) with an increased awareness of the Spirit's activity by the rest of Christendom. In light of this, Holm proposes a new self-understanding of tongues-speech that is not only sensitive to its biblical witness and cultural impact, but risks reshaping Pentecostal identity for a post-modern generation. Thus, like Studebaker, Holm carries on the ongoing debate with one of the historic and defining doctrinal distinctives of Classical Pentecostalism. Although he does not directly engage the global voices of the Pentecostal movement, his contribution assumes them, and thus sits in the context of an awareness that much of global Pentecostalism does not fit neatly into conformity with the Classical Pentecostal doctrine of Spirit baptism and speaking in tongues.

In the third section, Byron Klaus and Ivan Satyavrata draw on global Pentecostalism and the nature of globalization to propose new ways of thinking about Pentecostal leadership, ministry, and mission in the North American setting and beyond. Their goal is to suggest ways that an awareness and appreciation of the global movement can help re-envision Pentecostal leadership and ministry primarily, but not exclusively, in the North American setting.

Klaus articulates the theology and corresponding practice that fuelled early Pentecostal missions and that can invigorate contemporary Pentecostal leadership and ministry. He addresses the challenge of preaching the gospel in a way, on the one hand, that does not reduce the gospel and ministry to a religious consumer option or naively borrow corporate marketing strategies and, on the other hand, that treats humans as loved and empowered by God and not as objects of consumption and economic exploitation, as do so many of the cultural forces of the world. He also outlines characteristics that will serve Pentecostal leaders in the global North and South.

Satyavrata's three essays were originally delivered as the three-part lecture series "Following the Wind and Riding the Wave: Pursuing the Hogan Legacy into the Second Pentecostal Century," while he was serving as the 2009–2010 J. Philip Hogan Professor of World Missions at Assemblies of God Theological Seminary. Satyavrata draws on J. Philip Hogan's seminal and influential ministry with the Assemblies of God in order to point a way forward for Pentecostals to embrace mission strategies that are effective in the dynamic context of globalization. He describes the issues facing Pentecostal missions in the context of globalization, such as human migration to urban centers, multiculturalism, and religious plurality, and ways to respond to these issues that reflect the unique characteristics of Pentecostal ministry and missions, such as embracing technological innovation, responding compassionately and effectively to the exploitation of human beings that is a by-product of some dimensions of globalization, and developing "creative access avenues" to areas closed to traditional missionary activities.

David Reed's essay completes the volume by interacting with the contributors. His essay probes further implications raised by the volume and evaluates the constructive proposals set forth in sections two and three.

BIBLIOGRAPHY

Anderson, Allan. *An Introduction to Pentecostalism: An Introduction to Global Charismatic Christianity*. 2004. Reprint, New York: Cambridge University Press, 2006.

Bergunder, Michael. *The South Indian Pentecostal Movement in the Twentieth Century*. Grand Rapids: Eerdmans, 2008.

Browning, Don S. "Globalization and the Task of Theological Education in North America." *Theological Education* 23 (1986) 3–59.

Cox, Harvey. *Fire from Heaven: The Rise of Pentecostal Spirituality and the Reshaping of Religion in the Twenty-First Century*. Reading, MA: Addison-Wesley, 1995.

Delgado, Sharon E. *Shaking the Gates of Hell: Faith-Led Resistance to Corporate Globalization*. Minneapolis: Fortress, 2007.

Dempster, Murray W., Byron D. Klaus, and Douglas Petersen, editors. *The Globalization of Pentecostalism: A Religion Made to Travel*. Oxford: Regnum, 1999.

Droogers, André. "Globalisation and Pentecostal Success." In *Between Babel and Pentecost: Transnational Pentecostalism in Africa and Latin America*, edited by André Corten and Ruth Marshall-Fratani, 41–61. Bloomington: Indiana University Press, 2001.

González, Justo L. *The Changing Shape of Church History*. St. Louis, MO: Chalice, 2002.

Hastings, Adrian. "Introduction." In *A World History of Christianity*, edited by Adrian Hastings, 1–6. Grand Rapids: Eerdmans, 1999.

———, editor. *A World History of Christianity*. Grand Rapids: Eerdmans, 1999.

Held, David, Anthony G. McGrew, David Goldblatt, and Jonathan Perraton. *Global Transformations: Politics, Economics and Culture*. Cambridge, UK: Polity, 1999.

Hobsbawn, E. J. "The World Unified." In *The Globalization Reader*, edited by Frank J. Lechner and John Boli, 58–62. Malden, MA: Blackwell, 2003.

Hollenweger, Walter J. *Pentecostalism: Origins and Developments Worldwide*. Peabody, MA: Hendrickson, 1997.

Hylson-Smith, Kenneth. *To the Ends of the Earth: The Globalization of Christianity*. London: Paternoster, 2007.

Jenkins, Philip. *The Next Christendom: The Coming of Global Christianity*. Oxford: Oxford University Press, 2002.

Lechner, Frank J., and John Boli, editors. *The Globalization Reader*. 2nd ed. Malden, MA: Blackwell, 2003.

Martin, David. *Pentecostalism: The World Their Parish*. New York: Blackwell, 2002.

Miller, Donald E., and Tetsunao Yamamori. *Global Pentecostalism: The New Face of Christian Social Engagement*. Berkeley: University of California Press, 2007.

Nachtigall, Patrick. *Faith in the Future: Christianity's Interface with Globalization*. Anderson, IN: Warner, 2008.

Sánchez Walsh, Arlene M. *Latino Pentecostal Identity: Evangelical Faith, Self, and Society*. New York: Columbia University Press, 2003.

Scholte, Jan Aart. *Globalization: A Critical Introduction*. 2nd ed. Houndmills, Basingstoke, UK: Palgrave Macmillan, 2005.

Shaull, Richard, and Waldo Cesar. *Pentecostalism and the Future of the Christian Churches: Promises, Limitations, Challenges*. Grand Rapids: Eerdmans, 2000.

Shenk, Wilbert R. "Introduction." In *Enlarging the Story: Perspectives on Writing World Christian History*, edited by Wilbert R. Shenk, vi–xvii. Maryknoll, NY: Orbis, 2002.

Tomlinson, John. *Globalization and Culture*. Chicago: University of Chicago Press, 1999.

Ukpong, Justin S. "Reading the Bible in the Global Village: Issues and Challenges from African Readings." In *Reading the Bible in the Global Village: Cape Town*, edited by Justin S. Ukpong et al., 9–39. Leiden: Brill, 2002.

Wallerstein, Immanuel. "The Rise and Future Demise of the World Capitalist System: Concepts for Comparative Analysis." *Comparative Studies in Society and History* 16 (1974) 387–415.

Walls, Andrew F. "Eusebius Tries Again: The Task of Reconceiving and Re-Visioning the Study of Christian History." In *Enlarging the Story: Perspectives on Writing World Christian History*, edited by Wilbert R. Shenk, 1–21. Maryknoll, NY: Orbis, 2002.

PART ONE
Pentecostalism and Globalization

1

The Roots of Pentecostal Globalization
Early Pentecostal Missions

ALLAN ANDERSON

THE MISSIONARY NATURE OF PENTECOSTALISM

EARLY PENTECOSTALISM WAS INHERENTLY a missionary movement that took its message out into all the world within the shortest possible time. This paper focuses on early Pentecostal missionaries during the first two decades of the twentieth century, their global spread and the extreme difficulties they encountered.[1] There is a tendency in telling missionary stories to paint these pioneers in glossy, bright colors, neglecting the dark side of their ministries and the trials they often succumbed to. Early Pentecostals sometimes saw these severe trials as failures inconsistent with the truths they proclaimed. As one example, the Azusa Street revival newspaper *Apostolic Faith* did not publish the deaths of some of its missionaries and their children. Although some of our methods and medicines have improved since those days, we still face many of the issues encountered by these pioneers who, though dead, yet speak. The astonishing rapidity at which early Pentecostalism spread in the early twentieth century and those responsible for it warrant our attention and give insight into the present global movement now in almost every country on earth.

---

1. Some of this paper is adapted from Anderson, *Spreading Fires*.

At least four prominent factors created impetus for the international movement of hundreds of independent Pentecostal migrants in the early twentieth century. First, this was a time of unprecedented communication links, when the extensive migration of peoples was facilitated by the new colonial steamship and railway networks that had made travelling vast distances possible. It has been estimated that European powers together controlled some 85 percent of the world's surface by 1914. The beginning of the twentieth century was a time when international trade, migration, and capital flows were increasing so that Europe and North America could increase wealth and produce industrial goods for profit at the expense of their colonies.[2] As a result of this rampant imperialism, the nineteenth century had seen a single global economy emerge. The movement of goods, people, and money linked the most remote and still pristine parts of the world with the bureaucratic nation-states of Europe and the USA. The development of railway and steamship lines accelerated at the turn of the century, with the result that previously unreachable areas were now accessible to European and American traders, colonizers, and of course, missionaries.

Second, the premillennial eschatology of these Pentecostals posited the urgent task of world evangelism at the end of time before the imminent return of Christ. The demise of postmillennialism in nineteenth-century evangelicalism with its optimistic view of a coming "golden age" of material wealth and progress was replaced by an increasingly pessimistic premillennialism that believed that the world would get progressively worse until the return of Christ. Therefore, the missionary task was to rescue individuals from imminent peril rather than seek to transform society. One missionary writing from China expressed this well, as she said at the beginning of a new year that their hearts were "thrilling with the thought 'He is coming soon.' Oh! may we win many souls for the Master. . . . How evident it is that we are in the last days; the general indifference, coldness, deadness, & iniquity waxing worse & worse. Yet, praise God, here & there—a gleam of light."[3] But this premillennialism was not entirely pessimistic, for there was a certain tension between the negative view of the world and the very positive view of the place of Pentecostals in it. The outpouring of the Spirit in the last days made mission and evangelizing the nations possible. The eschatologi-

---

2. Said, *Culture and Imperialism*, 6.
3. Jenny Boyd to T. H. Mundell, Kaihua, January 8, 1919.

cal link between revival and missions was expressed by the founder of the China Inland Mission, James Hudson Taylor, who had apparently declared ten years before his death that "the next great series of events on the world's stage of action would be a great war between Russia and Japan in which Russia would be defeated. Then would follow the greatest spiritual revival the world has ever known, and soon after would follow the coming of Jesus."[4] This was a remarkable prophecy, but the last part had not been fulfilled, at least not as soon as Taylor thought. Pentecostals believed that they were in that revival and that their mission work was a direct consequence of it. These eschatological expectations motivated them in their task and filled the earliest reports of their activities.[5]

Third, at least in the case of American Pentecostals, they had a firm belief in their experience of Spirit baptism by which they had been given "foreign languages" to preach the gospel to the nations of the world. This will be considered later.

Fourth, these missionaries often met up with other, more experienced missionaries once in the field, especially when they discovered that God had not given them the ability to speak any language that people could understand. Missionary networks like those of the Christian and Missionary Alliance were very significant in the spread of Pentecostal ideas throughout the world and especially in the largest missionary regions of China and India. *The Bridegroom's Messenger* reported the astonishing news from India in December 1908 that sixty missionaries had received Spirit baptism and fifteen missionary societies had "witnesses to Pentecost" in twenty-eight stations throughout the country.[6] All this had happened in the space of only one year.

The rapid growth of Pentecostalism is directly attributable to the efforts and vision of its pioneers—who were by no means always Westerners. Pentecostalism was probably more dependent on "national workers" than any other missions were at the time, because of its emphasis on the empowering ability of the Spirit to equip ordinary believers for missionary service without requiring prior academic qualifications. Several of the first Pentecostal missionaries from the Azusa Street mission were African Americans who went to Liberia in 1907—some of them laid down their lives there—but these too have been ignored by

---

4. Quoted in *Word & Work* 30:5 (May 1908) 142.
5. Anderson, *Spreading Fires*, 219–23.
6. *Bridegroom's Messenger* 27 (December 1, 1908) 2.

historians, until Robeck's 2006 work.⁷ Many other early Pentecostal leaders in Africa, India, and China were similarly obliterated from historiography because their mass movements were later regarded as heterodox. Although missionaries from the West went out in independent and denominational Pentecostal missions, the overwhelming majority of missionaries have been national people "sent by the Spirit," often without formal training. This was a fundamental difference between Pentecostal and "mainline" missions. In Pentecostal practice, the Holy Spirit is given to every believer without preconditions. One of the results of this was, as Saayman observes, that "it ensured that a rigid dividing line between 'clergy' and 'laity' and between men and women did not develop early on in Pentecostal churches" and even more significantly, "there was little resistance to the ordination of indigenous pastors and evangelists to bear the brunt of the pastoral upbuilding of the congregations and their evangelistic outreach."⁸ Expatriate missionaries depended totally on their "native workers"—they would have failed without them. This was one of the reasons for the rapid transition from "foreign" to "indigenous" church that took place in many Pentecostal missions, even when foreign missionaries held on tightly to reins of power. Leaders tended to come from lower and uneducated strata of society and were trained in an apprentice-type setting where their charismatic leadership abilities could develop. Being the only ones who could communicate effectively with local people, they developed their leadership abilities while the foreign missionaries sometimes sat helplessly on one side.

One of the most important factors in the early spread of the Pentecostal message was the printed page, especially the periodicals. By 1908 not only were there numerous Pentecostal periodicals in North America (the most prominent being *The Apostolic Faith*), but Alexander Boddy in Sunderland, England had begun publishing *Confidence*, and there were Pentecostal papers in China, Japan, and India.⁹ By March 1909 in Atlanta the editor of *Bridegroom's Messenger*, Elisabeth Sexton, was reporting that "besides the many published in the United States and

---

7. Robeck, *Azusa Street Mission and Revival*.

8. Saayman, "Some reflections on the Development of the Pentecostal Mission Model in South Africa," 43.

9. Mok Lai Chi's *Pentecostal Truths* published in Hong Kong; M. L. Ryan's *Apostolic Light* in Japan; and Ramabai's *Mukti Prayer Bell* and Max Wood Moorhead's *Cloud of Witnesses* in India. See *Pentecost* 1:2 (Sept 1908) 4.

Canada," Pentecostal papers were being printed in ten other countries.[10] As Sexton put it (quoting Scripture) in December 1908, "the field is the world," and this paper, just over a year old, was already circulating in twenty-three countries. It exhorted prayer that the paper would "carry Pentecostal messages speedily to the utmost parts of the earth."[11] By 1910, *Confidence* reported that it was circulating in over 46 countries.[12] Because missionary activity was the very essence of the early Pentecostal movement, these periodicals had dedicated pages for reports from the mission field and some prioritized this.

Early Pentecostals placed an emphasis on missions as a result of the experience of Spirit baptism. The promise of Acts 1:8 was that when the Holy Spirit was received people would become witnesses to the "uttermost parts of the earth." This was not an option; it was the only way that the Great Commission could be fulfilled and it had to be sought in haste before it was too late and Jesus had returned. As Indianapolis Pentecostal leader and first General Secretary of the (USA) Assemblies of God (AG), J. Roswell Flower put it in 1908, "When the Holy Spirit comes into our hearts, the missionary spirit comes in with it; they are inseparable . . . carrying the gospel to hungry souls in this and other lands is but a natural result."[13] Pentecostal Missionary Union (PMU) director Cecil Polhill expressed the conviction in the same year that for any revival to endure it must have "the true Missionary Spirit." The "Pentecostal Blessing" he declared "must go right through the world" and was "the very best thing in the world for the Mission Field." The gift of the Spirit was a "Missionary Gift." The PMU had been founded on the conviction that "every true Pentecost means missionary service to the ends of the earth."[14] Alexander Boddy wrote in a similar vein that a true "Pentecost" meant "a growth of the Missionary Spirit," that "the indwelling Christ is an indwelling Missionary" who had sent Pentecostals to go, and when they obeyed "He goes with us in the power of the Holy Ghost to preach a great and a full Salvation for Body, Soul, and Spirit."[15]

10. *Bridegroom's Messenger* 33 (March 1, 1909) 1.
11. *Bridegroom's Messenger* 27 (December 1, 1908) 1.
12. *Confidence* 3:12 (Dec 1910) 284–85.
13. Quoted by McGee, "Pentecostals and their Various Strategies for Global Mission," 206.
14. *Confidence* 2:1 (Jan 1909) 15; 2:6 (June 1909) 129; 3:8 (Aug 1910) 198.
15. *Confidence* 3:8 (Aug 1910) 199.

MISSIONARY WOMEN

One cannot give a paper on the globalization of early Pentecostalism without considering the vitally important role of women, which has often been neglected.[16] The African American worker Lucy Farrow, who was not only a leader at Azusa Street but also one of the first Pentecostal missionaries to reach Africa (Liberia), or Lucy Leatherman, the first Pentecostal missionary in the Middle East, have largely been written out of the histories.[17] Similarly, the Indian reformer and Mukti Mission founder Pandita Ramabai was arguably the most significant woman involved in early Pentecostalism and as much a missionary as any Western one. Ramabai and the revival movement she helped lead were almost completely ignored because she did not start a Pentecostal denomination and, perhaps, because the revival she led was not in the Western world.[18]

The end of the nineteenth and the beginning of the twentieth century was an important period for changing social and religious expectations in the Western world regarding the role of women. By the 1880s, training schools for evangelical missionary women were being founded, and women like Carrie Judd Montgomery and Maria Woodworth-Etter, both of whom became Pentecostal, were preaching in mass meetings on a regular basis. Montgomery's *Triumphs of Faith* was a significant vehicle for giving expression to women preachers, and the majority of articles appearing there were written by women. It published an article "Should Women Prophesy?" in 1886 giving a spirited defense of the rights of women in ministry.[19] The remarkable and sudden surge in the number of missionary candidates offering themselves for overseas service from the 1890s onwards was partly attributable to changing attitudes towards single women becoming missionaries in evangelical circles. Many, perhaps most, of these missionary candidates were women. Coming from societies where their role was rapidly changing from a purely domestic function to that where women could embark on certain professional careers (at least in the middle classes), these women had volunteered for one of the few careers available in an ecclesiastical world that was

---

16. Wacker, "Are the Golden Oldies Still Worth Playing?" 95.
17. Anderson, *Spreading Fires*, 152–53 and 159.
18. Anderson, *Spreading Fires*, 77–101.
19. *Triumphs of Faith* 6:12 (Dec 1886) 270–73.

still very much male-dominated. By 1900, published figures indicated that women Protestant missionaries were already 45 percent of the "foreign missionary" force. It is also significant that this same source gave the number of "native laborers" at over three times the total number of "foreign missionaries."[20] Grant Wacker has estimated that two-thirds of the missionaries and half the travelling evangelists and healers in early American Pentecostalism were women.[21] Women played an enormous role in the early Pentecostal movement as leaders and missionaries throughout the world, even though they faced enormous theological and social prejudice in their task.[22]

Many of the early "native workers" were also women. *Word and Work* reprinted an article speaking of the enormous contribution made to Christian mission by the Indian women Pandita Ramabai, Soonderbai Powar, and Shorat Chuckerbutty. It declared that "the best work done in India to-day" was "upon purity principles of faith and prayer, and no leaders there are more mightily anointed than many of the native women." These were "women of peerless purity and power, the Deborahs of the darkened Empire." Each of these women was a "Spirit anointed prophetess of purity and faith principles" who had exposed herself to dangers on behalf of the "oppressed and perishing." Prayer had prevailed, and the work had "developed into a permanent institution owned by God," the report concluded.[23] These Indian women were outspoken in their demands for the equality of women in an unjust society, and of course, they had had the shining example of Pandita Ramabai who had led the way.[24] Ramabai had not only led a Pentecostal revival that preceded the events in Azusa Street, but her Mukti Mission was the center to which many Western Pentecostal missionaries to India went for training. It was visited by several well-known Pentecostals from the West, including T. B. Barratt, Carrie Judd Montgomery, A. G. and Lillian Garr, and Daniel Awrey. At a convention in Rochester, New York in 1918, one of Ramabai's American assistants spoke of the contribution such Indian women had made to Pentecostalism. She pointed out that they were "so filled with the Spirit and so taught of God" that expatriate missionaries

20. *Word & Work* 22:11 (Nov 1900) 337.
21. Wacker, *Heaven Below*, 160.
22. Ibid., 158.
23. *Word & Work* 26:3 (Mar 1904) 84.
24. Quoted in *Latter Rain Evangel* 5:6 (Mar 1913) 24.

had "received Pentecost through their gracious ministry," and had "been willing to learn the deeper truths of God through their words and holy examples."[25]

Shorat Chuckerbutty was a Bengali and like Ramabai, a Brahmin with an MA degree—unusual for Indian women at that time. She became a Pentecostal in early 1910 with co-worker Dorothea Chandra and her center in Allahabad became another center for the spread of Pentecostalism. Daily services were held there when many were reported converted and baptized in the Spirit, including three very significant missionaries: general secretary of the YWCA Agnes Hill, Eva Groat (a Pentecostal missionary in India for many years) and the English missionary Alice Luce of the CMS (later Assemblies of God missionary to Mexicans in the USA), their testimonies appearing in Pentecostal periodicals. In 1911 Chuckerbutty organized a Pentecostal convention there in which more missionaries and other Christian workers received Spirit baptism.[26] Lillian Garr wrote of Chuckerbutty and Chandra, "it is beautiful to see how true these two Indian sisters are to this blessed Truth. There is absolutely no compromise on their part and yet they are kept filled with a tender love to all who oppose."[27] Agnes Hill spoke at the Stone Church in Chicago in 1912, where she described this as a place where a "great many" received Spirit baptism. She made the interesting observation that the time had come "when those from Christian nations going to that country can receive spiritual blessings from the Indians." There was "no monopoly of the grace of God," she continued, and she was so pleased that "God baptized Sister Chuckerbutty first." Both Alice Luce and she had gone to Chuckerbutty's center "and received the baptism in the Holy Spirit through the prayers of an Indian woman, glory to God for the great sisterhood there is!"[28] Cecil Polhill visited Chuckerbutty's center in Allahabad in 1914.[29]

---

25. *Trust* 17:7 (Sept 1918) 11.

26. *Bridegroom's Messenger* 57 (March 1, 1910) 1; 61 (May 1, 1910) 4; 62 (May 15, 1910) 3; 77 (January 1, 1911) 4; 80 (February, 15 1911) 2–3; 141 (October 1, 1913) 1; *Confidence* 3:5 (May 1910) 113–14; *Upper Room* 1:10 (May 1910) 5; 2:5 (May 1911) 6; *Latter Rain Evangel* 9:7 (Apr 1917) 18.

27. *Bridegroom's Messenger* 66 (July 15, 1910) 3.

28. *Latter Rain Evangel* 5:4 (Jan 1913) 11.

29. *Confidence* 7:3 (Mar 1914) 60.

The use of women with charismatic gifts was widespread throughout the Pentecostal movement and resulted in a much higher proportion of women in Pentecostal ministry than in any other form of Christianity at the time. This accorded well with the prominence of women in many pre-Christian religious rituals in Africa and parts of Asia, contrasting again with the prevailing practice of older churches that barred women from entering the ministry or even from taking any part in public worship. But in spite of all the important practical involvement of women in the leadership of Pentecostal churches and missions during this period, Pentecostal churches were not yet ready to come to terms with the theological implications of women in ministry. There were strong male, conservative voices in Pentecostalism advocating a restriction on the opportunities for women in ministry. The praxis of Pentecostal missions and the stated position of the supporting churches did not always harmonize. But this was a time when women were still not fully franchised, educational opportunities were still denied them, and a general patriarchal attitude prevailed globally. Although the degree of gender discrimination has improved since those days, some Pentecostal denominations are still struggling with these issues and sometimes make decisions and actions limiting and quenching this most important ministry of women, who form the large majority of the church worldwide and without whose ministry Pentecostalism would have failed.

MISSIONARY TONGUES

The present proliferation of Pentecostalism and indeed its inherent character are fundamentally because this was a missionary movement of the Spirit from the start. The purpose of this new "Apostolic Faith" was clear in the Azusa Street revival: to stand for "the restoration of Apostolic faith, power and practice, Christian unity, the evangelization of the whole world preparatory to the Lord's return, and for all of the unfolding will and word of God." The followers of this new movement were convinced that they had "the simple but effective Scriptural Plan for evangelizing the world,"[30] namely, the gift of foreign languages. Pentecostalism, in common with other Christian revivalist movements at the time, held that their ecstatic manifestations were evidence of the end-time outpouring of the Spirit given to evangelize the world within

---

30. *Word & Work* 29:4 (Apr 1907) 117.

the shortest possible time. Pentecostals would seek to identify which particular language they had been given (usually through some member of the assembly who would be "familiar" with a foreign language), and then they would make arrangements to go to that country as soon as possible. Following the earlier ideas of Charles Parham and William Seymour, the first American Pentecostals almost universally believed that when they spoke in tongues, they had spoken in known languages by which they would preach the gospel to the ends of the earth in the last days. There would be no time for the indeterminable delays of language learning. Early Pentecostal publications were filled with these missionary expectations, often referring to their tongues as the "gift of languages."

The going out from Azusa Street was immediate, in ever-widening circles. In the first issue of *The Apostolic Faith* (September 1906), the full expectation of early American Pentecostals was that through Spirit baptism they could speak "all the languages of the world" in order to preach the gospel "into all the world."[31] The rather haphazard sending "by the Spirit" resulted in several Azusa Street missionaries itinerating from place to place, and from country to country. One of the earliest and most remarkable was Lucy Leatherman, a wealthy doctor's widow and former student at A. B. Simpson's Missionary Training School in Nyack, New York. She had received Spirit baptism at Azusa Street, where she believed she had spoken Arabic and was called to go to Palestinian Arabs. She travelled from country to country sending back reports to several Pentecostal papers and she was among the first group of missionaries reported as having left Los Angeles for Jerusalem via the east coast in August 1906. Among the languages this group believed they were able to speak through Spirit baptism were Turkish and Arabic, but there were no reports of them ever being understood by their hearers.

Those more skeptical about the fantastic claims that were being made, like Alexander Boddy in England, cautioned great care with regard to so-called "missionary tongues." In a 1911 article in his paper *Confidence*, Boddy wrote that those who felt that they had "a call to the Foreign Mission Field because they believe that they speak in Chinese, Indian, or African languages, etc." should "be very careful not to go before God" and "before leaving home they should take steps to verify the fact that they really have a complete language in which at all times they can preach the Gospel". Boddy said that he felt justified in saying that

31. *Apostolic Faith* 1 (Sept 1906) 1.

"from among the very many who have gone abroad after the Pentecostal blessing we have not yet received one letter stating that they have this miraculous gift in any useful fullness."[32] He had initiated this debate almost three years earlier in 1908, by publishing letters from the first Pentecostal missionaries to South China, T. J. McIntosh and A. G. Garr, discussing the issue that had already caused some considerable controversy and made mockery of Pentecostals in the eyes of other missionaries. This debate seemed to be occasioned by an attack by a missionary in Macao, who had apparently investigated the claims of the Garrs and the McIntoshes and stated that "at no time has there been any *known* tongue spoken, all has been an *unknown* utterance."[33] Boddy firmly stated his position, which would become the accepted tradition of Pentecostalism, that many of those who had gone out expecting to speak a foreign language had not at the time realized that the gift of tongues was "not the gift of any known language in its entirety." Boddy was "sure that God honoured their zeal" and had "permitted them to be a blessing though not as they expected." He said that the Lord had given some of them language interpreters and they had all "reached English speaking people with their Pentecostal message, while missionaries with whom they came in contact were encouraged to seek the Baptism of the Holy Ghost."[34]

Despite all these setbacks for missionary tongues, Boddy voiced the prevalent optimism of Pentecostal leaders when he described the "Hall-Marks" of Pentecostal baptism in August 1909. The fifth "Hall-Mark" was what he called the "Missionary Test." He wrote that although missionaries had been disappointed when they found out that "they could not preach in the language of the people, and in spite of mistakes made chiefly through their zeal," God had blessed and "now more than ever the Pentecostal Movement is truly a Missionary Movement." This "increasing band" of Pentecostal missionaries had "more training now" and were "going out ... to preach Christ and Him crucified to the heathen people, often in very hard places, amidst terrible difficulties."[35] Nevertheless, Boddy and other Pentecostal believers seemed to cherish the thought that there would be occasions when the "tongues of the nations" would be spoken, and the belief in missionary tongues lingered on. As late as

32. *Confidence* 4:1 (Jan 1911) 8.
33. Quoted in Robeck, *Azusa Street*, 246.
34. *Confidence* 1:2 (May 1908) 21.
35. *Confidence* 2:8 (Aug 1909) 181.

1913, Congo missionary Alma Doering claimed to have heard a tongues speaker in the last Sunderland convention speaking a language of Central Africa with which she was familiar.[36] One Pentecostal missionary in China, Sophia Hansen, claimed to speak Chinese miraculously by the Spirit from 1908–1916.[37]

But even when the "languages" did not appear, it was the fundamental experience of Spirit baptism that motivated them to mission. Although many misunderstandings arose from the belief in missionary tongues, the primary motivation behind this was the conviction that the Spirit had been given to enable the nations of the earth to be reached with the gospel. As *The Apostolic Faith* declared, it was "the baptism with the Holy Ghost which is the enduement of power, that will make you a witness to the uttermost parts of the earth."[38] People went to Azusa Street from Europe and went back with the "baptism," and Pentecostal missionaries were sent out all over the world, according to one estimation reaching over twenty-five nations in two years.[39] But the tide was changing. Thomas Junk in China expressed the increasing pragmatism of Pentecostal missionaries in the field when he wrote, "Although He [God] hasn't given the language outright, He has wonderfully blessed us in the learning of it."[40] Bernt Berntsen also wrote from China that some missionaries in Beijing had returned home because they "did not get the language" and the emphasis had shifted in his mission to language learning.[41] In fact, these same language-less Pentecostals depended on "native workers" who had acquired English and often other languages. They were certainly better linguists than most of the Western missionaries were. Their mission schools focused on teaching English to national people, especially children, in order to communicate their message. In many cases, the nationals acquired a foreign language much quicker than the foreign missionaries did.

The theological link between Spirit baptism and missions has always been made in the Pentecostal movement. It is very important

---

36. *Confidence* 6:7 (July 1913) 143 and *Latter Rain Evangel* 5:10 (July 1913) 15.

37. Anderson, *Spreading Fires,* 63.

38. *Apostolic Faith* 6 (Feb–Mar 1907) 1.

39. Faupel, *The Everlasting Gospel*, 212–16; Robeck, "Pentecostal Origins in Global Perspective," 176–77.

40. *Bridegroom's Messenger* 26 (November 15, 1908) 4; 32 (February 15, 1909) 1.

41. *Bridegroom's Messenger* 51 (December 1, 1909) 3.

to understand the significance of this, because just as Spirit baptism is Pentecostalism's central, most distinctive doctrine, so mission is Pentecostalism's central, most important activity. The missionary in India working with Ramabai, Minnie Abrams, explained that Spirit baptism should "make us world-wide" and "enlarge us." Jesus Christ had said "that repentance and remission of sins should be preached in His Name to all nations, beginning at Jerusalem," which was "the program that He laid out for us." Christ had said that "He would endue us with power from on high that we might be able to do it."[42] Abrams was probably the first to give a detailed exposition of Spirit baptism linking spiritual gifts with missions. Pentecostals were given gifts of the Spirit in order to engage in service to others. This was their mission to the world. As she put it, the "full Pentecostal baptism of the Holy Ghost" had not been received unless someone had received both the fruit of the Spirit and the gifts of the Spirit as outlined in 1 Corinthians 12. These gifts alone "enabled the early church to spread the knowledge of the gospel, and establish the Christian church so rapidly."[43] This fundamental and inseparable link between Spirit baptism, spiritual gifts, and missions remained the central plank of the whole structure of Pentecostalism in its early years.[44]

The fact is that from Azusa Street and other centers, Spirit-filled missionaries were sent out to places as far away and diverse as China, India, Japan, Argentina, Brazil, all over Europe, Palestine, Egypt, Somaliland, Liberia, Angola, and South Africa—all within two years.[45] This was no mean achievement, and was the beginning of what is arguably the most significant global expansion of a Christian movement in the entire history of Christianity. The primary motivation for this was that these Pentecostals believed they had received the Missionary Spirit who had empowered them to go to the nations. Although the belief in "missionary tongues" had originated with Parham, it took a new revival movement to put these teachings into practical effect and create a missionary migration movement of extraordinary proportions, whose primary motivation was the baptism of the Spirit and whose stated intention was to reach every nation on earth within the shortest possible time.

42. *Latter Rain Evangel* 3:8 (May 1911) 8.
43. *Word & Work* 33:8 (Aug 1911) 244.
44. *Flames of Fire* 12 (July 1913) 3.
45. Faupel, *Everlasting Gospel*, 182–86, 208–9, and 212–16; and Anderson, *Spreading Fires*, 288.

MISSIONARY HARDSHIPS

The migrants who carried the Pentecostal message all over the globe were mostly poor, untrained, and unprepared for what awaited them. Most of them fully intended to go permanently to the places they believed they were called to, and many did not return. Anna Deane Cole from Birmingham, Alabama arrived in Hong Kong in 1910 to work with her aunt Anna Deane in a children's school. She remained there for 52 years, writing: "I would not go to America if I had my passage paid. I am here until God says move on."[46] A missionary woman from the Rochester Bible Training School in New York State who left for India in 1913 said similarly, "I am going out expecting never to return, for since, as we trust, the coming of the Lord is near, my work is for India, and I shall not return, except by a clear word from Him."[47] This was the indomitable spirit in which some of these missionaries departed from their homelands. There was also an underlying fierce individualism and independence that often came with their experience of Spirit baptism. Sometimes it empowered ordinary, oppressed, and disadvantaged people to resist the status quo and those who were an institutional part of it. These early missionaries went out to live "on the faith line," to bring "light" into "darkness," and in some cases they had no fixed plans for their arrival and certainly none for their return—for they were led to their destinations by the Spirit, and the Spirit would show them what to do when they got there. As one of these missionaries, May Law, put it, speaking of her team in Hong Kong: "Three young women, and one of mature years, left their homes of wealth, and comfort . . . and their beautiful native State of Washington, for dark S. China."[48] Two of these three young women died there from tropical diseases in the next four years. This was the tragic fate of many of these unprepared missionaries who would refuse to take medicines, because to do so would show a lack of faith in divine healing. Some of them went to these faraway places leaving behind wives and children and sometimes they took their families with them only for them to perish from smallpox or malaria soon after arriving there. The sacrifices made by these missionaries were in some cases quite extreme. Many were independent, without financial or organizational backing

---

46. *Bridegroom's Messenger* 56 (February 15, 1910) 1; 59 (April 1, 1910) 4; 108 (April 15, 1912) 1.

47. Miss C. B. Herron, *Trust* 12:8 (Oct 1913) 2.

48. Law, *Pentecostal Mission Work in South China*, 2.

and related only in a loose way to small Pentecostal congregations in their home country. After all, the Spirit had set them free from human ecclesiastical institutions.[49]

Many missionaries did not return to their homelands and died on the field. Although he disappears from the records, Thomas Junk, another Azusa Street missionary, was probably one of these, whose measure of commitment to China was poignantly expressed in a letter he wrote in 1910. A Christian had asked him to return to the USA "and tell personally of the work and the need here if he, the brother, paid the expenses." He replied, "No, dear brother, no, I cannot afford to waste the time and money that way. My work is here till Jesus comes or I am called home. I never shall see the home land again till I see it from the clouds."[50] Some missionaries went out "by faith" without any income, going out with very little and "trusting God" to supply the necessary finances, usually through home contacts and periodical support. In return, the missionaries provided long and regular newsletters that were reproduced in order to raise funds back in the homeland. Disasters befell many of them. The Batman family of five all died within weeks of arriving in Liberia and a team of fourteen that went with M. L. Ryan to Japan without financial support all returned to the USA within a short time. Liberia was to be the burial ground for many Pentecostal missionaries. All together, ten missionaries in one Pentecostal mission in Cape Palmas died of tropical diseases in the first eight years and some returned home.[51] Many more Pentecostal missionary children were buried on the field here and in other tropical lands. Their parents wrote anguished letters to their supporting churches mixing bewilderment with grief.

The first Pentecostal missionaries certainly did not have it easy. Pentecostal leaders had to pull in the reins on overly excited and poorly prepared missionaries who became both a burden and an embarrassment to the fledgling movement. John G. Lake wrote an exasperated letter home from South Africa in 1909 about sending missionaries without funds—as one young American had arrived in Cape Town without the necessary minimum of a hundred dollars and a guarantee of support.[52] Long-term missionaries expressed their disquiet at the wholesale mi-

49. *Confidence* 3:6 (Jun 1910) 145.
50. *Bridegroom's Messenger* 59 (April 1, 1910) 2.
51. Anderson, *Spreading Fires*, 158–61.
52. *Pentecost* 1:7 (June 1909) 3.

gration of untrained, poorly funded, and inexperienced "missionaries" from Pentecostal churches in the Western world. Lake's views were not isolated.[53] This was a widespread problem during the first decade of Pentecostal missions. The issue was the expense involved in providing for the return fare and the effect this had on the morale and activities of remaining missionaries. Clearly, the leading of the Spirit in individual lives was becoming a challenge. Poor planning and organization, exacerbated by several globetrotting adventurers, were a strain on the limited finances of the fledgling movement. One of the reasons for the formation of the American Assemblies of God (AG) in 1914 was to better organize missions, and to "discourage wasting money on those who are running here and there accomplishing nothing."[54] The problem, however, was not solved (in most cases) by the 1920s, and Pentecostal missionaries continued to suffer from poor financial support and insufficient organization.

One cannot talk about missions without also mentioning money. Most of the early Pentecostal missionaries were entirely dependent upon supporting churches, individuals, and especially the periodicals for their financial support. They did not have it easy and often there is oblique reference in their letters to the financial hardships experienced. Some were forced to return home through inadequate support; some were greatly weakened through inadequate food supplies as they faced the ravages of tropical disease and unsanitary living conditions. Because so many of these missionaries opened up schools and orphanages, the support needed was for many more than the missionaries themselves, and they shared whatever they had with the children and workers in their care. Missionaries were restricted in their travelling and ability to move around and often they were unable to return for furlough because of the cost of purchasing the passage home. Some chose not to return at all. Special appeals were sometimes made in the periodicals for those missionaries unable to make ends meet through a lack of financial support.[55]

Minnie Abrams addressed the financial difficulties faced by "faith missionaries" and appealed for better support for Pentecostal missionaries, who had left on ships from their homelands "with such joy and gladness in the midst of shouts and hallelujahs." But once reaching their destination, she charged, these missionaries had "literally been starved

---

53. *Upper Room* 2:3 (Nov 1910) 7.
54. *Word & Witness* 9:12 (Dec 1913) 1.
55. *Bridegroom's Messenger* 127 (February 15, 1913) 2.

in foreign lands" and some had had "to live on roots or anything they could get, because those hallelujahs did not sink down into the heart."[56] Paul Bettex's heart-rending letter describing his wife's death in Canton put part of the blame on the lack of financial support they were receiving from the American churches:

> When weak and faint for lack of food for days, I saw my earthly treasure coming to an end of her strength, I prayed agonizingly day by day for means to provide the much needed milk and cheap fruit she craved. I prayed and wrestled in agony with God because I knew and felt that five dollars might mean life or death to my dearest—but no help came. In those hours of spiritual conflict, I seemed to see the home saints in their comfortable homes looking on to see how long we could hold out without breaking. We had covenanted to fight it out to the death and she did.[57]

This tragic event seemed to spark off more intense calls for better organization of the number of new missionaries going out and their financial support. The periodicals described awful conditions of financial hardship like this one faced by Pentecostal missionaries on the field in an attempt to raise more funds for missionaries, but these appeals were not often successful in what was still a fledgling movement in the "homeland." It seems that there were far more missionaries going out from Pentecostal churches than there were adequate funds to support them. Some missionaries went out in haste, one writing to *Word & Witness* that he had been in China for eight months and had only received twelve dollars in support. The editor, E. N. Bell added a rather caustic note: "This is because the brother did not get the support of the brethren in the home land before going."[58] The *Latter Rain Evangel* made several earnest appeals for better organization in missionary support and had a telling comment on cases like that of Nellie Bettex, that Pentecostal people were "grossly neglectful of our missionaries when they have not sufficient food to eat." This amounted to "indifference and lack of system in our giving" and had resulted in some missionaries who had gone out "expecting the Pentecostal movement to stand behind them have been compelled to connect themselves with some missionary society in order to stay on the field." Then the paper honed in on the specific tragedy of

56. *Latter Rain Evangel* 2:6 (Mar 1910) 17.
57. *Latter Rain Evangel* 5:4 (Jan 1913) 17.
58. *Word & Witness* 9:11 (Nov 1913) 4.

Nellie Bettex, whose "constitution was undermined by prolonged lack of food," and this "deeply stirs our hearts, and we can only hope that she has not died in vain." It went on:

> Whether or not she has been a martyr to our lack of system in supporting our missionaries, let us earnestly pray that it may be a trumpet call to us all to "keep not silence and give Him no rest" until we establish some method for the adequate support of the members of our Lord's body in heathen lands.[59]

Still the letters from missionaries reflected the financial difficulties they were facing on the field. Two young men from the Persian Pentecostal church in Chicago faced considerable hardship and persecution during the eighteen months they iterated in their homeland, and had to return to the USA through lack of financial support.[60] Another report on what was now called "the missionary problem" was published of missionaries living on one meal a day of "wild sago, boiled in water without salt and eaten without milk and sugar."[61] Mrs. D. L. McCarty, in Uttar Pradesh in India, wrote of the single women missionaries who did not want to join her because she had "no comforts, no proper building to live in." She lived in a "good mud house, but the ceilings are not high," and she ate "only native vegetables," but she said, "I get along well." She also wrote that she expected to stay in that village location "till Jesus comes."[62] J. M. L. Harrow placed the cause of death of two of his team in Liberia on the "lack of nourishing food."[63]

Calls for a more effective form of missionary organization began to be made.[64] By 1913 several periodicals were taking up the cause of the missionaries' financial hardships. Elisabeth Sexton published discussions relating to the appalling situation and lack of good financial management of funds sent to missionaries. Meanwhile, in the USA (unlike in Britain) there was resistance to the setting up of any organization for united missionary effort, doctrinal disputes had exacerbated the problem and

---

59. *Latter Rain Evangel* 5:4 (Jan 1913) 18–19.
60. *Latter Rain Evangel* 5:11 (Aug 1913) 4.
61. *Latter Rain Evangel* 5:12 (Sept 1913) 13.
62. *Latter Rain Evangel* 5:10 (July 1913) 22–23.
63. *Bridegroom's Messenger* 134 (June 1, 1913) 3.
64. *Latter Rain Evangel* 5:8 (May 1913) 24.

large financing of building projects in mission fields was missing.[65] In 1918 Blanche Appleby spoke at the AG's Missionary Conference giving graphic details of the Pentecostal missionaries' difficult and unsanitary living conditions in South China, where not only were their homes small and crowded but there was a lack of privacy, adequate sanitation, and healthy food.[66] These early Pentecostal missionaries were certainly finding their situation tough and some were getting bolder in letting their needs be known. The meeting forming the AG in April 1914 stated that one of the reasons for the organization was to better understand the needs of the mission field and see that missionaries were given fair treatment in support.[67] The war years did not improve the situation, even though the USA was not directly involved in the war until 1917. In 1916 American missionaries all over the world were feeling the pinch, one writing from Liberia that "the means for carrying on the work is the least we have known since the beginning." Yet on the same page the leader of this mission, Harrow, was appealing for more missionaries to join him.[68] Many missionaries had to return home for want of support for basic essentials. The AG reported that monthly income for missionaries in 1916 was one-third what it was two years earlier and published a special issue on missions in the hope of bolstering financial support. This was indeed a crisis, as there were "missionaries who are on the field suffering for the need of actual bread and butter." They were unable to return home because there was "no money to travel" and unable to continue on the field because there was "nothing to live on." There was "only one thing to do" and that was "to starve and die, unless the Pentecostal people awake out of their lethargy, renew their consecration and bend their energies anew to come up to the help of the Lord for these worthy missionaries."[69] The choice could not have been starker. Pentecostal missions were in crisis. The initial enthusiasm for getting missionaries out to the nations was waning seriously. In fact, the numbers of Pentecostal missionaries was increasing, but the supply of finances was not keeping up with the need, and prices were escalating.

65. *Bridegroom's Messenger* 131 (April 15, 1913) 2; 134 (June 1, 1913) 3.
66. *Latter Rain Evangel* 10:9 (June 1918) 19–23.
67. *Word & Witness* 9:12 (Dec 1913) 1.
68. *Weekly Evangel* 143 (June 10, 1916) 12.
69. *Weekly Evangel* 144 (June 17, 1916) 2.

By September 1917, when the AG held a missionary conference, important questions were being asked about the practice of Pentecostal missionaries going in the power of the Spirit without adequate training. Elisabeth Sisson, a former missionary and one of the most respected and experienced Pentecostal speakers and writers, addressed the issues in an article published in *The Weekly Evangel*. She wrote of "much criticism" that the early Pentecostal missionaries had received because of alleged wasted money and lives of "rash running into pioneer fields of novices in missionary operations." They had not stopped to learn the lessons from the past—and if they had, they would have avoided many disasters. But God had "poured out His Spirit so mightily and so suddenly" and this had been accompanied by "such a missionary uprising among those of lowliest walks of life"—while at home so few had understood "the missionary pull and its responsibilities." The failures of the missionaries had arisen because they had not received adequate prayer, sympathy, and financial support from their home base. Through the neglect of the Pentecostals at home, she charged, they had "really murdered many of our most precious missionary pioneers."[70]

Early Pentecostal missionaries were bombarded with challenges arising from the fact that they were often people without any experience, training, or adequate support going to distant lands simply because the Spirit had told them to. There were many drop-outs, deaths, and pitiful stories as a result. Of course, there were also success stories of people who had accomplished much in a short time and some who persevered for many years. Still, these were yet early days, and the Pentecostal missionary movement was barely a decade old. The many divisions that followed these early days ensured that Pentecostalism would become one of the most diverse and diffuse movements in the entire history of Christianity and perhaps, not so paradoxically, it became the fastest expanding Christian movement of all time.

---

70. *Weekly Evangel* 209 (6 Oct 1917) 2–3.

BIBLIOGRAPHY

Anderson, Allan. *Spreading Fires: The Missionary Nature of Early Pentecostalism.* Maryknoll, NY: Orbis, 2007.
Faupel, D. William. *The Everlasting Gospel: The Significance of Eschatology in the Development of Pentecostal Thought.* Sheffield: Sheffield Academic, 1996.
Law, E. May. *Pentecostal Mission Work in South China: An Appeal for Missions.* Falcon, NC: Falcon, 1915.
McGee, Gary B. "Pentecostals and their Various Strategies for Global Mission: A Historical Assessment." In *Called and Empowered: Global Mission in Pentecostal Perspective,* edited by M. A. Dempster, Byron D. Klaus, and Douglas Petersen, 203–24. Peabody, MA: Hendrickson, 1991.
Overy, Richard, ed. *The Times History of the World.* 2nd ed. London: Times Books, 1999.
Robeck, Cecil M. Jr. *The Azusa Street Mission and Revival: The Birth of the Global Pentecostal Movement.* Nashville: Nelson, 2006.
———. "Pentecostal Origins in Global Perspective." In *All Together in One Place: Theological Papers from the Brighton Conference on World Evangelization,* edited by H. D. Hunter and Peter D. Hocken, 166–80. Sheffield: Sheffield Academic, 1993.
Said, Edward W. *Culture and Imperialism.* London: Vintage, 1994.
Saayman, Willem A. "Some Reflections on the Development of the Pentecostal Mission Model in South Africa." *Missionalia* 21 (1993) 40–56.
Wacker, Grant. "Are the Golden Oldies Still Worth Playing? Reflections on History Writing among Early Pentecostals." *Pneuma* 8 (1986) 81–100.
———. *Heaven Below: Early Pentecostals and American Culture.* Cambridge, MA: Harvard University Press, 2001.

Early Pentecostal Periodicals Cited

Apostolic Faith (1906–1907)
Apostolic Light (1907)
Bridegroom's Messenger (1908–1913)
Confidence (1908–1914)
Flames of Fire (1913)
Latter Rain Evangel (1910–1918)
Mukti Prayer Bell (1907)
Pentecost (1908–1909)
Pentecostal Truths (1908–1917)
Triumphs of Faith (1886)
Trust (1913–1918)
Upper Room (1910–1911)
Weekly Evangel (1916–1917)
Word & Witness (1913)
Word & Work (1900–1911)

2

The Fruits of Pentecostal Globalization
Current Trends and Challenges

Allan Anderson

GLOBALIZATION AND DEFINING PENTECOSTALISM

Pentecostalism has come a long way since the heady days of its beginnings. One of the challenges facing us today is how to define the terms "Pentecostal" or "Pentecostalism." I want to start by considering how it is that we do our research, and use some personal illustrations in doing so. Simple definitions will not do justice to a bewildering plethora of movements scattered throughout the world. Nevertheless, they can be described as having "family resemblance."[1] Wittgenstein argued that family resemblance does not mean that there is something that all have in common, but that all have certain similarities and relations with each other. Describing or defining something must allow for "blurred edges," so an imprecise definition can still be meaningful.[2] Defining Pentecostalism may be considered in this way. There are Pentecostal churches meeting in living rooms, classrooms and rudimentarily constructed shelters as well as in enormous buildings. There are churches among all classes and ethnic categories, Western or Northern churches, Eastern and Southern churches, and urban and rural churches. All these

---

1. In this paper, "Pentecostal," "charismatic," and "neocharismatic" will be used as both nouns and adjectives.

2. Wittgenstein, *Philosophical Investigations*, 66, 71.

churches show a variety of theological positions from fundamentalist to liberal; and there are churches that combine several of these types and positions.

Pentecostalism today is both fundamentally and dominantly a global phenomenon. Its significant growth in North America occurs among Hispanics, Asians, Africans, and other minorities. More than three-quarters of its members in the world today are not "white," and this proportion continues to increase. In recent years, Pentecostalism has expanded most remarkably in sub-Saharan Africa, the Asian Pacific rim, and especially Latin America. Many, if not most, of the rapidly growing Christian churches in the majority world are Pentecostal in nature and operate independently of Western Pentecostalism.[3] Within less than a century, Pentecostal and charismatic Christianity in all its diversity has expanded into almost every country on earth. Today it has become extremely significant both inside and outside the older "historic" churches, and is probably the fastest growing religious movement(s) of the twenty-first century.

Theologian David Bosch has borrowed the term "paradigm" from Thomas Kuhn's natural scientific theory to describe the series of "paradigm shifts" Christianity has undergone during its history. These paradigm shifts happen when eventually most people in a field of study realize that a generally accepted theory is no longer tenable and replace or augment it with a new theory. Studies of world Christianity have gone through such drastic changes.[4] We now operate in a very different global context where Western powers are no longer seen as congenial benefactors, but often as aggressors and intruders. Racism, sexism, and patriarchalism are no longer tolerated by those embracing this paradigm. Environmental woes and globalization have made the planet vulnerable but united in common concerns. Freedom of religion is regarded as a right in many countries, and this has sometimes led on the one hand to doubts about whether evangelism and/or proselytism are valid activities, and on the other, has served to stimulate such activities. This new paradigm shift has profoundly affected the approach to the academic study of Christianity as a whole as well as changing the definitions we use, and the study of Pentecostalism is no exception. Academics also

---

3. The term "majority world" is adapted from the *New Internationalist* and refers to the continents of Asia, Africa, South America, the Pacific islands, and the Caribbean.

4. Bosch, *Transforming Mission*, 1–11.

operate under different paradigms that profoundly affect the way they study and define Pentecostalism.[5] Part of our new task in the twenty-first century is to reflect on the role of the majority world in the transformation of Christianity, or what Andrew Walls has called "the change in Christianity's centre of gravity."[6]

Researchers of Pentecostalism must acknowledge their own personal paradigms, presuppositions, and predilections that influence *what* they study and write about, and *how* they do it. In all academic writing, authors have their own agendas and influences that determine the nature of their work. For example, my own academic view has been influenced by two decades of activism in Southern African Pentecostalism and my reading of such paradigm-shifting texts as those of Walter Hollenweger.[7] I am an insider, having spent most of my adult life in Pentecostal and charismatic churches, being indoctrinated in the 1970s into a particular form of Pentecostal theology and having spent twenty-three years as a Pentecostal minister. I have had what my theological background might describe as experiences of God through the Spirit; I sometimes pray in tongues and share the confessional stance of Pentecostals. It is also true that the more one studies and reflects on these movements, the more one discovers the dark and seamier side of Pentecostalism. Yet while I become more critical, this does not prevent me from appreciating strengths, sharing a worldview, and admitting that these influence my analyses. Mine could be described as an "insider" paradigm that makes my academic and theologically-founded reflection quite different from those "outsider" paradigms that might not admit to the influence of divine agency. This means that I sometimes have to refer to testimonies and accounts of healing and miracles at face value, as they were narrated. Because of my personal experiences, the boundaries between truth, confession, and science are blurred. A researcher must in any case take others' experiences as they are reported and offer an interpretation.

The paradigms we use to do research fundamentally change what and how we write, and how we make our definitions. Most so-called "Pentecostal theology" has been written by American insiders and emerges from a paradigm serving a particular interest group, often with denominational pressures, and intent to preserve a "pure" Pentecostal

5. Droogers, "Essentialist and Normative Approaches."
6. Walls, *Missionary Movement*, 145.
7. Hollenweger, *Pentecostals* and *Pentecostalism*.

theology. Although "etic" observers sometimes make use of these studies, their scholarly orientation is completely different. The emic/etic distinction is basic to understanding this discussion.[8] I think that "Pentecostalism" is best understood broadly to include both its historical and social connections and its theological focus on the Holy Spirit. This broad sweep includes "charismatic" churches that are part of older denominations and independent ones that have arisen in recent years. Seen from this perspective, Pentecostalism is not a movement with a distinct beginning, nor a movement based on a particular theology—it is rather a series of movements that took several years and different formative ideas and events to emerge.[9] I demonstrated in the former essay, "The Roots of Pentecostal Globalization," that at the beginning of the twentieth century, what became known as "Pentecostalism" was in a process of formation, and did not become a distinct form of Christianity until at least a decade after the start of the revival and missionary movements out of which it emerged. Pentecostalism then (as now) was a polynucleated and variegated phenomenon, best seen from its pneumatological center as related movements, where the emphasis was on the experience of the Spirit and the exercise of spiritual gifts.[10]

Developments in the late twentieth century amounted to a veritable revolution within Christianity that has precipitated a resurgent interest in pneumatology and spirituality. Whereas older Protestant churches in the North bemoan their ever-decreasing membership in the early twenty-first century and possible demise in the West, a most dramatic church growth has continued to take place in the South, especially as a result of Pentecostalism. To give some examples: during the 1990s, it was estimated that the majority world mission movement had grown at seventeen times the rate of Western missions. Countries like South Korea, Nigeria, Brazil, and India have become major Christian missionary sending nations, many of whose missionaries are Pentecostal.[11] Over half the world's Christians today live in developing and poor countries, where forms of Christianity are very different from those found in Europe and North America. These Christians have been profoundly affected by sev-

---

8. See further discussion in Anderson, "Varieties, Taxonomies and Definitions."

9. Anderson, *Spreading Fires*, 4, 291.

10. Anderson, *Vision of the Disinherited*, 152.

11. Jaffarian, "Are There More Non-Western Missionaries than Western Missionaries?" 132.

eral factors, including the desire to have a more contextual and culturally relevant form of Christianity, the rise of nationalism, a reaction to what are perceived as "colonial" and foreign forms of Christianity, and the burgeoning Pentecostal and charismatic renewal. These factors play a major role in the formation of independent churches throughout the world, but especially in the global South.

Like many other religious movements in the 1990s, Pentecostalism was affected by the sudden fall of the Iron Curtain in Central and Eastern Europe, as will be demonstrated in this paper. But it is more difficult to establish the influence of the dramatic events of 1989–1991 on the growth of Pentecostalism in the South in the last decade of the twentieth century, except in an indirect way. Its accelerating growth was already set in motion in the 1970s and has continued unabated ever since. Undoubtedly, the forces of globalization and the movement towards a "universal culture" were at work in this shift in religious demographics.[12]

Pentecostalism was also fast becoming an alternative meta-culture within an even larger global culture in an increasingly polarised world, and offered membership in a global religious community that was more accessible than the culture requiring the elusive wealth of the West. When the "Cold War" ended, the competition between the USA and the Soviet Union that had brought large amounts of money and benefits to prop up governments favorable to one or the other in the southern continents ceased. This meant that poverty accelerated, and nations and peoples were looking for alternative sources of highly valued international connections. This was particularly the case in Africa, where entrepreneurial religious leaders found that religion was a way to attain an affluent lifestyle—here, Pentecostalism's potentially anarchistic ecclesiastical structures offered freedom to run an independent church like a large and highly successful corporation. The easiest international connections to obtain were religious ones, and the most successful preachers were those who could demonstrate and establish such links. Pentecostalism with its transnational and polynucleated networks and ability to recreate itself in any cultural context was poised in the 1990s to provide these global connections.

---

12. Ryan, "Growth of a Global Culture," 64.

A GLOBAL TOUR

According to the much-quoted but hugely speculative figures of Barrett et al., there were 68 million "Pentecostals/Charismatics/Neocharismatics" in the world in 1970. By 2000 this figure had risen exponentially to 505 million, and in just eight years (by 2008) another 100 million were added to total an estimated 601 million. This figure is projected to rise to almost 800 million by 2025.[13] I quote these figures to indicate the probability that Pentecostalism and its associated movements has continued to grow at a rate that accelerated dramatically in the last quarter of the twentieth century. In all its variety as an alternative, enthusiastic, and non-traditional form of Christianity, this was undeniably the fastest growing religious movement in the twentieth century and probably of all time. Much depends, however, on what is included in these statistics. The half-billion plus figures are considerably inflated by including such large movements as African and Chinese independent churches and Catholic Charismatics. But even if these figures are inaccurate and over-inflated, no one who has visited megachurches in the global South or in North America can deny the significance of Pentecostalism in the twenty-first century's religious landscape and the large crowds of people who attend its many churches. Considering that this movement had a miniscule number of adherents at the beginning of the twentieth century, it has been an astonishing event. The many varieties of Pentecostalism have contributed to the transformation of the nature of global religion itself and its adherents are often on the cutting edge of the encounter with people of other faiths and often so in a confrontational way. The future of Christianity and the nature of global religion are affected by this seismic change in the character of the global Christian faith at the close of the twentieth century.

After the 1970s, large independent Pentecostal communities sprang up in many parts of the world, often forming international networks and loose associations, which have occasionally been organized into new denominations. As indicated previously, in the South they are often the fastest growing movements and churches within Christianity, appealing especially to the younger and better-educated urban population, and some of these churches promote a "prosperity gospel," which can at times reproduce the worst forms of consumer capitalism in Christian guise.

---

13. Barrett, Johnson, and Crossing, "Missiometrics 2008," 30.

Some have suggested that this is a form of "Americanization,"[14] but there is also the danger of generalizing and failing to appreciate reconstructions and innovations made by Pentecostals in adapting to a very different social context. Many of the rapidly growing Christian churches in the majority world are Pentecostal and operate independently of Western Pentecostalism. In the last fifteen years of the twentieth century, when the eyes of the world were focused on the dramatic events in the former Soviet Union and Warsaw Pact countries, Pentecostalism was expanding most remarkably in other parts of the world. In Latin America, the astounding growth caused David Stoll to ask whether the continent was turning Protestant.[15] In some Latin countries Pentecostalism today challenges Catholicism as the largest Christian community. It is thought that more Pentecostals attend church on any given Sunday in Latin American cities like Sao Paulo, Brazil than attend mass in Catholic churches. In Brazil, Chile, Guatemala, and Nicaragua, Pentecostals far outnumber all other Protestants, and in Guatemala may soon be the majority of the population.[16] Pentecostals have also grown rapidly in the Caribbean, particularly in Jamaica, Puerto Rico, and Haiti.[17]

On the African continent, Pentecostalism is now one of the most prominent forms of Christianity, especially in West Africa. This has also profoundly affected older mission churches that have become "pentecostalized" as a result. One of the most dramatic examples of the new Pentecostalism is to be found in Nigeria. In the south-west, on the road between Lagos and Ibadan, is the sprawling headquarters of the Redeemed Christian Church of God, called "Redemption Ground," where vast crowds of over a million attend the monthly "Holy Ghost night" presided over by their leader Enoch A. Adeboye. One of the largest enclosed church buildings in the world, seating 50,000 persons, is found at another impressive campus outside Lagos called "Canaan Land," headquarters of Living Faith World Outreach, founded by David Oyedepo, also known as "Winner's Chapel." A Christian university and private school offering tuition for all ages adorn this multifaceted complex that unashamedly espouses a prosperity gospel. From West Africa the new Pentecostalism spread rapidly eastwards and southwards throughout

14. Brouwer, Gifford, and Rose, *Exporting the American Gospel*.
15. Stoll, *Is Latin America Turning Protestant?*
16. Cox, *Fire from Heaven*, 168.
17. Martin, *Tongues of Fire*, 51.

Africa's cities in the 1990s. Holding services that are usually emotional, enthusiastic, and loud (especially as most make use of electronic musical instruments even in poorer, rural areas), this has become a major expression of Christianity in Africa, emerging all over the continent.

In parts of Asia the developments have been similar. Pentecostalism continues to expand remarkably in India, South-East Asia, and East Asia. In India, vigorous missionary and church planting activities, sometimes in the face of severe persecution, characterize Pentecostal churches, especially in South India. In 2007 I attended a graduation service of a seminary in Kottayam, Kerala, of the Indian Pentecostal Church of God, the largest independent Pentecostal denomination in India, where most of some seventy graduates were being commissioned to go to North India as missionaries. I was told that this was common practice in the several South Indian Pentecostal seminaries. Some of the largest crowds in Indian Christianity have attended meetings of the healing evangelist D. G. S. Dhinakaran (1935–2008) from Tamil Nadu, the best known and most influential charismatic evangelist there. Dhinakaran remained a member of the Church of South India and his "Jesus Calls Ministry," now led by his son Paul, conducts extensive healing campaigns all over India. Like the Oral Roberts University in Tulsa, Oklahoma, it has a sprawling headquarters campus in Tamil Nadu with a prayer tower and university.[18]

Remarkable things are occurring in China, the most populous nation on earth. Chinese Christianity is dominated by a Pentecostal type of spirituality that has followed a different trajectory because of its relative isolation, but this is not unconnected to global events. The 1989 tragedy of Beijing's Tiananmen Square had the unexpected consequence of greater freedom of religion, facilitating the rapid growth of unregistered Pentecostal and Pentecostal-like independent churches. These have an often uneasy relationship with both the Communist Party and the officially-recognised China Christian Council. Chinese Pentecostals have a burden to reach the vast Chinese nation in China itself and throughout the Chinese diaspora. In the "Back to Jerusalem" movement they have elaborate plans to evangelize along the old silk trading route into the heartland of Islam.

The extent of South Korean Pentecostalism is now legendary. The largest local Christian community in the world in the 1970s and 1980s

---

18. Bergunder, "Ministry of Compassion," 160–61.

was a Pentecostal one: the Yoido Full Gospel Church in Seoul founded by David Yonggi Cho. There are now several charismatic churches in this city with memberships exceeding 10,000. In Singapore, the independent City Harvest Church is the largest church in that city, appealing especially to the city's youth. Opulent buildings like these Asian examples, holding thousands of worshippers, reflect the emerging Pentecostal middle class in some regions, or at least house those aspiring to be so. However, Pentecostals globally are still predominantly grassroots movements appealing initially to the disadvantaged and underprivileged, whose desire for upward social mobility is nurtured and sometimes realized by Pentecostalism's support of an alcohol-free, thrifty, and industrious lifestyle. Pentecostalism has become the preference of the poor in places like Latin America, where liberation theology has declared God's preference *for* the poor.

PENTECOSTALISM IN EUROPE

In contrast to the other continents, Europe has a Pentecostal movement that is quite small and only a few countries have significant Pentecostal populations. According to one statistic, only four (in descending order: Ukraine, Britain, Romania, and Russia) had Pentecostal populations of more than 400,000 in 2000, and three of these were in Eastern Europe.[19] These figures, however, were estimates of numbers of so-called "classical" Pentecostals with origins at the beginning of the twentieth century, and did not include "charismatics" in older churches or the several new churches that began in the 1990s, now a significant part of Christianity in some European states. David Martin takes issue with the common secularization theories in explaining the "exceptionalism" of Europe, and suggests that there are other equally important factors contributing to the low numbers. Pentecostalism is less likely to succeed in the developed world because it "represents the mobilization of a minority of people at the varied margins of that world, whereas in the developing world it represents the mobilization of large masses." The USA is the obvious exception to this, but Pentecostalism flourishes there because of that country's well-established Protestant pluralism and voluntarism. He suggests further that in Europe, Pentecostalism does not do as well

---

19. Johnstone and Mandryk, *Operation World*.

where there is a strong state church, unless there has been a significant minority of "free churches," as is the case in Romania and Ukraine.[20]

Pentecostalism in Europe differs from the North American movement in several important aspects. Although it also had its roots in the radical evangelical missionary and pietistic holiness movements of the nineteenth century, it did not have the pluralistic milieu that characterized American Christianity. There were stronger formative influences coming from the Keswick movement in England and its more Reformed position, from Pietism in the state churches in northern Europe, and from revival movements at the beginning of the twentieth century. There was also greater resistance on the part of state churches to new forms of Christianity, at least until the 1980s, and in some countries this prejudice has been hard to shake off. Only with the proliferation of the so-called "migrant" Pentecostal churches in Europe has there arisen a new interest. Classical Pentecostalism has been relatively more successful in Eastern Europe, where it grew, especially after the Second World War, in the face of severe restrictions and persecution from Communist regimes.

During the Soviet years, most Pentecostals were forced to merge with evangelicals and Baptists in state-controlled structures, and those that failed to cooperate were seen as "anti-revolutionary" and severely punished, often imprisoned and exiled to Siberian work camps. In the Baltic states and Russia, Pentecostal influence first came from missionaries from neighboring Scandinavia, from the Englishwoman Eleanor Patrick, and from the Latvian William Fetler (1883–1957), under whose ministry there was a significant charismatic movement among Latvian Baptists. Pentecostals in the Baltics, like those in other parts of the former Soviet Union, are now divided between those independent churches with links to Western Pentecostal denominations, neopentecostals, and "eastern Pentecostals" mainly founded by Russians and Ukrainians and resistant to any influence from the West.[21]

There are over 300,000 Pentecostals in Romania. The Pentecostal Apostolic Church of God is the largest denomination, founded in 1922 by George Bradin and later (1929 and 1950) uniting with other groups, the last occasion at the behest of the Communist government. This was largely a rural phenomenon until the 1950s, when it began to spread to urban areas, and it now has flourishing city churches. A "fraternal

---

20. Martin, *Pentecostalism*, 67–70.
21. Teraudkalns, "Pentecostalism in the Baltics," 91–108.

agreement" with the Church of God (Cleveland) was negotiated in 1980, and since 1996 the church has been known as the Pentecostal Union. In the immediate aftermath of the revolution in December 1989, in which the Communist dictator Ceausescu was executed, evangelicals and Pentecostals were given permission to hold public evangelistic rallies in several Romanian cities, which thousands attended, and many conversions were reported. Clearly, there was a new religious freedom unprecedented in the previous four decades.[22]

The highest number of Pentecostals in any European nation, an estimated 780,000 in 2000, was in Ukraine, where the Evangelical Pentecostal Union is probably the largest Pentecostal denomination in Europe, with some 370,000 members in 2000. The great majority of the Ukrainian and Russian churches are fiercely independent, have a conservative dress code and morality, and eschew formal links with the West.[23]

One cannot speak of Pentecostalism in the Ukraine without reference to the remarkable story of the Nigerian pastor Sunday Adelaja. He is the leader of a congregation in Kiev numbering twenty thousand members called "The Embassy of the Blessed Kingdom of God for all Nations." It was founded in 1994 and is possibly the largest single congregation in Europe. Adelaja first went to the Belarus State University in Minsk in 1986 on a scholarship to study journalism, and did not return to Nigeria because of the instability in that country at the time. He relocated to the Ukraine in 1993 and started the church a year later. He preaches in Russian and has Ukrainian assistants, the vast congregation is nearly all Ukrainian and his organization actively plants churches all over Eastern Europe.[24]

Russia was a vast mission field for early Pentecostals. By 1927, when the first Pentecostal Congress for the Soviet Union took place and Ivan Voronaev was appointed president of the Union of Christians of Evangelical Faith, there were an estimated 80,000 Pentecostal members enjoying the favor of the Communist state that had liberated them from Orthodox persecution. But after the passing of the anti-religious laws

---

22. Johnstone and Mandryk, *Operation World*, 536; Ceuta, "Pentecostal Apostolic Church of God in Romania," 74–87; and Pandrea, "Historical and Theological Analysis of the Pentecostal Church in Romania," 109–35.

23. Hollenweger, *Pentecostals*, 267–69, 274, 281; Durasoff, *Bright Wind of the Spirit*, 227; and Johnstone and Mandryk, *Operation World*, 540, 644.

24. Adelaja, "Go to a Land That I Will Show You!" 14, 37–55; and Asamoah-Gyadu, "African Pentecostal on Mission in Eastern Europe," 297–321.

in 1929–1930, Voronaev and eight hundred pastors were arrested and sent to Siberian concentration camps. Soon after his release in 1935, Voronaev disappeared and was later presumed dead. The Pentecostal churches continued to grow in the face of persecution. In 1944 they united with the Baptists to form the All Union Council of Evangelical Christians and Baptists, which joined the World Council of Churches in 1961. Tensions within this union over the forbidding of tongues in public worship resulted in a large number of Pentecostals setting up their own organization, the Christians of the Evangelical Faith (Pentecostal), which unsuccessfully approached Soviet leaders Kruschev (in 1957) and Brezhnev (in 1965) for religious freedom. The recognition was finally accomplished in 1991 under Mikhail Gorbachev's *glasnost* policies at the very end of the Soviet Union. By 2000 this Russian Pentecostal group had more than 100,000 members. Another Pentecostal association of churches in Russia of equal size refused to register for government recognition. Its leader, Bishop Ivan Fedotov was imprisoned for nineteen years during the Soviet regime. These churches continued to expand and by 2000 there were some 400,000 Russian Pentecostals.[25]

The Apostolic Church in Hungary is part of the Evangelical Pentecostal Fellowship. Here, since the fall of Communism in 1989, the Faith Church led by Sàndor Nèmeth has arisen, growing to some 10,000 members in Budapest in less than twenty years, with branches in other Hungarian cities. Some of the new churches like this one, emerging since the collapse of Communism, have succeeded in attracting large crowds to their services and number their membership in the thousands. One of the reasons for the relative success of these new charismatic groups is their openness to the forces of globalization; this is in sharp contrast with the tendency towards self-isolation and puritanical dress codes that still characterize many of the Eastern European older Pentecostal groups after many years of repression. The Latvian scholar Teraudkalns observes:

> Most Classical Pentecostals still live and worship in the context of painful memories of being ridiculed and persecuted. It has left a lasting impact on the ways in which people tend to act. Marginalization by force, in some cases, has turned into the pro-

---

25. Anderson, *Introduction to Pentecostalism*, 98–102.

> cess of marginalizing by choice ... However, there are positive signs of change.[26]

Although there has been more freedom for Pentecostals in Central and Eastern Europe since the disintegration of Communism, this has also presented challenges. Pentecostal expansion in the 1990s has met with stiff opposition. There, the role of resistance to Pentecostalism that characterized the Communist era has been taken up by both the newly emerging secular governments and especially by the dominant Orthodox Christianity. The latter has struggled to re-establish its hegemony in newly emerging secular democracies—and in some cases, like that of the post-Communist Russian Orthodox Church, has been quite effective. The flip side is that new Pentecostal and charismatic groups from the West on a quest for mission have entered former Communist countries with aggressive evangelistic techniques provoking opposition from Orthodox churches and national governments. The institutionalizing of those Pentecostal denominations that had been forced to share their identity with evangelicals and Baptists and the creation and expansion of Pentecostal theological colleges has resulted in a more inward-looking Pentecostal movement in some former Communist countries. The Pentecostal churches in these countries are in danger of becoming dependent on Americans for theological education, although there are also signs of resistance to any such dependency. The situation is still in a state of flux, and the next few years will determine the direction that Pentecostal Christianity will take in Eastern Europe. Most of Pentecostalism there, however, is largely independent of expatriate missionaries, and the future of European Pentecostalism still looks promising. It may be that renewal stimulated by Pentecostal and charismatic forms of Christianity will help rescue the church from pending oblivion in this so-called "post-Christian" continent.

TRENDS AND CHALLENGES IN THE GLOBALIZATION OF PENTECOSTALISM

Finally, to avoid the impression of reductionism in considering the reasons for the changes in global Christianity that have occurred in the late twentieth century, some of the characteristics of Pentecostalism that have made it attractive in global communities are outlined. Although

---

26. Teraudkalns, "Pentecostalism in the Baltics," 107.

socio-political and historical factors undoubtedly had a role in the spread of Pentecostal Christianity in the 1990s, the religious factors were probably even more significant. The ability of Pentecostalism to adapt to and fulfill religious aspirations continues to be its main strength. A belief in a divine encounter and the involvement or breaking through of the sacred into the mundane, including healing from sickness, deliverance from hostile evil forces, and perhaps above all, a heady and spontaneous spirituality that refuses to separate "spiritual" from "physical" or "sacred" from "secular," are all important factors in Pentecostalism's growth. There are undoubtedly other factors, but these five are given as preliminary suggestions.

Infectious Enthusiasm

For Pentecostal Christians, Christian worship is a joyful experience to be entered into with the whole person. This free, exuberant Christianity is attractive not merely because it is a cultural trait of Africans or Latin Americans to be enthusiastic, rhythmic, and noisy. (One has only to be at a European football match to see that Europeans can have the same enthusiasm.) A new emphasis on the role of the Spirit in the worship, work, and witness of the church is one of the main reasons for this enthusiasm. The experience of the Spirit's presence is seen as a normal part of daily life and is brought to bear upon all situations. God's salvation is seen in different manifestations of God's abiding presence through the Spirit, divine revelations that assure us that "God is there" to help in every area of need. As Ghanaian theologian Asamoah-Gyadu puts it, referring to African Pentecostalism:

> One of the major contributions of African Christians, particularly Pentecostals and charismatics, to Western Christianity is the attention it [sic] draws to the fact that Christianity is about experience and that the power of God is able to transform circumstances that Western rationalist theologies will consider the preserve of psychology and scientific development.[27]

These holistic, ecstatic, and experiential religious practices are found throughout the world today. The boisterous antiphonal singing, simultaneous and spontaneous prayer, and rhythmic dance are found throughout global Pentecostalism, emphasizing the freedom, equality,

---

27. Asamoah-Gyadu, "Reversing Christian Mission," 4.

community, and dignity of each person in the sight of God. The experience of the power of the Spirit is for Pentecostals a unifying factor in a global society still deeply divided, and can be the catalyst for the emergence of a new society where there is justice for all and hope for a desperately violent world.

Positive Attitude to Mission

With their enthusiasm, Pentecostals have a positive attitude to their mission. From its beginning, Pentecostalism has been a highly migratory, missionary movement.[28] Many Pentecostals are unencumbered by out-of-date ecclesiastical structures and hierarchies. With a sense of divine call to do something important for God, they place primary emphasis on being "sent by the Spirit" and depend more on what is described as the Spirit's leading than on formal structures. People "called by God" are engaging in mission in other countries because they believe that the Spirit has directed them to do so, often through some spiritual revelation like a prophecy, a dream, or a vision, or even through an audible voice perceived to be that of God. The result is that Pentecostals approach their ministry and involvement in the church with abandoned commitment, often with self-sacrifice, enduring hardship in order to see their divine vision realized. Not all have the success they dream of, but their dedication to the mission of the church is exemplary. The existence of vibrant African Pentecostal churches in Europe since the 1990s implicitly urges European Christians to seriously reconsider the effectiveness, content, and relevancy of the church's mission. In the processes of its vigorous expansion, Pentecostalism as a whole sees the "world" as the space to move into and "possess" for Christ. Transnationalism and migration do not affect the essential character of migrant Pentecostals, even though they may have to steer a precarious course between contradictory forms of identity resulting from the migratory experience. Pentecostals make full use of opportunities to proclaim the gospel in word and deed in order to evangelize and minister to what they see as the felt needs of people. This often results in the growth of their churches.

---

28. Anderson, *Spreading Fires*, 65–68.

Leadership Based on Calling

There is a fundamental historical difference between the nature of church leadership in the mission of Pentecostal churches and that of older churches. In Pentecostal practice, the Holy Spirit is given to every believer without preconditions. One of the results of this is that the dichotomy between "clergy" and "laity" does not usually exist.[29] Until comparatively recently, Pentecostals have had no tradition of formal training for "ministers" as a class set apart. Pentecostal leaders are those whose primary qualifications have been a "call of God" and an ability to preach effectively. This is still the case. Many of the most successful Pentecostal churches today are led by leaders with little or no training in theology. A strong emphasis on charismatic leadership is a feature of Pentecostalism today and is accompanied by inevitable problems (especially the emergence of dictatorial leaders), but it results in churches that are often well organized, and where the emphasis is on hearing the "word of God," relevant to the daily needs of the hearers.

Salvation in the "Here and Now"

The phenomenon of growing Pentecostal churches indicates that there are unresolved questions facing the church, such as the role of "success" and "prosperity" in God's economy, enjoying God *and* his gifts, including healing and material provision, and the holistic dimension of "salvation now." Many African Pentecostal migrants to Europe and North America see financial success and prosperity as evidence of the blessing of God and the reward for faith in difficult financial circumstances. However, this "prosperity" is also seen as the means for advancing the work of God and for the ability to give generously to the needy. The "here-and-now" problems being addressed by these churches are problems that still challenge the church as a whole.[30] One Nigerian preacher in the USA put it like this:

> We live in rather difficult times; dreams are constantly being dashed against the rocks of adversity. People desperately need to know that things will get better ... We preach that there is hope for tomorrow beyond yesterday's failure ... We preach that mir-

---

29. Saayman, "Some Reflections on the Development of the Pentecostal Mission Model in South Africa," 43.

30. Anderson, *African Reformation*, 175–86.

acles still happen! God still fixes shattered lives. Often, the only thing that prevents a suicide from taking place is one word of hope or comfort. This message of hope transcends race, culture, class and creed. Everybody needs hope. A church that preaches a message that gives people hope, encouragement and healing will never lack for attendance.[31]

The remarkable global growth of Pentecostalism in the midst of incredible economic, political, and natural adversity and the corresponding decline in membership among older churches means that there might be something that Pentecostals are doing from which other Christians can learn. And conversely, there might be something that the older churches failed to do or did wrongly that has resulted in their decline. Important questions are raised about the relevance of the faith and life of older churches.

The Church as Community

Pentecostal and charismatic churches see themselves as God's people, called out from the world around them with a distinct mission. They have a sense of identity as a separated community whose primary purpose is to promote their cause to those outside. "Church" for them is the most important activity in life, and Christianity is brought to bear upon every situation. The churches of migrant Pentecostals in the Western world for them have practical functions—whether obtaining a permit to remain in the country, receiving employment, dealing with racism and rejection, finding financial help, getting advice regarding marriage and family affairs, or obtaining relief from sickness and other afflictions seen as the attack of Satan. In short, the church is a caring, therapeutic community and at once a refuge from the storms and difficulties of a new life and an advice center for every possible eventuality. Many European churches, influenced by their individualistic and secular society, have largely lost this sense of therapeutic community and belongingness that is so much a central characteristic of Pentecostal Christianity.

CONCLUSION

With its offer of the power of the Spirit to all regardless of education, language, race, class, or gender, Pentecostalism has been a mission move-

---

31. Adefarasin, "Kingdoms of This World," 144.

ment that has subverted the conventions of the time. Unlike older forms of Christian mission, its methods were not so dependent on Western specialists and trained clergy and the transmission of Western forms of Christian liturgy and leadership. The author of *The Secular City*, Harvey Cox, in his 1995 book *Fire from Heaven*, reversed his well-known position on secularization and wrote of Pentecostalism as a manifestation of the "unanticipated reappearance of primal spirituality in our time" that would reshape religion in the twenty-first century.[32] Pentecostalism developed its own characteristics and identities in different parts of the world during the twentieth century without losing its transnational connections and international networks. The growth of churches that provide total environments including international connections for members, widespread use of the mass media, the setting up of new networks that often incorporate the word "international" in their title, and frequent conferences with international speakers that reinforce transnationalism are all features of this multidimensional Pentecostalism, which promotes this global meta-culture constantly. The opening up of what was formerly a closed world to Western forms of Christianity after the fall of the Iron Curtain has rapidly accelerated the expansion of this transnational movement. The extent to which globalization and migration in the late twentieth century have affected the shape of this very significant global religious player is something that requires a much more careful analysis than this paper offers. The shapes of the new Pentecostalisms that have emerged as a result of the globalization process, how they differ from the older networks of denominational Pentecostalism, and specifically what the features of this global shift of center to the South mean for Pentecostalism have yet to be precisely described. Another area that needs further investigation is the extent to which Pentecostalism has permeated and affected the beliefs, values, and practices of other Christians. Only when these investigations have taken place will we be better able to understand those external forces that forge the religious identities of people in our contemporary societies and the increasingly important role of Pentecostalisms in this pluralistic world.

---

32. Cox, *Fire from Heaven*, 83.

BIBLIOGRAPHY

Paul Adefarasin, "The Kingdoms of This World." In *Out of Africa*, edited by C. Peter Wagner and Joseph Thompson, 130–50. Ventura, CA: Regal, 2004.

Adelaja, Sunday. "Go to a Land That I Will Show You!" In *Out of Africa*, edited by C. Peter Wagner and Joseph Thompson, 37–55. Ventura, CA: Regal, 2004.

Anderson, Allan. *African Reformation: African Initiated Christianity in the Twentieth Century*. Trenton, NJ: Africa World, 2001.

———. *An Introduction to Pentecostalism: Global Charismatic Christianity*. Cambridge: Cambridge University Press, 2004.

———. *Spreading Fires: The Missionary Nature of Early Pentecostalism*. London: SCM; Maryknoll, NY: Orbis, 2007.

———. "Varieties, Taxonomies and Definitions." In *Studying Global Pentecostalism: Theories and Methods*, edited by Allan Anderson, Michael Bergunder, André Droogers, and Cornelius van der Laan. Berkeley: University of California Press, forthcoming.

Anderson, Robert Mapes. *Vision of the Disinherited: The Making of American Pentecostalism*. Peabody, MA: Hendrickson, 1979.

Asamoah-Gyadu, J. Kwabena. "An African Pentecostal on Mission in Eastern Europe: The Church of the 'Embassy of God' in the Ukraine." *Pneuma* 2 (2005) 297–321.

———. "Reversing Christian Mission: African Pentecostal Pastor Establishes 'God's Embassy' in the Ukraine." Unpublished paper, May 2004.

Barrett, David B., Todd M. Johnson, and Peter F. Crossing. "Missiometrics 2008: Reality Checks for Christian World Communions." *International Bulletin of Missionary Research* 32, no. 1 (2008) 27–31.

Bergunder, Michael. "'Ministry of Compassion:' D. G. S. Dhinakaran—Christian Healer-Prophet from Tamil Nadu." In *Christianity is Indian: The Emergence of an Indigenous Christianity*, edited by Roger Hedlund, 158–74. Delhi: ISPCK, 2000.

Bosch, David J. *Transforming Mission: Paradigm Shifts in Theology of Mission*. Maryknoll, NY: Orbis, 1991.

Brouwer, Steve, Paul Gifford, and Susan D. Rose. *Exporting the American Gospel: Global Christian Fundamentalism*. New York: Routledge, 1996.

Ceuta, Ioan. "The Pentecostal Apostolic Church of God in Romania." *Journal of the European Pentecostal Theological Association* 13 (1994) 74–87.

Cox, Harvey. *Fire from Heaven: The Rise of Pentecostal Spirituality and the Reshaping of Religion in the Twenty-First Century*. London: Cassel, 1996.

Droogers, André. "Essentialist and Normative Approaches." In *Studying Global Pentecostalism: Theories and Methods*, edited by Allan Anderson, Michael Bergunder, André Droogers, and Cornelius van der Laan. Berkeley: University of California Press, forthcoming.

Durasoff, Steve. *Bright Wind of the Spirit: Pentecostalism Today*. London: Hodder & Stoughton, 1972.

Hollenweger, Walter J. *The Pentecostals*. London: SCM, 1971.

———. *Pentecostalism: Origins and Developments Worldwide*. Peabody, MA: Hendrickson, 1997.

Jaffarian, Michael. "Are There More Non-Western Missionaries than Western Missionaries?" *International Bulletin of Missionary Research* 28:3 (2004) 131–32.

Johnstone, Patrick, and Jason Mandryk. *Operation World: 21st Century Edition*. Carlisle, UK: Paternoster, 2001.

Martin, David. *Pentecostalism: The World Their Parish*. Oxford: Blackwell, 2002.
———. *Tongues of Fire*. Oxford: Blackwell, 1990.
Pandrea, Rodica. "A Historical and Theological Analysis of the Pentecostal Church in Romania." *Journal of the European Pentecostal Theological Association* 21 (2001) 109–35.
Ryan, Alan. "The Growth of a Global Culture." In *The Oxford History of the Twentieth Century*, edited by Michael Howard and William Roger Louis, 63–76. Oxford: Oxford University Press, 1998.
Saayman, Willem A. "Some Reflections on the Development of the Pentecostal Mission Model in South Africa." *Missionalia* 21.1 (1993) 40–56.
Stoll, David. *Is Latin America Turning Protestant?* Los Angeles: University of California Press, 1990.
Teraudkalns, Valdis. "Pentecostalism in the Baltics: Historical Retrospection." *Journal of the European Pentecostal Theological Association* 21 (2001) 91–108.
Walls, Andrew F. *The Missionary Movement in Christian History: Studies in the Transmission of Faith*. Maryknoll, NY: Orbis; Edinburgh: T. & T. Clark, 1996.
Wittgenstein, Ludwig. *Philosophical Investigations*. Oxford: Blackwell, 2001.

3

The Impact of Globalization on Pentecostals in Canada

Michael Wilkinson

In this chapter I will be arguing that globalization offers a very important optic to view significant social and cultural change. Globalization can be defined simply as an awareness of the world as a single place. The view of the world as a single place, however, is not without controversy. For some, it is a world to be embraced with new open borders, free trade, and political freedom. For others it means the loss of culture and diversity. In some cases globalization is interpreted as Americanization or Westernization that must be stopped. The process of globalization includes world-wide transformations of social structures, culture, and social institutions. All religions are adjusting to social change, including Pentecostals in Canada. Worldwide, Pentecostalism is experiencing something of a transformation even as it intends to transform the world.

The transformation for Pentecostals revolves around the changing role of religion in global society, the pluralization of religions and their legitimacy in Canada, and internal debates over what Pentecostals believe, how they practice their faith, and whether it is authentic and authoritative. Specific cases will examine the responses of Canadian Pentecostals to social issues, multiculturalism and new immigrants, organizational change, and theology. For Canadian Pentecostals, an ongoing discussion on the nature of Spirit baptism, cultural diversity, and organization will need to occur. However, the discussion must move beyond the pragmatic response of denominations with policy to a more reflective theologizing on these important issues.

THEORIZING RELIGION AND GLOBAL SOCIETY

There are two important theorists of religion and globalization who help frame my view. Peter Beyer and Roland Robertson have written extensively on the topic and each provides important frames of reference for my analysis. More specifically, Robertson's idea of the universal and the particular helps me to understand the changing nature of Pentecostalism as it is globalized and localized.[1] Beyer's view of religion and global society raises other important issues.[2] In this case his view that globalization has an effect upon religions so that they wrestle with specific questions about what they believe, how they practice their faith, and whether it is authentic or authoritative is instructive. What I present is not the whole of Beyer's view of religion as a differentiated global system. For my purposes here I will only reference those aspects of Robertson and Beyer as they pertain to my objectives.[3]

Roland Robertson's view of globalization is that the world is increasingly interconnected, and throughout the world humans are conscious of this new social and cultural reality. Key to Robertson's theory is that globalization is a long historical process characterized by an increasing awareness of the world as a single place.[4] However, the singularity of the world does not mean cultural homogeneity. Rather, what we see and experience in the world is a certain kind of homogeneity as well as heterogeneity. "Glocalization" is one term that tries to capture this idea of sameness and difference.[5] It also points to the key concepts of universalization and particularization in his theory. More precisely, Robertson speaks of it as the universalization of the particular and the particularization of the universal.

What Robertson is attempting to illustrate is the simultaneity of the global and the local, which he calls "glocal" to highlight the dialogical na-

---

1. Robertson, *Globalization*.

2. Beyer, *Religions in Global Society*.

3. It is more accurately an example of appropriation or disembedding whereby I have found one aspect of his theory helpful for framing the issues surrounding the issue of localizing Pentecostalism. See Giddens, *Consequences of Modernity*, 21–29.

4. Robertson, *Globalization*, 57–60 and Scholte, *Globalization*, 85–120.

5. Robertson, *Globalization*, 173–74.

ture of the two points. The spread of particular social forms around the planet comprises their universalization. However, these universal forms do not simply spread to other local sites. They are also transformed as they are particularized, which in turn distinguishes them from the original. The new particular form thus becomes particularized in other locations or universalized throughout the planet, which continues the process. For Robertson, the global is expressed as local and the local as global. This feature of Robertson's theory is somewhat easy to illustrate with Pentecostalism. The development of Pentecostalism throughout the twentieth century and its global quality must be understood as universal and particular. The kind of Pentecostalism that emerges in the United States has a particular form. Missionaries who carry it throughout the world and share it with new converts discover that it is particularized or localized so that it in turn takes on a local or indigenous context. However, Pentecostalism does not simply stay the same in the local. It is continuously transformed through cultural interaction, social networks, and migration. African Pentecostalism transplanted in North America in the late twentieth century illustrates another moment in history when Pentecostalism returns and is localized and particularized once again. Thus Pentecostalism is best understood in a plural sense as "Pentecostalisms," with ongoing transformation characterizing the globalization process.

The transformation of Pentecostalism, however, should not be viewed without some controversy. At stake are the histories, theologies, and organizations of Pentecostals worldwide. Universalization raises questions about power, authority, and conflict as Pentecostalism is particularized. At the local level there are debates about the nature of beliefs and practices as the various expressions of Pentecostalism worldwide intersect. Global Pentecostalism is not represented by uniformity. Rather, it is characterized by flows of belief and practice that move back and forth across cultures, in and through the churches, and in and out of the lives of its practitioners.[6] It also points to the hybrid quality of Pentecostalism.[7] The sacred *scape* of Pentecostalism highlights what is universal or global about the faith.[8] It also points to controversy and debate about the particular expressions of Pentecostalism.

6. Wilkinson, "Religion and Global Flows."
7. Nederveen Pieterse, *Globalization and Culture*.
8. Arjun Appadurai introduced the idea of "scapes" to discuss global flows of ethnicity, for example, as ethno-scapes. "Scape" is used metaphorically as in landscape. See

Peter Beyer's work focuses on the systematization of religion in global society and the formation of religion as a sub-system.[9] At stake is the formation of the category of religion as well as the construction of the various religions within the category. Furthermore, the religions of the world have to articulate the ways in which they will engage or relate to the other spheres of global society such as economics and governance. Beyer's theory relies substantially on the work of Niklas Luhmann and his view of systems and differentiation, the structure of global society, institutional function, programme, and communication.[10] It is not possible to deal with all of these issues here, so what follows is a focus on what Beyer calls "programme" or what may be understood as the culture of a religion.[11]

For Beyer, one consequence of the globalization of religion is the process whereby each religion in the world has to come to terms with the nature of its beliefs, its relationship to other religions, and the relationship between similar expressions of a faith. In this case, for the purpose of this chapter, it means globalization acts upon Pentecostals in such a way that they must come to terms with orthodoxy, orthopraxy, authenticity, and authority. In other words, what do Pentecostals believe, how will they practice their faith, and who gets to say which expression of Pentecostalism is the correct one? These internal or cultural debates among Pentecostals are especially heightened in a global world where the interaction and engagement of Pentecostals occurs more frequently. It is also apparent with the migration of Pentecostals from one region of the world to another. Additionally, it is evident in the missionizing practices of Pentecostals, who carry their faith from one region to another and discover it cross-fertilizes with other faith expressions in new and unique ways. All of this illustrates the kinds of debates, tensions, and transformations occurring throughout the world and not just among Pentecostals. This global perspective also raises our attention to ways in which Pentecostalism in North America is transforming. There are consequences of globalization for North America and Canada

---

Appadurai, *Modernity at Large*. David Lyon applies the idea to religion and talks about sacred-scapes as characteristic of globalization. See Lyon, *Jesus in Disneyland*.

9. Beyer, *Religions in Global Society*, 62–97.
10. Luhmann, *Differentiation of Society* and *Social Systems*.
11. Beyer, *Religions in Global Society*, 88–90.

specifically that need to be investigated and understood for their own particularities.[12]

DEBATING PENTECOSTALISM

These various debates about the universal and the particular, the global and the local, are evident in some of the most important Pentecostal writers today. While these authors do not write from an explicit globalization framework, their theologizing is illustrative of a globalization process. While there are other important voices in the globalization of Pentecostalism literature, I will limit my observations to three authors and their ideas: Frank Macchia, Amos Yong, and Allan Anderson. Each of these authors illustrates internal debates and the contested nature of Pentecostalism in global society, especially as it relates to a theology of Spirit baptism, pluralism and other religions, and finally questions about organization and Pentecostal-Charismatic Christianity as a global movement.

Frank Macchia's latest work on Spirit baptism is an excellent example of the way in which Pentecostals are re-imagining Pentecostal theology.[13] Specifically, Macchia is concerned with differences among Pentecostals worldwide on the nature of Spirit baptism. Further, he makes great efforts to show how Spirit baptism was and continues to be the defining doctrine of Pentecostalism. However, he recognizes that there are divisions, or a disunity, over this doctrine. Macchia states:

> I want to explore from this broad eschatological framework how Spirit baptism might function as an organizing principle of a Pentecostal theology. It may thus be possible to heal the fractures of Pentecostal theology and contribute to the global Pentecostal conversation about the significance of life in the Spirit for theological reflection. I speak as only one voice for a given context. The use of the word "global" in the subtitle is meant as an invitation for others to converse with me from contexts very different from my own.[14]

Nowhere does Macchia claim there will emerge a universal view of Spirit baptism. In this sense he recognizes multiple views, or the

12. Wilkinson, *Spirit Said Go*, and "What's 'Global' about Global Pentecostalism?" 1–13.
13. Macchia, *Baptized in the Spirit*.
14. Ibid., 17.

particularization of Spirit baptism, to use Robertson's terms. He does argue, however, that Spirit baptism is the central metaphor that unites Pentecostals from a variety of contexts. He also recognizes that Spirit baptism is contentious as a doctrine. What he desires is a conversation to begin so that there may be healing among Pentecostals who have argued over the finer points of Spirit baptism. As a way forward he sees his project as an ecumenical one and not ecclesiological. That is, he does not see his position confined to the debates of a single denomination. It is a global exercise that calls for all Pentecostals worldwide to theologize on this important theme.

Macchia hopes that his work will help Pentecostals move beyond the impasse of competing notions of Spirit baptism, recognizing that there is room in the metaphor to embrace so-called competing views of Spirit baptism as empowerment or initiation. To do so he argues for an eschatological viewpoint of hope and love that ought to move Pentecostals beyond the differences as represented in competing denominations. Spirit baptism, therefore, is defined metaphorically as a central unifying theme for Pentecostal theology. His ecumenical challenge is to bring together the views of Spirit baptism in Paul and Luke so that it functions more broadly than has been defined by Classical Pentecostals,[15] especially if it is to continue as a central theme among Pentecostals. While not stated explicitly, there is an underlying assumption that the central theme of Pentecostalism may be at risk of either losing its distinctiveness or expanding so as to be more inclusive. In either case, the response of denominational leaders and theologians to Macchia's work is still to be assessed. Further, the central theme of Pentecostalism, Spirit baptism, will most likely change or transform as it is contextualized in different places throughout the world. I will return to the implications for Canadian Pentecostals later.

The second challenge of globalization for Pentecostals is best represented in the work of Amos Yong and his assessment of Pentecostal theology in relationship to world religions.[16] This too is an important theme in the globalization literature. As Beyer argues, global society is increasingly characterized by the functional differentiation of social

---

15. See Stronstad, *Charismatic Theology of St. Luke*. Macchia does not disagree with Stronstad's interpretation of Luke and he does refer to it as an excellent example of a work that treats Spirit baptism in the Classical Pentecostal tradition.

16. Yong, *Beyond the Impasse*.

systems like religion. Religion as a subsystem of global society, however, consists of all the world's religions. In spite of the vast differences of the world's religions, and the innovation with new religions appearing, all religions will be shaped by this new global reality. Each religion will have to find its voice as it defines what is distinct about it as a religion. But all religions in global society will be influenced by the systematization of the planet, including a specialized form of communication for religion. Yong recognizes this challenge and through his analysis of Pentecostalism he argues persuasively for a Pentecostal theology that can adequately deal with the contemporary reality of a global society characterized by plurality and competing visions of orthodoxy, orthopraxy, and legitimacy.

The way in which Yong deals with this issue is to show how inter-religious dialogue, for example, is possible with a theology that recognizes the pneumatological role of the Spirit at work in the world. Specifically, Yong does not see plurality and questions of religious legitimization as a threat. Rather, they are opportunities to listen and hear where the Spirit is at work, even in the other faiths of the world. This too is a consequence of a globalized world. Yong is not suggesting that all religions are the same. He holds to a particularized view of Pentecostalism. Yet, there is something universal about religion and especially the role of the Spirit to be active and alive in all people of the world regardless of their faith commitments. For Yong, Pentecostal theology needs to have an ear to hear what the Spirit is saying in the world and through the world's religions.

In some sense Yong offers a "liberal" or ecumenical perspective. However, it is still a "conservative" or traditional perspective as he is not suggesting all religions are the same.[17] Beyer too, in his global view, does not suggest all religions are the same. Only, argues Beyer, is the development of a category or subsystem called religion universal. The category consists of all the different religions in the world. Yong's work has important significance for Canadian Pentecostals who live in a country that recognizes plurality and polyethnicity. It celebrates multiculturalism as an ideological expression of Canadian values. It also enshrines those values in official government policy that promotes and encourages

---

17. See Beyer, *Religion and Globalization*. Beyer makes a distinction between "liberal" and "conservative" responses to social issues in global society. The continuum reflects a range of responses as illustrated by religious responses to issues in other spheres like economics.

cultural diversity. How ought Pentecostals in Canada to respond to a multicultural society? I will return to this point later.

Finally, the work of Allan Anderson and his focus on Pentecostal-Charismatic Christianity moves us past specific denominational histories toward a focus on Pentecostalism as a movement.[18] This too has important implications for how we conceive of Pentecostalism. It raises questions about the organization of Pentecostals as well as the future of organizations. Is it possible that denominations and the organization of Pentecostalism will become less important? If so, what might the future of Pentecostalism look like? Will organizations disappear? Or does Pentecostalism's character change so drastically when organized that something is lost? The early Pentecostal movement in Canada faced many issues over organizing and the Hebdens are an excellent example of those who argued against the organization of Pentecostalism.[19] Can we conceive of Pentecostalism as movement *and* organization?

Anderson does not directly deal with the question of organization and Pentecostalism but his strategy of defining Pentecostalism as a movement is consequential. More specifically, Anderson wants to de-center the notion that Pentecostalism emerges in the USA and spreads throughout the world in some uniform, if not homogeneous, form, so that encounters with Pentecostals who do not look or act like those in the USA are suspect or perhaps even written out of a global history. Anderson goes to great length to argue that non-Western Pentecostals played important leadership roles in the worldwide spread of Pentecostalism. He argues persuasively that these non-Western Pentecostals need to be written into the histories to show diversity and difference, or in the words of Robertson, the particularization of Pentecostalism, including the legitimization of different Pentecostalisms. One effect of defining Pentecostalism as a movement, even if unintended, is the destabilizing of denominations and organizations, especially the Assemblies of God in the USA. Here the universalizing history of this one denomination is challenged. Anderson's work, however, also illustrates another trend in the sociology of religion. It is the movement away from examining religious life organized around denominations towards the local congregation as the central organizing principle or towards the social move-

---

18. Anderson, *Introduction to Pentecostalism*.

19. Miller, "Canadian Azusa," 5–29; and Di Giacomo, "Pentecostal and Charismatic Christianity in Canada," 15–38.

ment character of religion. Will denominations disappear? Not likely. But as an all-encompassing mode of organization, even for Pentecostals in Canada, denominationalism will decline in importance and the scholarship of those who continue to define and investigate Pentecostalism as a movement will have an influence.

IMPLICATIONS FOR PENTECOSTALISM IN CANADA

Did We Change Our Position? Spirit Baptism and Theological Debate

The work of Macchia on Spirit baptism is instructive in several ways. First, it raises questions about the nature of Spirit baptism, including the centrality of Spirit baptism among Pentecostals. Second, it acknowledges a variety of viewpoints and positions on Spirit baptism among Pentecostals throughout the world. Third, it is an open invitation to revisit the doctrine and to ask important questions about it. Finally, it illustrates how internal debates about theology are related to globalization. One effect of the global systematization of religion is internal theologizing about orthodoxy, and in this case, about the central metaphor of Pentecostal belief. Of further interest for sociologists will be the response of Pentecostals to this invitation to theologize, to open up a discussion about Spirit baptism.

For some there will be a willingness to engage Macchia's ideas and to rethink the nature of Spirit baptism. Classical Pentecostals have long held that Spirit baptism follows salvation and is an experience that empowers those baptized to proclaim the good news of the Kingdom of God. The initial evidence doctrine among Classical Pentecostals subscribes to a view that "speaking in tongues" or glossolalia is the first sign (and the most important evidence for some) that one has experienced Spirit baptism. Macchia opens up a window to rethink and review this position. Initial evidence is not the position many Pentecostal and Charismatic Christians hold, including those in the historic mainline churches and the evangelical churches like the Vineyard Fellowship or the Toronto Airport Christian Fellowship.

However, if Classical Pentecostals like those represented in the Pentecostal Assemblies of Canada (PAOC) were to even consider discussing the issue, where would they begin? Is there a forum for discussing the nature of Spirit baptism? Or is the risk too high to suggest the possibility of change? Will their constituency feel betrayed if the position is to be reconsidered? How would the PAOC negotiate theological differences? Is it possible to rethink Spirit baptism in such a way that the doctrine could be expanded to embrace other Pentecostal views? This seems to be what Macchia is suggesting. At the very minimum, he is arguing for a healthy dialogue that holds Spirit baptism as central to Pentecostal belief and practice but one that is expanded to include Pauline notions of initiation, hope, and divine love for ecumenical unity.

Steven Studebaker has also raised questions about Spirit baptism and the focus on tongues, which in his view reduces the role of the Spirit.[20] Studebaker's objective is to move Pentecostal theology forward to a more expansive or inclusive pneumatological view centered upon the Trinity and grace. Following Clark Pinnock, Studebaker argues persuasively for a Pentecostal theology that articulates more fully the role of the Spirit without compartmentalizing or reducing Spirit baptism to tongues. Studebaker conceives of the Spirit as the essence of grace and not merely one of the gifts of grace.

In the 1970s Ronald Kydd wrote "I'm Still There" to articulate the central ideas held by the PAOC on Spirit baptism. One of the reasons for writing the booklet, says Kydd, is "that some students have come to Bible College with significant reservations about our belief that tongues are the initial evidence of the baptism in the Holy Spirit."[21] Kydd engages some of the major criticisms surrounding the doctrine by people like Rodman Williams, George Montague, and Clark Pinnock. However, he does say, "I don't wish to throw up walls between us and those who hold opinions on the questions which differ from ours, but I do want to have another look at the relevant Scriptures."[22] Not since his work has any PAOC venue or publication addressed this important topic. In light of the work of Macchia, Studebaker, and others on Spirit baptism, Canadian Pentecostals like those in the PAOC will need to articulate some kind of response.

The One True Faith or One among Many? Legitimacy and Pluralization

The second point for discussion revolves around Yong's work and his openness to dialogue and engagement with other religions. To do

---

20. Studebaker, "Beyond Tongues," 46–68.
21. Kydd, "I'm Still There," 4.
22. Ibid., 6.

so Pentecostals in Canada will have to think clearly about a theology that legitimizes interfaith dialogue. They will also have to think clearly about the context of Canada as a multicultural and multi-faith society. Multiculturalism carries many meanings.[23] It not only describes the demographic diversity of Canada, it also has a prescriptive meaning outlining a set of ideals for promoting diversity. Politically, multiculturalism refers to government initiatives and policies about diversity. Finally, it also has a practical component to it as minority groups can apply for funding to support a range of festivals, activities, and community groups. Multiculturalism, however, has shifted from the language of non-English and non-French ethnic groups to now include any minority group. What might the Spirit be saying in and through minority groups in Canada, to follow Yong's pneumatological hermeneutic?

While pluralism is a threat to some, in 1995 I wrote about my experience working on a major university campus in Canada and how the value of pluralism shaped all religious group activity.[24] At the time some PAOC friends expressed a concern that working with a multi-faith group might lead to compromise. Is it possible to work with non-Christian groups for a common cause? My stance is still the same today as then. Pluralism represents an opportunity to engage Canadian society. However, Pentecostals will need to consider their theological viewpoints about multiculturalism and inter-faith dialogue. If Yong is correct, there are many theological resources available within a pneumatological framework in a multicultural society like Canada.

Diversity is also a reality among Pentecostals and not just between them and other religious and cultural groups. Increasingly, Pentecostals are arriving in Canada from Africa, Asia, and Latin America.[25] In the PAOC, for example, essentially all of its growth in the 1990s was due to immigration. This too is a consequence of globalization and changes in government policy on immigration. As cultural diversity increases among Canadian Pentecostals, it will require ongoing evaluation. However, cultural diversity needs to be thought through theologically and not just from the pragmatic perspective of denominations and organizational policy. There seems to be a real lack of theologizing among Canadian Pentecostals on diversity, ethnicity, and multiculturalism.

23. Fleras and Elliott, *Engaging Diversity*.
24. Wilkinson, "Pluralism," 24–28.
25. Wilkinson, *Spirit Said Go*.

The End of Denominations? Pentecostalism as Global Movement

Finally, globalization raises questions about religious organization and especially the role of denominations. Sociologists of religion have long examined these issues. H. Richard Niebuhr, writing in the 1920s, was quite critical of denominationalism.[26] He saw denominations furthering the social, racial, and economic divisions in the USA. He believed that denominationalism divided Christians and that Christianity divided offered no hope to a world in need of the Kingdom of God. Niebuhr was critical of all denominations, including the upper class historical churches and the lower class disinherited, by which he no doubt had in mind the Pentecostals.[27] Niebuhr did not have in mind an ecclesiological solution. He did not see church union as an answer. But he was ecumenical. He maintained:

> The road to unity is the road to repentance. It demands a resolute turning away from all those loyalties to the lesser values of the self, the denomination, and the nation, which deny the inclusiveness of divine love. It requires that Christians learn to look upon their separate establishments and exclusive creeds with contrition rather than with pride. The road to unity is the road of sacrifice which asks of churches as of individuals that they lose their lives in order that they may find the fulfilment of their better selves. But it is also the road to the eternal values of a Kingdom of God that is among us.[28]

Denominations did not disappear, and throughout the middle of the twentieth century identity and denominationalism continued to shape the character and quality of many Christians. In the early 1970s Andrew Greely wrote the book *The Denominational Society* arguing that denominationalism was quite strong in the USA and any weakening of denominations would threaten the religious fabric. However, in the 1980s denominationalism began to take a back seat with the rise of televangelism, new religious movements, and the rapid growth, if not popularity, of Pentecostalism. New Charismatic wings were developing that raised questions about the borders and boundaries of Pentecostalism. Evangelical groups were claiming to be Pentecostal although in practice only and not in name. This too raised questions about defining and

26. Niebuhr, *Social Sources of Denominationalism*.
27. Ibid., 30–33.
28. Ibid., 284.

locating Pentecostals if they were in fact not located within identifiable denominations.

Studies of congregations and communities of Charismatic Christians also moved the focus away from denominations. Sociologists of religion claimed that the congregation was the primary unit of religious community.[29] Notwithstanding Poloma's study of the Assemblies of God,[30] increasingly attention was given to the study of Pentecostalism as culture or movement, including topics on healing, prophecy, prayer communities, gender, and local congregations, especially those that demonstrated phenomenal growth.[31] This does not, however, suggest that denominations have disappeared.

Robert Wuthnow argues that denominations have not declined or disappeared.[32] Rather, they continue to be important sources of religious organization. However, Wuthnow does point out that they are no longer the only source of religious organization. Furthermore, I would contend that, with the growth of special purpose groups, non-denominational groups, and other kinds of religious groups, the competition for money, time, and other resources among people of faith will put pressure on denominations. This is especially true of the PAOC, as financial pressure has resulted in a number of changes for the denomination including downsizing of a national office, changes in missionary funding strategies, and reduction in office personnel. Consequently, Pentecostals in Canada will need to rethink how they organize, especially at the level of denominations, networks, congregations, special purpose groups, and movements.

CONCLUSION

In conclusion, globalization is best understood as a reconfiguration of the world that requires us to think about the development of global society. The systematization of the world assumes that specialized spheres of economics, politics, and religion are emerging. However, globalization is not a uniform process and there is much debate about the nature

29. Warner, "Place of the Congregation."
30. Poloma, *Assemblies of God at the Crossroads*.
31. For example, see the following: McGuire, *Ritual Healing in Suburban America*; Poewe, *Charismatic Christianity as a Global Culture*; Griffith, *God's Daughters*; and Csordas, *Sacred Self*.
32. Wuthnow, *Restructuring of American Religion*, 71–99.

of social change, economics, politics, and religion. For religious groups, there is debate about the nature of global society, the relationship between religions, how religions will interface with other spheres of global society, as well as internal debates over orthodoxy, orthopraxy, and authority. Furthermore, within religious families there is much diversity, so that Pentecostalism is best understood as "Pentecostalisms." Significant Pentecostal voices are currently writing on themes that illustrate these tensions. Specific debates over Spirit baptism, cultural and religious diversity, and denominationalism all point to important areas for reflection and theological development. Canadian Pentecostals are not immune to these global trends and need to articulate, if not rethink, a Pentecostal theology with reference to our contemporary world.

BIBLIOGRAPHY

Anderson, Allan. *An Introduction to Pentecostalism: Global Charismatic Christianity.* Cambridge: Cambridge University Press, 2004.

Appadurai, Arjun. *Modernity at Large: Cultural Dimensions of Globalization.* Minneapolis: University of Minnesota Press, 1996.

Beyer, Peter. *Religion and Globalization.* London: Sage, 1994.

———. *Religions in Global Society.* New York: Routledge, 2006.

Csordas, Thomas J. *The Sacred Self: A Cultural Phenomenology of Charismatic Healing.* Berkeley: University of California Press, 1994.

Di Giacomo, Michael. "Pentecostal and Charismatic Christianity in Canada: Its Origins, Development, and Distinct Culture." In *Canadian Pentecostalism: Transition and Transformation*, edited by Michael Wilkinson, 15–38. Montreal/Kingston: McGill-Queen's University Press, 2009.

Fleras, Augie, and Jean Leonard Elliott. *Engaging Diversity: Multiculturalism in Canada.* 2nd ed. Toronto, ON: Nelson Thomson, 2002.

Giddens, Anthony. *The Consequences of Modernity.* Stanford, CA: Stanford University Press, 1990.

Greeley, Andrew M. *The Denominational Society: A Sociological Approach to Religion in America.* Glenview, IL: Scott, Foresman, 1972.

Griffith, R. Marie. *God's Daughters: Evangelical Women and the Power of Submission.* Berkeley: University of California Press, 1997.

Kydd, Ronald. *I'm Still There: A Reaffirmation of Tongues as the Initial Evidence of the Baptism in the Holy Spirit.* Toronto, ON: Pentecostal Assemblies of Canada, 1977.

Luhmann, Niklas. *The Differentiation of Society.* New York: Columbia University Press, 1982.

———. *Social Systems.* Stanford, CA: Stanford University Press, 1995.

Lyon, David. *Jesus in Disneyland: Religion in Postmodern Times.* Malden, MA: Polity, 2000.

Macchia, Frank. *Baptized in the Spirit: A Global Pentecostal Theology.* Grand Rapids: Zondervan, 2006.

McGuire, Meredith B. *Ritual Healing in Suburban America*. New Brunswick, NJ: Rutgers University Press, 1988.

Miller, Thomas. "The Canadian Azusa: The Hebden Mission in Toronto." *Pneuma* 8 (1986) 5–29.

Nederveen Pieterse, Jan. *Globalization and Culture: Global Mélange*. Lanham, MD: Rowman & Littlefield, 2004.

Niebuhr, H. Richard. *The Social Sources of Denominationalism*. 1929. Reprint; New York: Meridian, 1957.

Poewe, Karla, editor. *Charismatic Christianity as a Global Culture*. Columbia: University of South Carolina Press, 1994.

Poloma, Margaret. *The Assemblies of God at the Crossroads: Charisma and Institutional Dilemmas*. Knoxville: University of Tennessee Press, 1984.

Robertson, Roland. *Globalization: Social Theory and Global Culture*. London: Sage, 1992.

Scholte, Jan Aart. *Globalization: A Critical Introduction*. 2nd ed. New York: Palgrave MacMillan, 2005.

Stronstad, Roger. *The Charismatic Theology of St. Luke*. Peabody, MA: Hendrickson, 1984.

Studebaker, Steven M. "Beyond Tongues: A Pentecostal Theology of Grace." In *Defining Issues in Pentecostalism: Classical and Emergent*, edited by Steven M. Studebaker, 46–68. McMaster Theological Studies Series 1. Eugene, OR: Pickwick Publications, 2008.

Warner, R. Stephen. "The Place of the Congregation in the Contemporary American Religious Configuration." In *American Congregations*, edited by J. P. Wind and J. W. Lewis, 54–99. Chicago: University of Chicago Press, 1994.

Wilkinson, Michael. "Pluralism and the Implications for Intercultural Ministry." *Eastern Journal of Practical Theology* 9.2 (1995) 24–28.

———. *The Spirit Said Go: Pentecostal Immigrants in Canada*. New York: Peter Lang, 2006.

———. "Religion and Global Flows." In *Religion, Globalization and Culture*, edited by Peter Beyer and Lori Beaman, 375–89. Leiden: Brill Academic, 2007.

———. "What's 'Global' about Global Pentecostalism?" *Journal of Pentecostal Theology* 17 (2008) 96–109.

Wuthnow, Robert. *The Restructuring of American Religion*. Princeton: Princeton University Press, 1988.

Yong, Amos. *Beyond the Impasse: Toward a Pneumatological Theology of Religions*. Grand Rapids: Baker Academic, 2003.

PART TWO

Implications of Global Pentecostalism for Pentecostal Theology

4

Globalization and Spirit Baptism

Steven M. Studebaker

I became a Christian in a fairly traditional Classical Pentecostal church—Forest Grove Assembly of God. My experience with the church reflects the Classical Pentecostal paradigm (i.e., Spirit baptism is an experience subsequent to salvation that empowers the person for witness and is accompanied by the initial evidence of speaking in tongues). At a men's Bible study sponsored by Forest Grove AG, I accepted Christ as Savior and later the same evening experienced Spirit baptism and spoke in tongues. Moreover, the church preached and practiced Spirit baptism, speaking in tongues, and a certain vision of holiness. Sunday evening services typically reached their crescendo in an exuberant and extended altar service. During these altar times, people were invited to, and often did, receive Spirit baptism with the sign of speaking in tongues.

While earning my BA at Northwest University (an AG institution), I attended Calvary Temple. Calvary Temple was an Assemblies of God church, but its style of preaching and its worship service was more discernibly evangelical than Pentecostal. Although the church formally endorsed the Classical Pentecostal doctrine of Spirit baptism and Pentecostal emphases were not intentionally downplayed, they were not a matter of emphasis within the life of the church.[1]

After I graduated with the BA from Northwest, I served as youth pastor and associate pastor in two Assemblies of God churches. The first

---

1. Robert P. Menzies identifies "the assimilation of the Pentecostal movement into mainstream Evangelicalism" as the source of the current self-identity crisis within Pentecostalism ("Evidential Tongues," 111).

was Avondale Christian Center in Woodinville, WA and the second was Virginia Assembly of God in Virginia, MN. Both churches formally affirmed the Classical Pentecostal doctrine of Spirit baptism. However, Avondale was more a garden variety evangelical church than a Classical Pentecostal one like the church in which I became a Christian and received my initial understanding of Pentecostalism. Virginia Assembly of God reflected more of a charismatic set of emphases than Classical Pentecostal ones. The church was also marked by diversity: some insisted on tongues as the initial evidence of Spirit baptism, some were open to multiple signs of Spirit baptism and were not insistent on the simultaneous manifestation of the sign and experience of Spirit baptism, while others were not particularly interested in Spirit baptism per se, but more broadly in ecstatic and at times sensational altar experiences. My ministry at Virginia coincided with the popularity of the Toronto Airport Vineyard revival and the Australian revivalist Rodney Howard Browne and many of the people sought to import the experiences that characterized these ministries to the church in Virginia.

I attended graduate school in the Chicago area and at different times attended three Assemblies of God churches. We initially attended Waukegan Assembly of God. This church was caught up in the Brownsville Revival and sent buses with church members on pilgrimage to Brownsville and sought to kindle a similar revival in our church. Although the Brownsville Revival occurred within an Assemblies of God church (a Classical Pentecostal church), the revival shared more in common with the Third Wave and various charismatic revival movements that emerged in the 1990s than with the Classical Pentecostal emphases on Spirit baptism and speaking in tongues. The Third Wave and charismatic revival movements are characterized by spiritual power encounters, a broad spectrum of charismatic manifestations, and healings and deliverance ministries. We then attended Hanover Park Assembly of God, which styled itself as a "Pres-tecostal" church (a combination of Presbyterianism and Pentecostalism). Hanover Park was hardly distinguishable from a lively evangelical church save for the occasional charismatic expression. Spirit baptism and speaking in tongues were not intentionally subdued, but the leadership intentionally sought to foster an "evangelical" style of worship and preaching. In a church change necessitated by a move to Kenosha, WI, we attended Racine Assembly of God, which in style and emphasis was very similar to Hanover Park.

Both congregations were Classical Pentecostal churches and formally affirmed the Classical Pentecostal doctrine of Spirit baptism, but they also did not make the historic distinctive doctrine a distinguishing feature of the everyday life of the church, its ministries, and preaching.

After I completed my doctoral program, I accepted a position as Assistant Professor of Theology at Emmanuel College in Franklin Springs, GA, which is affiliated with the International Pentecostal-Holiness Church. We attended the historic Springs Church, which is next to the college and affiliated with the same denomination. The IPHC is a Wesleyan-Holiness denomination, which means that it affirms three works of grace—conversion, entire sanctification, and baptism in the Holy Spirit. Although the IPHC is distinct from the Assemblies of God and other two-stage (i.e., conversion and Spirit baptism) Pentecostal groups, its theology of Spirit baptism is the Classical Pentecostal one. However, as in my experiences in most of the other Pentecostal churches I have attended, the doctrine of Spirit baptism did not play a significant role in the church. The worship and ministry style of the church reflected the Third Wave and charismatic revival emphases of high-octane spiritual experience, which sometimes included speaking in tongues. However, the church did not understand tongues in the Classical Pentecostal way of initial evidence, and saw tongues as merely one of many ways to experience the Holy Spirit.

My hunch is that many Pentecostals in North America have encountered a similar variety within Pentecostal churches.[2] The important

---

2. Classical Pentecostal theologians and leaders have also noted the loss of the Classical Pentecostal emphasis on Spirit baptism, tongues, and missions in contemporary North American Pentecostal churches: e.g., Anderson, "Baptism in the Holy Spirit," 4, and Watt, "Dangers." Although his study considers the British Assemblies of God and Elim Pentecostal Church, William K. Kay's documentation of significant ambivalence over the necessity of tongues as the sign of Spirit baptism seems to parallel the situation in North America; see Kay, "Initial Evidence." Earl Creps's research in Pentecostalism, mostly among Assemblies of God pastors and students, shows that significant members of the AG no longer maintain a Classical Pentecostal understanding of the Spirit Baptism and initial evidence; Creps calls this group "Post-distinctive Pentecostals" (Creps, "Postmodern Pentecostals," 33–36). Margaret M. Poloma also documents the emerging disconnect between the Assemblies of God's doctrine of the Spirit baptism and initial evidence and the affirmation and experience of these doctrines (and broader charismatic experience) among AG pastors and parishioners (Poloma, "Symbolic Dilemma," 108–15). Her conclusion is, "Hope for the future of a unique Pentecostal identity as reflected in ritual is not bright for the white American sector of the movement" (ibid., 115).

point to note is that all of the above churches fall under the category of Classical Pentecostalism, but the doctrine of Spirit baptism (which historically has been the defining doctrine of Classical Pentecostalism) has different meanings and roles in each church. Notwithstanding the fact that they all have a Classical Pentecostal doctrine of Spirit baptism in their doctrinal statements in the church office, at the more important level of the Sunday morning worship service they exhibit diverse understandings of the meaning and role of the doctrine. In other words, a divide exists between the actual practices and the formally stated beliefs of many Pentecostal churches. Moreover, how do we know when to label/call/categorize/classify a church as Pentecostal? Should we only classify as "Pentecostal" Forest Grove Assembly of God because it is the only one of the churches that actually practiced a Classical Pentecostal doctrine of Spirit baptism and speaking in tongues? If we take this route and decide to classify as "Pentecostal" only churches that actually believe and practice a Classical Pentecostal understanding of Spirit baptism, then what should we call the other churches? The diversity of the global Pentecostal movement can help us to engage these sorts of issues and questions that (1) get to the heart of the function of the Classical Pentecostal doctrine of Spirit baptism as the distinctive doctrine of Pentecostalism and that (2) seek to discern the theological meaning of Spirit baptism within the diverse forms of the Pentecostal movement. Although this essay does not intend to take on the formidable task of defining Pentecostalism, the present essay more or less follows Allan Anderson's inclusive definition of Pentecostalism as "all churches and movements that emphasize the working of the gifts of the Spirit, both on phenomenological and on theological grounds."[3] With that in mind, the first step toward engaging the above issues is the recognition of the global diversity within Pentecostalism.

RECOGNIZING THE GLOBAL DIVERSITY OF PENTECOSTALISM

The rise and global expansion of Pentecostalism is one of the most notable stories of Christianity in the twentieth century and first years of the twenty-first century. Pentecostalism in its various forms has attracted more than 602 million adherents. Within the span of a century,

---

3. Anderson, *Introduction to Pentecostalism*, 13.

Pentecostalism has grown from scattered bands of revival seekers to a global movement that comprises nearly one-third of Christians worldwide. Although Pentecostalism started primarily as a movement within North American conservative Protestantism, it is now a global phenomenon that transcends confessional boundaries. Indeed most Pentecostals now live outside of North America. For instance, as of 2007 the worldwide number of Pentecostals, Charismatics, and Third Wavers or charismatic type Christians was approximately 602 million and roughly two-thirds of these were non-white and non-Western. Furthermore, the majority of those classified as Pentecostal in these statistics are not so in the Classical Pentecostal sense (of the 602 million perhaps about fifteen percent are Classical Pentecostals).[4] Illustrative of the global growth of Pentecostalism is David Yonggi Cho's (1936–) Yoido Full Gospel Church in Seoul, Korea with 700,000 members. In the above respect, Pentecostalism may have come full circle from the interracial and ecumenical experience of the Spirit at Azusa Street to a global multicultural and trans-denominational movement of the Spirit.

The worldwide Pentecostal groups operate in spiritual gifts and participate in charismatic forms of worship, ministry, and personal spiritualities, but do not necessarily hold to the doctrines of Spirit baptism as a subsequent work of grace and speaking in tongues as its initial evidence.[5] For example, the South American Chilean Pentecostal movement and the large Brazil for Christ Evangelical Pentecostal Church (Igreja Evangélica Pentecostal 'Brasil para Cristo') embrace the experience of Spirit baptism, but do not insist on the doctrine of initial evidence. Among Pentecostal groups in Britain and Europe, such as the Elim movement, the doctrine of initial evidence has never been accepted as the exclusive sign of Spirit baptism, and among groups such as the Assemblies of God in Great Britain and Ireland that do formally hold to the doctrine, it is losing widespread support.[6] Thus, a consideration of the role and status of the Classical Pentecostal doctrine of Spirit baptism should be carried on in light of the global diversity of Pentecostalism.

---

4. Barrett, Johnson, and Crossing, "Missiometrics 2007," 32.

5. E.g., Clark notes that the issue of tongues has not played the sine qua non role of identifying authentic Pentecostalism among South African Pentecostals as it has among Western Pentecostals ("Initial Evidence," 208).

6. Anderson, *Introduction to Pentecostalism*, 65, 73, 94–95, and Bush, "Development."

POSSIBLE RESPONSES TO THE DIVERSITY WITHIN PENTECOSTALISM

For Pentecostals in North America, an important question is: what does the global diversity within Pentecostalism mean for the Classical Pentecostal doctrine of Spirit baptism? What are some possible responses to the fact that the doctrine of Spirit baptism, which has been understood as the distinctive doctrine of Pentecostalism within North America, is not characteristic of the majority of global Pentecostalism? In the following paragraphs I discuss three possible responses to the diversity exhibited in global Pentecostalism in respect to the Classical Pentecostal doctrine of Spirit baptism.

One option when we confront the diversity within the worldwide Pentecostal movement is to reject *as Pentecostal* people, movements, and churches that do not adopt the Classical Pentecostal understanding of Spirit baptism. Therefore, we would need to reject as Pentecostal all Charismatics and Third Wavers who do not adhere to the Classical Pentecostal view of Spirit baptism. If the Classical Pentecostal understanding of Spirit baptism is taken as the essence of Pentecostalism (which includes the belief that Spirit baptism is a distinct work of the Spirit subsequent to salvation with the initial evidence of speaking in tongues), then movements that do not hold these beliefs, whether in North America or elsewhere, would need to be classified as something other than "Pentecostal." They could be called "Charismatic," but this would assume that Pentecostalism and the Charismatic movement are distinct experiential movements and theological trajectories.[7]

The problem with this option is that it is inconsistent not only with the global diversity of Pentecostal movements and experiences but also with the variety of North American Pentecostalism, out of which Classical Pentecostalism arose. Moreover, if the Pentecostal movement, both in its variety of expressions in North America and global contexts, is understood as a work of the Holy Spirit, then this first option is out of step with the Holy Spirit (Gal 5:25). If Pentecostal experience is taken seriously in theological terms, which the doctrine of Spirit baptism intends to do, then Pentecostal experience suggests a theological

---

7. E.g., Kurt Koch's rejection of the revivals in West Timor as Pentecostal revivals because speaking in tongues was not central to the revivals (see Anderson, *Introduction to Pentecostalism*, 130–31). Gordon Anderson also implicitly makes a case for this perspective; see Anderson, "Baptism in the Holy Spirit."

account that is inclusive of the plurality of Pentecostal experience that arises from the Spirit of Pentecost. Thus, this first option would result in a hardening and narrowing of the boundaries of Pentecostalism that seems to be inconsistent with the expansive nature of the Spirit's work in the Pentecostal movement. I will develop at more length the theological implication of the plurality of Pentecostal experience for the doctrine of Spirit baptism later in the paper.

A second response to the global diversity of Pentecostal experience is to reject the identification of a specific doctrine or theology as the essence of Pentecostalism and to classify its essence as a unique type of charismatic experience.[8] The advantage of locating the essence of Pentecostalism in charismatic experience and not a particular doctrine such as Spirit baptism is that it can more effectively accommodate diverse movements under the category of Pentecostalism than can the doctrinal approach. However, Simon Chan warns that the phenomenological approach to Pentecostalism runs the risk of being too inclusive with the result that the term "Pentecostal" becomes ambiguous and amorphous.[9] An additional downside of this approach is that it forestalls, or at least diminishes the importance of, the task to understand the Pentecostal experience of the Spirit in theological categories because theology and doctrine become epiphenomena to the more foundational charismatic experience.

A third response is for contemporary North American Pentecostals to let global Pentecostalism remind them of the diversity within the history of North American Pentecostalism. I want to recommend this third response because remembering the plurality within the North American Pentecostal experience of the Spirit can help us to make theological sense of the current diversity within North American Pentecostalism and to understand the role of the doctrine of Spirit baptism within Pentecostalism. I develop the rationale for this third response in the next section of the paper.

---

8. E.g., Anderson, *Introduction to Pentecostalism*, 13–14, 187–88; Cox, *Fire from Heaven*; Hollenweger, *Pentecostalism*; Land, *Pentecostal Spirituality*, 23–32. Hollenweger does not reduce the essence of Pentecostalism to charismatic experience, but he was a key figure in the trend to locate its essence in something other than a specific doctrine, especially the Classical Pentecostal doctrine of Spirit baptism.

9. Chan, "Whither Pentecostalism?" 579.

FROM GLOBAL TO LOCAL PENTECOSTAL DIVERSITY

The discussion of the diversity of early North American Pentecostalism and particularly its implication for the doctrine of Spirit baptism needs to recognize three overlapping horizons of diversity. These are (1) the global origins of Pentecostalism, (2) the pluralism of early North American Pentecostalism, and (3) the pluralism of the Charismatic and Third Wave movements.

The Global Origins of Pentecostalism

Recent studies on global Pentecostalism have highlighted the global points of origin for the Pentecostal movement and thereby have effectively challenged the habit of North American interpretations of Pentecostalism to privilege the North American sources of the movement.[10] In support of global origins of Pentecostalism, Allan Anderson cites the revivals in Korea (1903), China (1908), and India (in Tamil Nadu in 1860–1865, in Travancore in 1873–1881, and with Pandita Mukti's Mission in 1905–1907), all of which predated and/or were not connected with the Azusa Street Revival. He also highlights that news of Mukti's Indian and other Pentecostal revivals in Venezuela and Norway sparked the Pentecostal revival in Chile that led to the formation of the Chilean Methodist Pentecostal Church under the leadership of Willis Hoover.[11]

The recognition that early Pentecostalism emerged in various revivals around the world and sometimes independently of each other seriously questions the notion that Azusa Street (or even more broadly, North American Pentecostal revivals) was the epicenter and source of the worldwide Pentecostal movement. Recognizing the diverse historical origins of Pentecostalism has a twofold consequence for Pentecostals in North America: (1) North American Pentecostals cannot assume that they are the only historical progenitors of worldwide Pentecostalism and (2) consequently they cannot arrogate to themselves a privileged status as the official interpreters of the movement.

---

10. E.g., Anderson, "Revising Pentecostal History" and Creech, "Visions of Glory." For an interpretation that supports the traditional idea of a North American source for the global Pentecostal movement, see Robeck, "Pentecostal Origins."

11. Anderson, "Revising Pentecostal History," 152–56.

The Pluralism of Early North American Pentecostalism

Recent scholarship on North American Pentecostalism has questioned the traditional paradigm that a common theology and experience characterized the early North American Pentecostal movement. Douglas Jacobsen suggests that the notion of a unified theology and set of practices in early Pentecostalism that later fragmented into the current diversity within the movement is problematic because "the origins of the Pentecostal movement are too scattered and fluid to support the ideal of original unity that the term 'fragmentation' implies."[12] He further comments that the formation of distinct Pentecostal groups was more of a process of,

> simple differentiation rather than declension from unity ... [and that] this means that there is no meta-model of Pentecostalism—no essence of Pentecostalism or normative type—that can provide an infallible rule against which to judge all the various particular renditions of Pentecostal faith and theology to determine precisely which is the most Pentecostal and/or the least Pentecostal.[13]

The different emphases evident in the ministries of Charles Fox Parham and William J. Seymour are a case in point. Although they both initially adopted what is called the Classical Pentecostal doctrine of Spirit baptism and its insistence on speaking in tongues as the initial evidence (or "the Bible evidence") of Spirit baptism, Seymour later had reservations about the focus on speaking in tongues and in its place emphasized the formation of multicultural and ecumenical communities of sanctified Christians as signs of the baptism in the Holy Spirit.[14] Additionally, even within the early years of the Assemblies of God, now a stalwart defender of the Classical Pentecostal doctrine of Spirit baptism and initial evidence, an openness to flexibility on the necessity of speaking in tongues as the initial physical evidence of Spirit baptism was present among some of its leadership.[15] Thus, recent studies on the history of early Pentecostalism have made untenable unquestioned allegiance to the two interrelated myths that the worldwide Pentecostal movement

---

12. Jacobsen, *Thinking in the Spirit*, 10.

13. Ibid., 11–12.

14. Ibid., 78–79; Jacobsen, *Reader in Pentecostal Theology*, 53–54; Robeck, "William J. Seymour."

15. Robeck, "Emerging Magisterium?"

radiated from a North American center, either Topeka, Kansas or the Azusa Street Revivals in Los Angeles, and that the doctrine of Spirit baptism and speaking in tongues was the exclusive theological hallmark of the movement.

The Pluralism of the Charismatic and Third Wave Movements

In addition to the diversity within early North American Pentecostalism, the emergence of the Charismatic movement and the Third Wave indicate a lack of homogeneity within North American Pentecostalism. The Charismatic movement was the first major development after the consolidation around the doctrine of Spirit baptism achieved in Classical Pentecostalism. For the first half of the twentieth century, the North American Pentecostal movement remained a distinct subgroup within Protestant Christianity. However, in the 1950s Christians within the traditional mainline Protestant churches and Catholic Church not only came into the Pentecostal experience, they remained within their churches. Prior to the Charismatic renewal, church leaders and congregants who participated in Pentecostalism most often left their traditional churches and joined Pentecostal ones. Important initial figures in the rise of the Charismatic movement are Harald Bredesen (1918–2006), a Lutheran minister, and Demos Shakarian (1913–1993), who founded the Full Gospel Business Men's Fellowship International in 1951. The Catholic Charismatic renewal began at Duquesne University, Pittsburgh, Pennsylvania and the University of Notre Dame, South Bend, Indiana in 1967. Throughout the 1970s the renewal spread from America to Europe, Australia, Latin America, and Korea. Early leaders in the Charismatic renewal within the Catholic Church included Ralph Martin (1942–), Stephen Clark (1940–), and Cardinal Léon-Joseph Suenens (1904–1996), who was the papal representative to the Catholic Charismatic movement and helped to keep the movement within the ecclesiastical structures of the Catholic Church.

The significance of the Charismatic movement for the Classical Pentecostal doctrine of Spirit baptism as the defining doctrine of Spirit baptism is that the Charismatics did not always adhere to the Classical Pentecostal account of Spirit baptism. Henry I. Lederle documents that three distinct doctrinal accounts of Spirit baptism are present in the Charismatic movement. First, the Neo-Pentecostal view reflects the Classical Pentecostal notion that Spirit baptism is an experience subsequent to conversion, but is less insistent on the doctrine of tongues as the initial evidence of Spirit baptism. Second, the Sacramental interpretation links the reception of Spirit baptism with the sacrament of water baptism and sees later charismatic experience as the release and manifestation of the Spirit received in the earlier sacramental rite. Third, the Integrationist view understands Spirit baptism and charismatic experience as one dimension of the Christian life that is linked to Christian conversion-initiation and/or a late filling of the Spirit. A Charismatic theologian in his own right, Lederle proposes a fourth alternative that sees Spirit baptism as a biblical metaphor for conversion that highlights the charismatic dimension of the Christian life.[16]

The rise of the television and mega-crusade evangelists is also a significant aspect of the Charismatic movement.[17] Although some of them identified with a denomination (e.g., Jimmy Swaggart [1935-] was ordained by the Assemblies of God, a Classical Pentecostal denomination), they preached a message that transcended any one denomination and that emphasized faith, healing, and charismatic empowerment and gifting through the Holy Spirit. Thus, their message was broader than the Classical Pentecostal doctrine of Spirit baptism as a second work of grace accompanied by tongues and for the purpose of empowering believers for new levels of Spirit-empowered mission. Key figures in this realm of the Charismatic renewal were Oral Roberts (1918–2009), Jim and Tammy Faye Bakker (1940– and 1942–2007), Pat Robertson (1930–), Kenneth Hagin (1917–2003), and Kenneth Copeland (1937–).

The early 1980s saw the emergence of the most recent development within Pentecostalism: the Neocharismatic movement or Third Wave (the first and second waves being Classical Pentecostalism and the Charismatic Renewal). Key leaders in the rise of the "Third Wave" are C. Peter Wagner (1930–), who coined the term to refer to the spread of charismatic experience in evangelical churches, and John Wimber (1934–1997), who founded the Vineyard Christian Fellowship in Anaheim, CA, which is the movement's most visible organization. Wimber is known for his "Signs and Wonders" ministry that he advocated while lecturing in Wagner's class at Fuller Theological Seminary in the 1980s. The emphasis on spiritual renewal through the Holy Spirit without the traditional

16. Lederle, *Treasures Old and New*, 217–41.

17. Watt refers to this group of Pentecostals as the "Fourth Wave" ("Dangers," 381–82).

Pentecostal doctrine of Spirit baptism appealed to many within evangelical churches in North America and Britain. The Neocharismatic movement replaced the Classical Pentecostal emphasis on Spirit baptism for empowerment for witness with charismatic manifestations—e.g., "Signs and Wonders"—for church growth, and took charismatic spirituality to the evangelical churches.

Furthermore, Neocharismatics often have no clear connection with traditional Pentecostal and Charismatic Renewal churches, but nevertheless embrace charismatic forms of spiritual experience and worship. Perhaps the most significant theological feature of the Neocharismatic movement is its rejection of the doctrine that baptism in the Holy Spirit is subsequent to conversion and the accompanying doctrine of speaking in tongues as the initial evidence of Spirit baptism. Familiar manifestations of the Neocharismatic movement are the "Toronto Blessing" led by former Vineyard pastor John Arnott (1940–), the Brownsville Revival led by pastor John Kilpatrick in Pensacola, Florida (although the revival occurred at an Assemblies of God church, which is a Classical Pentecostal denomination, it reflects the ethos of the Neocharismatic movement), and the more recent revival in Lakeland, Florida.

The Classical Pentecostals, Charismatics, and Third Wavers exhibit three distinct views on Spirit baptism and speaking in tongues. Although Pentecostals and Charismatics generally agreed that an experience of Spirit baptism is available to believers beyond their conversion, they differed over the best ways to articulate the theological meaning of Spirit baptism and the normativity of speaking in tongues as the evidence of Spirit baptism. Participants in the Third Wave are less committed to or they reject outright the Classical Pentecostal and Charismatic theologies of Spirit baptism and tongues, even though they embrace a wide range of charismatic expressions and experiences.

Highlighting an additional dimension of diversity, Charles Peter Watt points out that the different Pentecostal groups hold distinct understandings of the purpose of Spirit baptism. The Classical Pentecostals believe that Spirit baptism empowers the believer primarily for evangelistic missions. Charismatics usually emphasize that Spirit baptism is for the purpose of renewing the church. Rather than having an outward missionary focus, Spirit baptism has an intra-ecclesial focus among Charismatics. Third and Fourth Wave (the Rhema and "faith" churches) Pentecostals seek Spirit baptism to gain personal spiritual power. Thus, not only do the different Pentecostal groups disagree over whether Spirit baptism is a subsequent work of grace and the necessity of tongues as its initial evidence, they also have quite distinct notions of its purpose: empowerment for missions, power to renew the churches, and spiritual power that fosters personal spiritual experience.[18]

The diversity within global and North American Pentecostalism outlined above carries with it at least two implications for the doctrine of Spirit baptism. First, North American Classical Pentecostals should not assume that their movement is the sole or even the primary source of worldwide Pentecostalism. Second and consequently, North American Classical Pentecostals should not expect their doctrinal formulations to possess a privileged status in defining the theological essence of the Pentecostal movement, either in its global or North American context. These two observations provide a transition point to the next topics of discussion: the source and role of the doctrine of Spirit baptism within Pentecostalism.

THE SOURCE AND STATUS OF SPIRIT BAPTISM IN NORTH AMERICAN PENTECOSTALISM

Spirit baptism enjoys the status of the distinctive doctrine of Classical Pentecostalism. Important for considering the status of Spirit baptism is the historical source of the doctrine. In the doctrine of Spirit baptism, did the Pentecostals develop a new theological formulation or recover a forgotten biblical doctrine? From a historical-theological perspective the answer should be affirmative to at least one of these questions in order for Spirit baptism to play the role of the distinctive doctrine of Pentecostalism. Moreover, from the perspective of systematic theology, the doctrine of Spirit baptism should express the unique and diverse nature of the Pentecostal experience of the Holy Spirit. The following discussion first treats the source of the doctrine of Spirit baptism and then addresses its role as the distinctive doctrine of Pentecostalism.

The Source of the Doctrine of Spirit Baptism

In respect to the sources of the Classical Pentecostal doctrine of Spirit baptism, Pentecostals did not develop it. Although it is now known as the doctrinal distinctive of Classical Pentecostalism, the idea of Spirit

---

18. Watt, "Dangers," 382, 385–86.

baptism as a work of grace subsequent to conversion was prevalent among late-nineteenth- and early-twentieth-century evangelical revivalists. To be sure, the Pentecostals added the notion of tongues as the initial evidence of Spirit baptism, but they borrowed the basic content of the doctrine along with the supporting interpretation of Acts from the evangelical revivalists.[19] The point is that the doctrine that Classical Pentecostals have taken as their distinctive doctrine is not unique to Pentecostals from a historical-theological perspective. In other words, Pentecostals did not create the doctrine of Spirit baptism nor did they recover a heretofore forgotten biblical doctrine, but rather borrowed it from the evangelical revivalists and holiness theologians.[20]

The derivative nature of the Classical Pentecostal doctrine of Spirit baptism invites the question: given that the doctrine of Spirit baptism does not arise out of the Pentecostal movement (excepting the insistence on speaking in tongues as its initial evidence), but rather is a theological concept the early Pentecostals adopted from the early-twentieth-century repertoire of theological notions, should the Classical Pentecostal view of Spirit baptism be understood as the sine qua non of Pentecostalism? I will respond to this question in the final section of the essay, but at this point turn to the question of what is the function or role of the doctrine of Spirit baptism in the Pentecostal movement.

The Role of the Doctrine of Spirit Baptism within Pentecostalism

The role of the doctrine of Spirit baptism within Pentecostalism is to give the recovery of the experience and manifestation of the Spirit a commensurate theological articulation. Although Jacobsen is correct that theological categories informed the Pentecostal experience of the

---

19. E.g., Torrey, "Baptism with the Holy Spirit," 12–16. For the doctrine of Spirit baptism in nineteenth-century Wesleyan-Holiness theology, see Knight, "John Fletcher's Influence," 26–27; Dayton, *Theological Roots of Pentecostalism*, 48–54; Dieter, "Nineteenth Century Holiness Theology," 68; Faupel, *Everlasting Gospel*, 79, 90; Reasoner, "American Holiness Movement's Paradigm Shift," 133, 143. For the Reformed evangelical background of Pentecostal theology, see Waldvogel (née Blumhofer), "'Overcoming' Life: Evangelical Contribution," and "'Overcoming Life': Evangelical Origins"; and Wessels "Spirit Baptism, Nineteenth Century Roots."

20. Dionson refers to Parham's adaption of the doctrine and terminology of Spirit baptism as a subsequent work of grace from Holiness theology as something that led Pentecostal theology into a *cul de sac* that prevents non-Pentecostals from recognizing the importance of the Spirit and charismatic experience for the Christian life ("Doctrine of the Baptism," 236).

Spirit, he is also right to note that Pentecostal theology as such was (and continues to be) an attempt on the part of the Pentecostals to make theological sense of their charismatic experience.[21] In this respect, the Pentecostal experience of the Spirit is the source of Pentecostal theological (inclusive of biblical) reflection. Furthermore, the Pentecostal movement has an intentional reforming impulse. The early Pentecostals, the Charismatics, and more recently the Third Wavers, sought to bring reform through a recovery of a fuller experience and manifestation of the Holy Spirit in the lives of Christians and Christian churches. Since Pentecostal experience has a renewal dimension, Pentecostal theology should too; Pentecostal theology should reflect the renewal nature of the movement and, therefore, offer a unique theological contribution to alternative Christian theologies.

Pentecostal theology then needs (1) to provide a theological articulation that captures the nature of the Pentecostal experience of the Spirit and (2) to develop a theology that embodies the reforming nature of Pentecostal experience. The key *theological* question in respect to the Classical Pentecostal doctrine of Spirit baptism is, does the doctrine succeed in giving the Holy Spirit a theological expression that corresponds both to the Pentecostal experience of the Spirit and to the reforming nature of that experience? The question of whether the Classical Pentecostal doctrine of Spirit baptism successfully gives the Pentecostal experience of the Spirit an adequate theological expression can be answered in several ways.

First, given the historical derivation of the doctrine the answer seems to be "no." Since the doctrine is not the product of Pentecostal theological reflection, identifying the doctrine as the distinctive doctrine of Pentecostalism is problematic because it neither arises out of the unique Pentecostal experience of the Spirit nor matches the reforming nature of the Pentecostal movement. That is to say, Pentecostal theology, if it captures the reform ethos of the Pentecostal movement, should also reform traditional theological categories, but since the Classical Pentecostal doctrine of Spirit baptism was adapted from the nineteenth-century Wesleyan-Holiness and Reformed revivalists it does not seem well suited to accomplish this task.

At the same time, Jacobsen points out, "Pentecostal experience has been circumscribed by theology, and Pentecostal theology has been

21. Jacobsen, *Thinking in the Spirit*, 2–12.

grounded in experience."²² What this means is that since many of the early Pentecostals came out of the Holiness and evangelical revival movements, they possessed a theology of Spirit baptism that provided the template for their Pentecostal experience. For instance, Charles Parham's students, who experienced one of the initial outpourings of the Spirit, were expecting a baptism in the Holy Spirit. Jacobsen remarks that "one could argue that [Parham's] theology had a more causal impact, even to the point of, in essence, creating the experience."²³ Alan Anderson, who prefers to define Pentecostalism in terms of charismatic experience rather than in terms of the doctrine of Spirit baptism, nevertheless recognizes that speaking in tongues "was the most distinctive and central preoccupation of early Pentecostal experience."²⁴ So, given that the doctrine of Spirit baptism as a distinct work subsequent to conversion provided the theological structure for much of Pentecostal experience in North America, the answer to the question, "does it successfully serve as the doctrinal distinctive of Pentecostalism?" is "yes."²⁵

The point is that from the perspective of historical theology, although the doctrine of Spirit baptism is hardly unique to Pentecostals, it nonetheless provided the theological foundation and structure for many of the early Pentecostal experiences in North America and around the world and, therefore, it seems legitimate to see it as a defining doctrine within the movement.²⁶ One may find less correspondence between the doctrine of speaking in tongues and the experience of Spirit baptism among Pentecostals (whether they are Classical Pentecostals, Charismatics, or Third Wavers), but will very likely find a consistent

22. Ibid., 2.

23. Ibid., 4.

24. Anderson, *Introduction to Pentecostalism*, 190.

25. The way the doctrine of Spirit baptism provides the theological structure of Pentecostal experience reflects George Lindbeck's theory of the "cultural-linguistic" nature of doctrine (*Nature of Doctrine*, 33–36). Although I think Lindbeck's theory is a useful way to assess the function of the doctrine within Pentecostalism, I agree with Shane Clifton's point that it is ultimately problematic for developing a Pentecostal theology because it appears to reduce doctrine to an intra-church language. However, theology endeavors to make claims that have reference to the real nature of the Christian life and redemption. See Clifton, "The Spirit and Doctrinal Development," 8.

26. E.g., Anderson chronicles that although significant "Spirit-type" churches arose in Africa without any connections to North American Pentecostalism, nevertheless many of the major African Pentecostal churches can be traced back to Pentecostal missionaries who spread out from the Azusa Street revival (Anderson, *Moya*, 26–29).

correlation between the experience of Spirit baptism and the Classical Pentecostal doctrine.[27] In other words, many Pentecostals will testify that they first came to Christ and were saved and later were filled or baptized with the Holy Spirit (i.e., they experienced Spirit baptism subsequent to their salvation and they experienced some form of Charismatic manifestation and ongoing transformation in their lives).

Adding further support to preferring the North American doctrinal distinctive of Classical Pentecostalism, Robeck maintains that evidence for the origins of Pentecostalism inevitably point to Azusa Street.[28] The logic that follows from an Azusa Street epicenter for the modern Pentecostal movement is: since Azusa Street was the radial source of the worldwide Pentecostal movement and the Classical Pentecostal doctrine of Spirit baptism and the experience it inspired was its primary export, then Classical Pentecostalism and its doctrine of Spirit baptism possess a privileged status in defining Pentecostalism. An initial assessment of the history of the Pentecostal movement suggests that the doctrine of Spirit baptism provided a theological paradigm for the early Pentecostal experience of the Spirit and that it played a key role in defining the theological distinctive of the movement's original denominations. Based on these two historical roles of the doctrine, the historical judgment that the Classical Pentecostal theology of Spirit baptism is the distinctive doctrine of Pentecostalism appears almost incontestable.[29]

However, a closer historical and theological consideration of both North American and global Pentecostalism suggests that the Classical Pentecostal doctrine of Spirit baptism does not hold privileged status for defining the theological distinctive of the movement. Within the North American setting, the Classical Pentecostal doctrine of Spirit baptism took some time to establish itself and reigned only until the mid-twentieth century, when the Charismatic movement began to modify the doctrine. Recourse to the fact that the largest North American Pentecostal denom-

---

27. Clifton points out that the Classical Pentecostal doctrine of Spirit baptism as a work subsequent to salvation arises out of the early Pentecostal experience of the Spirit. He notes that Parham's students perceived themselves as Christians, who then received an experience they identified as Spirit baptism and spoke in tongues, which they interpreted as the evidence of their Spirit baptism (Clifton, "Spirit and Doctrinal Development," 13).

28. Robeck, "Pentecostal Origins," 170–80.

29. The above point lends credibility to James R. Goff's thesis that Parham is the founder of the movement. See Goff, *Fields White unto Harvest*, 164.

inations (e.g., the Assemblies of God and the Pentecostal Assemblies of Canada) endorsed it does not seem the best argument and is perhaps, at worst, the theological and ecclesiastical form of the "might makes right" argument and, at best, a populist-democratic method of sorting out doctrinal truth. Furthermore, the Pentecostal movement has exhibited a variety of emphases, such as social and confessional transcending love in the Azusa Street Mission and the diverse charismatic experiences promoted in the Charismatic and Third Wave forms of Pentecostalism.

If the diversity within the Pentecostal movements is taken as theologically significant, then the Classical Pentecostal doctrine of Spirit baptism does not appear to be the best candidate for the defining doctrine of Pentecostalism. From a theological perspective, the two facts that the doctrine of Spirit baptism derived from previous non-Pentecostal sources and that other manifestations of the Spirit were accepted, such as the formation of multicultural and ecumenical communities of faith among the early Pentecostals, especially the Azusa Street revival, suggest that the Classical Pentecostal doctrine of Spirit baptism might not be adequate as the defining doctrinal category of worldwide Pentecostalism.[30]

IMPLICATIONS OF GLOBAL PENTECOSTALISM FOR SPIRIT BAPTISM

In this final section, I want to outline several implications of global Pentecostalism for the Classical Pentecostal doctrine of Spirit baptism. First, the Classical Pentecostal doctrine of Spirit baptism can function as the distinctive doctrine of *Classical Pentecostal denominations*, but not as a broader doctrinal category for global Pentecostalism. The reason for this is twofold. On the one hand, Classical Pentecostal groups have selected this doctrine as their theological distinctive and they have the prerogative to select what they think is their distinctive theology. Therefore, the Classical Pentecostal doctrine of Spirit baptism can serve as the defining characteristic of Classical Pentecostal denominations such as the Assemblies of God and Pentecostal Assemblies of Canada. On the other hand, since the Classical Pentecostal doctrine of Spirit baptism is not unique to Pentecostals from a historical-theological perspective and cannot integrate the plurality of the historic and contemporary empha-

---

30. In this respect, Hollenweger appears to be correct that Goff's preference of Parham over Seymour as the progenitor of Pentecostalism is an appropriate historical judgment, but the wrong theological one (Hollenweger, *Pentecostalism*, 23).

ses either in North American or worldwide Pentecostalism, it should not serve as a standard to evaluate anyone's status as a Pentecostal.

The global diversity within Pentecostalism seems to commend the above way of considering the role of the Classical Pentecostal doctrine of Spirit baptism as a defining doctrine of Pentecostalism. Since global Pentecostalism is diverse, doctrinal categories that do not accommodate that diversity should not be given the privileged status as *the* distinctive doctrine of all of Pentecostalism. Yet, specific movements within worldwide Pentecostalism should have the freedom to identify what they believe is the theological distinctive of their specific movements. Of course, a Classical Pentecostal could object that the present proposal begs the question because it implies that genuine Pentecostal experience occurs outside of ecclesiastical contexts that maintain Classical Pentecostal doctrine. However, the same line of reasoning can be applied to Classical Pentecostalism; namely, that in light of the diversity within North American and worldwide Pentecostalism, to assume a privileged status to the Classical Pentecostal doctrine of Spirit baptism likewise begs the question because it assumes its status as the defining and authenticating doctrine of genuine Pentecostalism.

Second, the doctrinal category of *Spirit baptism* may still serve as a defining and distinctive doctrine for Pentecostalism. But if it does, it will need to be understood in a way that is inclusive of the broad range of the experience of the Spirit within the global Pentecostal movement. Frank D. Macchia's proposal that takes Spirit baptism as a lens though which to interpret the full range of Christian thought and life and Amos Yong's case that Spirit baptism is a metaphor that is inclusive of the full range of Christian experience are examples of more expansive views of Spirit baptism that hold promise to serve as theologies of Spirit baptism that can account for the global diversity within Pentecostalism.[31]

Third, we need to consider the question: why are Pentecostal denominations reluctant to revisit the doctrine of Spirit baptism especially when it is widely recognized that many pastors and parishioners are ambivalent about the doctrine? Perhaps the situation is similar to that of politicians who avoid admitting that they have changed positions, because it carries with it the tacit recognition that they were wrong. Institutions avoid admissions of error and retractions because they undermine institutional authority. After all, what are Pentecostal

---

31. Macchia, *Baptized in the Spirit*; Yong, *Spirit Poured Out*, 81–120.

denominations expected to say? "We have been wrong on this point for a century, but we are pretty sure we have it right now."

Notwithstanding the obvious institutional inhibitions for revisiting the formulation of the doctrine of Spirit baptism, the implicit dogmatism entailed in this reluctance is out of step with the non-traditional and non-creedal ethos of the early Pentecostal movement. The resistance to re-consider the doctrine is also ironic.[32] The early Pentecostal experience of the Spirit and doctrine of Spirit baptism (which sought to give the Pentecostal experience of the Spirit an appropriate theological expression) was a protest against the quenching of the Spirit that the early Pentecostals perceived in the traditional churches. Now, a century later, many Pentecostals have become the type of dogmatic traditionalists against which their forerunners protested. The Apostle Paul encouraged the church of Galatia, "Since we live by the Spirit, let us keep in step with the Spirit" (Gal 5:25). Pentecostals have superlatively kept in step with the Spirit when it comes to openness to the manifestation of the gifts of the Spirit and empowerment for ministry. Perhaps it is time for them to show a similar willingness in respect to a theology of the Spirit.

CONCLUSION

This paper explores the implications of global Pentecostalism for the Classical Pentecostal doctrine of Spirit baptism. On the one hand, it has clearly served as a defining doctrine of many Pentecostals groups and provided the structure for Pentecostal experience. On the other hand, it does not reflect the theology and experience of many Pentecostals. These two facts suggest ramifications in the global Pentecostal movement for the Classical Pentecostal doctrine of Spirit baptism. First, the Classical Pentecostal doctrine of Spirit baptism can function as the doctrinal distinctive of the Classical Pentecostal subgroup of the broader global Pentecostal movement. Second, it cannot function as a meta-doctrine for defining worldwide Pentecostalism precisely because its theological categories do not accommodate the diverse experience of the Spirit

---

32. Clifton notes the potential irony of the unwillingness of Classical Pentecostalism to consider revision of the doctrine of Spirit baptism and its insistence on speaking in tongues as the initial evidence with the comment, "it would be ironic if a doctrine that was developed by Pentecostals as a means of describing their experience of the liberative power of the Spirit, and which accompanied their rejection of traditional dogmatisms, was itself to become dogmatically entrenched!" (Clifton, "Spirit and Doctrinal Development," 22).

within the global Pentecostal movement. Third, an expanded and more inclusive theology of Spirit baptism may enable this biblical metaphor to continue to play a defining theological role for global Pentecostal theology.

BIBLIOGRAPHY

Anderson, Allan. *An Introduction to Pentecostalism: Global Charismatic Christianity.* 2004. Reprint, New York: Cambridge University Press, 2006.

———. *Moya: The Holy Spirit in an African Context.* Pretoria: University of South Africa, 1991.

———. "Revising Pentecostal History in Global Perspective." In *Asian and Pentecostal: The Charismatic Face of Christianity in Asia,* edited by Allan Anderson and Edmond Tang, 147–73. Baguio City, Philippines: Regnum, 2005.

Anderson, Gordon L. "Baptism in the Holy Spirit, Initial Evidence, and a New Model." *Paraclete* 27 (1993) 1–10.

Barrett, David B., Todd M. Johnson, and Peter F. Crossing. "Missiometrics 2007: Creating Your Own Analysis of Global Data." *International Bulletin of Missionary Research* 31 (2007) 25–32.

Bush, Timothy A. C. "The Development of the Perception of the Baptism in the Holy Spirit within the Pentecostal Movements in Great Britain." *European Pentecostal Theological Association Bulletin* 11 (1992) 21–41.

Chan, Simon. "Whither Pentecostalism?" In *Asian and Pentecostal: The Charismatic Face of Christianity in Asia,* edited by Allan Anderson and Edmond Tang, 575–86. Baguio City, Philippines: Regnum, 2005.

Clark, Matthew S. "Initial Evidence: A Southern African Perspective." *Asian Journal of Pentecostal Studies* 1 (1998) 203–17.

Clifton, Shane. "The Spirit and Doctrinal Development: A Functional Analysis of the Traditional Pentecostal Doctrine of the Baptism in the Holy Spirit." *Pneuma* 29 (2007) 5–23.

Cox, Harvey. *Fire from Heaven: The Rise of Pentecostal Spirituality and the Reshaping of Religion in the Twenty-First Century.* Reading, MA: Addison-Wesley, 1995.

Creech, Joe. "Visions of Glory: The Place of the Azusa Street Revival in Pentecostal History." *Church History* 65 (1996) 405–24.

Creps, Earl. "Postmodern Pentecostals? Emerging Subcultures among Young Pentecostal Leaders." In *The Future of Pentecostalism in the United States,* edited by Eric Patterson and Edmund Rybarczyk, 27–47. Lanham, MD: Lexington, 2007.

Dayton, Donald. *Theological Roots of Pentecostalism.* Grand Rapids: Francis Asbury, 1987.

Dieter, Melvin E. "The Development of Nineteenth Century Holiness Theology." *Wesleyan Theological Journal* 20 (1985) 61–77.

Dionson, Narciso C. "The Doctrine of the Baptism in the Holy Spirit: From a Pentecostal Pastor's Uneasy Chair." *Asian Journal of Pentecostal Studies* 2 (1999) 233–42.

Faupel, David W. *The Everlasting Gospel: The Significance of Eschatology in the Development of Pentecostal Thought.* Journal of Pentecostal Theology Supplement Series, 10. Sheffield: Sheffield Academic, 1996.

Goff, James R. Jr. *Fields White unto Harvest: Charles F. Parham and the Missionary Origins of Pentecostalism*. Fayetteville: The University of Arkansas Press, 1988.

Hollenweger, Walter J. *Pentecostalism: Origins and Developments Worldwide*. Peabody, MA: Hendrickson, 1997.

Jacobsen, Douglas G. *A Reader in Pentecostal Theology: Voices from the First Generation*. Bloomington: Indiana University Press, 2006.

———. *Thinking in the Spirit: Theologies of the Early Pentecostal Movement*. Bloomington: Indiana University Press, 2003.

Kay, William K. "The 'Initial Evidence': Implications of an Empirical Perspective in a British Context." *The Journal of the European Theological Association* 20 (2000) 25–31.

Knight, John A. "John Fletcher's Influence on the Development of Wesleyan Theology in America." *Wesleyan Theological Journal* 13 (1978) 13–33.

Land, Steven J. *Pentecostal Spirituality: A Passion for the Kingdom*. 1993. Reprint, Sheffield: Sheffield Academic, 1997.

Lederle, Henry I. *Treasures Old and New: Interpretations of "Spirit-Baptism" in the Charismatic Renewal Movement*. Peabody, MA: Hendrickson, 1988.

Lindbeck, George A. *The Nature of Doctrine: Religion and Theology in a Post-Liberal Age*. Philadelphia: Westminster, 1984.

Macchia, Frank D. *Baptized in the Spirit: A Global Pentecostal Theology*. Grand Rapids: Zondervan, 2006.

Menzies, Robert P. "Evidential Tongues: An Essay on Theological Method." *Asian Journal of Pentecostal Studies* 1 (1998) 111–23.

Poloma, Margaret M. "The Symbolic Dilemma and the Future of Pentecostalism: Mysticism, Ritual, and Revival." In *The Future of Pentecostalism in the United States*, edited by Eric Patterson and Edmund Rybarczyk, 105–21. Lanham, MD: Lexington, 2007.

Reasoner, Victor P. "The American Holiness Movement's Paradigm Shift concerning Pentecost." *Wesleyan Theological Journal* (1996) 132–46.

Robeck, Cecil M., Jr. "An Emerging Magisterium? The Case of the Assemblies of God." *Pneuma* 25 (2003) 164–215.

———. "Pentecostal Origins from a Global Perspective." In *All Together in One Place: Theological Papers from the Brighton Conference on World Evangelization*, edited by Harold D. Hunter and Peter Hocken, 166–80. Sheffield: Sheffield Academic, 1993.

———. "William J. Seymour and 'The Bible Evidence.'" In *Initial Evidence: Historical and Biblical Perspectives on the Pentecostal Doctrine of Spirit Baptism*, edited by Gary B. McGee, 76–87. Peabody, MA: Hendrickson, 1991.

Torrey, R. A. "The Baptism with the Holy Spirit." In *"The Higher Christian Life": Sources for the Study of the Holiness, Pentecostal, and Keswick Movements*, edited by Donald W. Dayton, 9–20. New York: Garland, 1985.

Waldvogel (née Blumhofer), Edith L. "The 'Overcoming' Life: A Study in the Reformed Evangelical Contribution to Pentecostalism." *Pneuma* 1 (1979) 7–19.

———. "The 'Overcoming Life': A Study in the Reformed Evangelical Origins of Pentecostalism." PhD diss., Harvard University, 1977.

Watt, Charles Peter. "Some Dangers in the Globalisation of Pentecostalism: A South African Perspective." *Missionalia* 34 (2006) 381–82.

Wessels, Roland. "The Spirit Baptism, Nineteenth Century Roots." *Pneuma* 14 (1992) 127–57.

Yong, Amos. *The Spirit Poured Out on All Flesh: Pentecostalism and the Possibility of Global Theology*. Grand Rapids: Baker Academic, 2005.

5

Tongues and a Postmodern Generation of Pentecostals

RANDALL HOLM

WHILE TONGUES-SPEECH, AND IN particular the signature doctrine of "initial evidence," has been the brand distinction of thoroughly modern Classical Pentecostals, today many point to a growing restlessness with this traditional theological construct within the North American Pentecostal church. Ironically, this is not occurring because of a lack of interest or belief in tongues-speech, rather its impetus is largely the fusion of a growing Pentecostal indifference to the traditional tongues-speech construct with an increased awareness of the Spirit's activity in Christian communities across the globe.

At the risk of overextending biblical precedent, the current situation can be likened to the dilemma that confronted the religious leaders in Acts 3 who were threatened by the activities of Peter and John on the steps of the Jerusalem Temple. The Temple was a spiritual global hub with visitors coming from "every nation under heaven" (Acts 2:5). As the keepers of the gate, the religious leaders saw it as their self-acclaimed role to manage the activity of God *within* the Temple parameters. They could not afford to have God's Spirit "leak out" of the Temple on the Spirit's own agenda. Two millennia later the free movement of the Spirit, particularly when its diversity of local expressions collide through the process of globalization, continues to present the church with new opportunities and challenges. There are new opportunities in understanding and witnessing the work of God's Spirit and new challenges as churches endeavor to respond to that work in productive ways while addressing the fears and apprehensions that any change fosters. Given these dynamics I propose a new self-understanding of tongues-speech that seeks to remain sensitive to its biblical witness and cultural impact, but risks reshaping Pentecostal identity for a global post-modern generation.

INITIAL EVIDENCE AS "BIBLICAL" AND "MODERN" DOCTRINE

In his apologetic on spiritual gifts (1 Cor 12–14), the Apostle Paul thanks God that he speaks in tongues more than his contemporaries (1 Cor 14:18). His bold statement leaves many questions unanswered, but it nonetheless underscores the importance of tongues-speech for Paul. Today from a Pentecostal viewpoint tongues-speech is no less important. Not only has its reintroduction into active practice birthed the Pentecostal movement, but it has reinvigorated many main-line congregations with a new spiritual enthusiasm.[1] To be sure, the modern Pentecostal movement is more than "speaking in tongues," but it is no less than that either. Nonetheless, as we enter the twenty-first century the signs point to a growing uneasiness in the thought of Pentecostals about tongues-speech, at least in its traditional usage in North America. Some might even conclude that both tongues-speech and its nameplate "Pentecostal" are on the endangered species list.[2]

The reasons are many. On the plus side it is perhaps an indication that Pentecostals have finally achieved a measure of respectability. While many still question the Pentecostal evidential construct, which maintains a symbiotic relationship between tongues-speech and the baptism of the Holy Spirit, few deny the legitimacy of tongues as an expression (if not a little quirky) and practice of Christian spirituality. For some this might sound like good news with a net result of homogenizing denominational distinctives. To put it bluntly, with each passing week Baptists

---

1. Pentecostalism, a contemporary movement that formally began in the early twentieth century, is summarily described today as a religious faith "with exuberant worship; an emphasis on subjective religious experience and spiritual gifts; claims of supernatural miracles, signs, and wonders—including a language of experiential spirituality, rather than of theology; and a mystical 'life in the Spirit' by which they (adherents) daily live out the will of God" (Burgess and McGee, *Dictionary*, 5).

2. There is an irony here that is difficult to ignore. At a time when the word Pentecostal conjured images of people swinging from chandeliers, amidst the howling of worshippers, the signage "Pentecostal" proudly adorned most church assemblies. Now that the word Pentecostal no longer projects such pejorative images, the name is being replaced with a variety of less identifiable terms.

sound more and more Pentecostal and Pentecostals sound more and more Baptist.

But the real winds of change have little to do with doctrinal persuasion. Presently, the Western cultural shift from modernity to postmodernity has put considerably stress on the historic cornerstone of Pentecostal identity—tongues-speech as "initial evidence."[3] When Pentecostalism first burst onto the scene in Los Angeles in 1906, onlookers could be forgiven if they thought they were witnessing some sort of flashback to a pre-scientific era. In and of itself, tongues-speech does not partner well with modernity. But the language and logic of a *glossolalic* evidential construct is a thoroughly modern collaboration. Among modernity's truth claims is the assumption that *evidence* is something that can be empirically measured. With an emphasis on tongues-speech being the physical evidence of Spirit baptism, Pentecostals successfully incorporated the language of modernity by making tongues-speech the litmus test of Spirit baptism.[4] Any subsequent scriptural support for this construct was a bonus. The fact that tongues-speech is the only biblical manifestation mentioned that can stand up to the criteria of modern evidence is a moot point. Steeped in modernity, this evidential construct not only put Pentecostals on the map, it thrived on its own account as people sought to get their baptism, which was understood to mean "speak in other tongues."

Enter post-modernity and its ability to include non-evidential or non-linear narratives in quests for truth. Suddenly Pentecostals are wondering if their historical attention to the tongues-speech theological

---

3. From a sociological perspective, Pentecostals owe their sudden rise in popularity over the last one hundred years in no small measure to their doctrinal distinctive of "initial evidence," a doctrine that presented tongues-speech as the evidence that a believer was baptized with the Holy Spirit. How does one know they are "baptized with the Holy Spirit"?—they speak in tongues! The net result was that it set apart Pentecostals with a distinct identity and it kept the message of Spirit baptism front and center among its adherents. While many other denominational affiliations accept the legitimacy of spiritual gifts including tongues-speech, none outside of Pentecostal groups accept the tongues-speech theological construct (i.e., the doctrine of initial evidence).

4. The Bible incorporates much "sign" language, but this differs from the modern usage of evidence. Signs point beyond themselves, but they do not need to stand up to empirical verification. Evidence needs to be something tangible that can be measured, and, in the case of tongues, it not only pointed to the baptism in the Holy Spirit, it *became* the baptism in the Holy Spirit.

construct is not handcuffing the very presence of the Holy Spirit they wish to promote.⁵

MY STORY

As a third-generation Pentecostal, my own journey into this foray of Spirit activity started at an early age. I became a card-carrying tongue speaker some thirty-five years ago. As a teenager, I understood that Pentecostals at some point in time need the "baptism" with the accompanying evidence of speaking in tongues. I spoke in tongues. I had the "baptism in the Spirit."

Later, while attending a Pentecostal Bible College in the mid 1970s, I was further "baptized" into why God evidently chose this quirky gift to initialize believers into the baptism of the Holy Spirit. Evidently, God chose tongues as his "initial evidence" of Spirit baptism for the following reasons: (1) Tongues constitute a visible symbol of spiritual reality. (2) They are uniformly recognizable by all cultures. (3) They reflect the personality of the Spirit. (4) They symbolize the Spirit's complete control of the believer. (5) They reveal the Holy Spirit as the believer's source of truth and utterance. (6) They signify the honor that God has placed upon human speech. And, (7) they are a foretaste of heavenly speech.⁶ To this, as students, we could have added, "No tongues, no credentials" for ministry upon graduating. Fortunately that was not a pressure that concerned me; after all, I had my evidence before I went to college and I really had no reason to question any of it. My tradition accepted this explanation, why shouldn't I?

However, it was not long after my graduation that my own intellectual curiosity and the realities of pastoral ministry combined to raise some questions for which my previous college education offered little help. I spoke in tongues, now what? Or in my darker moments, I spoke in tongues, so what? And, in my quiet moments, I wondered what all

---

5. In terms of biblical analogy, one might make a comparison with Peter and John on the Temple steps post-ascension when they created a public disturbance by being implicated in the healing of a beggar. The religious leaders frowned on the gesture, given the fact that the disciples in question did not follow proper protocol. But the religious leaders understood the full import of this action. Could they bear the Spirit leaking out of the Temple into the streets on his own agenda?

6. Brumback, *What Meaneth This*, 35.

good Pentecostals wonder one time or another: whether tongues-speech could simply be learned behavior.

Fortunately, into this personal void Pentecostal theologian Frank Macchia's exploration into tongues-speech as an acoustic sacrament was a timely and crucial incursion into my own spiritual journey. In the same way a gothic cathedral says God is majestic, Macchia, drawing on the insights of anthropologist William Samarin and others, made the compelling case that tongues-speech says, "God is here."[7] This revelation came on the heels of my freshly minted MA degree from Laval University, a French Catholic institution. Not only did Macchia's thought resonate with my new appreciation and understanding of catholic sacramental theology, but it gave me for the first time a way for me to integrate tongues-speech into a richer holistic spiritual worldview that moved beyond the merely apologetic teachings that I received in my theological training a decade earlier.[8]

But while Macchia's insights allayed many of my own questions, I confess not all was resolved. Among other things, I still wrestled with making sense of what appeared to be a disparate functional biblical witness when it came to the subject of tongues-speech. Apparently tongues-speech can operate missionally as a way of instant communication with peoples of different known language groups; it can operate as a form of ecstatic prayer speech with God, of no known language group; it operates evidentially as a sign of Spirit baptism; and it can operate corporately as a source of prophetic inspiration when accompanied by the gift of interpretation. To be sure there are no shortages of systems by prominent Pentecostal theologians to explain such anomalies, but they did little to allay my own nagging questions. Are we talking about kinds of tongues? Is there a gradient scale of operation? Are Luke and Paul, the two primary protagonists on the subject of tongues-speech, simply addressing the same subject from different theological agendas?[9] Or is their experience of tongues that of two entirely different entities? Added

---

7. Macchia, "Sighs Too Deep for Words," 53. A sacrament is a manifestation or a sign that in some mysterious way confers grace upon the participant.

8. In Bible College during the 1970s on the issue of tongues-speech, most of our energies were spent defending the doctrine of initial evidence. Little attention was given to what tongues may contribute to spiritual life.

9. I confess the earlier debates over this question among members of the Society for Pentecostal Studies provided no end of memorable moments for me as a younger participant.

to all of this I still wondered silently about the divine nature of tongues-speech. Are the sounds emitted divinely imparted by God, or are they better classified as some sort of learned behavior? To be sure, if asked by the uninformed I knew the answers to these questions, but I was a long way from being satisfied with my own response.

Into this personal journey, during the course of the thirty-fifth annual meeting of The Society for Pentecostal Studies, came philosopher James Smith's paper, "Tongues and Philosophy of Language: Conceptual Production at the Limits of Speech." This opened for me another personal avenue of investigation. Engaging, in particular, the philosophers J. L. Austin and John Searle, Smith considered the conceptual and ethical implications of tongues by viewing tongues-speech through the lens of speech-act theory, where the emphasis shifts from what tongues-speech "means" to what tongues-speech "does." In summary, Smith invited us to consider tongues-speech as performative language that "arises out of resistance to given cultural norms and institutions."[10] In this case perhaps the very inherent dissonance in *glossolalic* prayer says in no uncertain terms, "all is not right." In the words of Smith, it is an "act of resistance" that I might add in corporate settings has the democratic additional benefit of stirring solidarity with others as they cry out to God to act on their behalf. From this perspective we might even imagine that the anomaly of missionary tongues-speech in Acts 2, where the disciples speak in actual foreign tongues that are, however, unknown to themselves, could be an act of resistance to a confused crowd that came to expect such authoritative boldness from those appropriately schooled—not from Galileans or anyone so uneducated. In this perspective, tongues-speech is more than just a language that needs translation; rather it is an event that requires interpretation—a theme that resonated with Macchia but in my judgment moves in a different, perhaps complimentary, direction. If tongues-speech functions as an acoustic *sacrament* for Macchia, an action of grace bestowed from God to the devotee, tongues-speech, at least from the perspective of speech-act, appears to function as an acoustic *icon*, where the emphasis is on perhaps a divinely sponsored, but thoroughly human initiation to transcend the ordinary and achieve something extraordinary.[11]

10. Smith, "Tongues and Philosophy of Language."

11. In the early church, iconic art enabled people to entertain God's presence providing it followed the accepted community rules governing icons. The community

From a Classical Pentecostal perspective Smith's hypothesis is bold and certainly not without controversy. And here, my interest is only partially roused by Smith's hypothesis of resistance, an emphasis that in my judgment has merit on its own. Rather, my interest is focused on his conclusion that the "linguistic" content of tongues-speech may be irrelevant to its overall purpose. I wondered if Smith was intentionally blurring the line between tongues-speech as a gift of divine origin, a classical Pentecostal mainstay, and tongues-speech as a tonal *human* act of resistance reflecting "sighs too deep for words." Or perhaps such a distinction is artificial?

At this point Smith admits he was in uncharted waters. In a departure from the speech-act theories of Austin and Searle who reserve the application of speech-act for language to that which is rule-governed, Smith stepped outside any conventional rules of language. But his suggestion that likewise the content of the tongues-speech is "basically irrelevant" raised the inevitable question from a Pentecostal perspective, "What are the consequences for Pentecostal spirituality?"[12] Can tongues-speech survive being "outed" as a learned language[13] providing the right accompanying elements are in place?[14] Could not any incoherent ecstatic utterance produce the desired effect? By shifting the attention of tongues-speech from the illocutionary act (what it does) to the perlocutionary effect (what it brings about) of incoherent speech, Smith's hypothesis certainly opens the door to such a possibility. For instance, could a Latin Mass duly performed in the appropriate sacred place for congregants who do not speak Latin be a form of tongues-speech, if it

---

stood behind the rules, and iconic art that failed to meet the standards was rejected. In a similar way, tongues-speech within Pentecostal circles follows a certain convention that must be respected. Linking the convention to the biblical text misses the point. While the convention does not ignore Scripture, it is the community that gives tongues-speech practice its definitive authority.

12. Unless of course we can claim that tongues-speech as an act of resistance is seen in its incoherent nature.

13. Or to rhetorically frame the question in another way, "are children two years of age aware that they are learning a language through mimicry?" If they understood this process of language acquisition would it make any difference in achieving their results? Would they think any less of their acquired speaking skills?

14. J. L. Austin, one of the chief architects of speech act theory, is clear that for a performative phrase to have a happy result, "the particular persons and circumstances in a given case must be appropriate for the invocation of the particular procedure invoked" (see *How to Do Things with Words*, 34).

has the desired effect of initiating a certain communion with God that some might define as Spirit baptism? Intrigued by Smith's hypothesis, I followed it with my presentation to the thirty-seventh annual meeting of the Society for Pentecostal Studies (2008). In particular, I solicited the writings of two leading Jewish thinkers of the twentieth century, namely Abraham Heschel and Martin Buber, to ponder the possibilities of a learned prayer language that we might identify as tongues-speech.[15]

KAVANAH AND ABRAHAM HESCHEL

The key to understanding Heschel's focus on prayer is found in the Jewish concept of *Kavanah* or what he describes as "the yielding of the entire being to one goal, the gathering of the soul into focus."[16] For Heschel, the act of prayer itself trumps its motive, and its content. Or, to put it into a contemporary illustration, the salary of professional athletes may be their impetus to play, but when true athletes are playing the idea of their salary is far from their mind. Winning is generally better than losing, but players would rather be playing on a poor team than sidelined on a good team. Athletes play for the love of playing or so we mere mortals like to believe. And so in Heschel, the primary purpose of prayer is not to inform, rather it is to partake or indulge. On this level, for Heschel, the language or linguistic content of prayer is generally incidental to the act of praying. And so Heschel concludes there is little difference in essence between prayer as a stammer and prayer as eloquent discourse. What is important is to move prayer beyond communication into communion with God—a transition that can be betrayed by the twisting phrases, traps, and decoys often inherent in formal language. Subsequently, for Heschel, even ritual prayer is often preferred over eloquent speech, insomuch as the ritual itself can divert attention away from self and allow the devotee an opportunity to present herself unadulterated before God. What is at stake is the ability of the devotee in the act of prayer to "simplify self and to make God relevant to oneself."[17]

God is the great ineffable, concludes Heschel. And as such, God cannot be presumed upon as if someone thinks she can master a response to God. Again, prayer is not a sermon delivered to God; it is "unbosom-

---

15 My choice in probing these two Jewish philosophers on this subject has been influenced by the work of Frank Macchia.

16. Heschel, *Quest for God*, 12.

17. Ibid., 17.

ing oneself to God."[18] Prayer is an action that is "guided by order and outburst, regularity and spontaneity, uniformity and individuality, law and freedom, a duty and a prerogative, empathy and self-expressions, insight and sensitivity, creed and faith, the word and that which is beyond words."[19] From this perspective, tongues-speech acting as a kind of post-language has a great deal of potential insofar as it deflects attention away from the means in the quest to draw closer to God.[20] In fact, Heschel is clear that we should not think of prayer as analogous to the give and take of human conversation. Prayer as *Kavanah* only makes ourselves communicable to him as we pour out our hearts before him. But neither is prayer simply silence. Prayer engages words/sounds. But prayer is not found in the words themselves.

In reading Heschel and studying early Pentecostal practice it is not difficult to make a connection between Jewish *Kavanah* and Pentecostal Spirit baptism as it is incarnated through tongues-speech. Both concepts describe a transcending state that climaxes in an ecstatic experience. In both cases, while words or sounds are the means into the "state of presence," the state is not defined by speech. It is a necessary passage that connects the two, but neither God nor humans are defined by it. From this perspective one can understand why many Jewish worshippers who do not speak Hebrew may still insist that their Shabbat liturgy remain in the Hebrew language. The rhythm and cadence of the language with its attachment to their long history is in a unique position to lift the worshipper into the place of God, a possibility that may even increase for those who cognitively do not understand the language.

Of course for classical Pentecostals, any notion that tongues-speech is less than a specific gifting from God is problematic. However, I suspect for Heschel that such a distinction is artificial. All language is a gift from

---

18. Ibid.

19. Heschel's description of prayer as noted here certainly resonates with anyone who has participated in or witnessed a chorus of people employing tongues-speech in corporate prayer. To the observant, the relative incoherent nature of tongues-speech is balanced with a specific coherent rhythm and structure.

20. I opt for the nomenclature "post-language" over either "a-verbal" or "primitive" to describe the ontology of tongues-speech. There is a layer of complexity in tongues-speech that may be overlooked in the other two descriptions, where primitive implies an effort to recapture the first century usage, and a-verbal implies a move away from language itself. By post-language, I am suggesting an organic language that simply refuses to be categorized by the rational discourse of finite minds.

God. The ability of humans to communicate with each other and make themselves communicable with God is a gift, whether the language follows known normative patterns of human speech or falls outside of them.

Heschel is instructive when he recounts Moses's encounter by God on Mount Sinai. For Heschel this encounter is not a single one-time occurrence that is never to be repeated; rather it is a paradigm of humanity's need of God and God's need of humanity. God who is unwilling to be left alone seeks to draw humanity by not only presenting himself, but equipping his creation to respond in kind. And when we as his creation suffer ourselves to dwell with God, some prefer to wear a mask to conceal God's emanating glory while others are content to blush when the ineffable in them stands before the ineffable beyond them.[21] Could tongues-speech be a blush in the presence of God when the mask is removed and we are left chasing words?[22]

Again, the emphasis is not on the nature of the language or its meaning, but on what it is, an ontology that I suggest is only made known through what it does in very specific contexts. And what it does is function as an icon that potentially allows those seeking after God to go through language into an audible transcendent communion with God—a state we could perhaps entertain as Spirit-baptism.[23]

At this stage, two caveats are in order. First, for the language form to duly function in this way, users must agree upon a certain accepted conventional context and procedure. Is this not what Paul, at least in part, is addressing in 1 Corinthians 12–14 with his emphasis on order? Or to put it more bluntly, I could speak in tongues out loud while shopping for groceries, or more precisely I could utter some phonemes but it would not likely be considered tongues-speech, at least on the Apostle Paul's or Luke's terms. The occasion is misplaced and any perlocutionary effect would be unhappy to say the least.[24] I feel the same way when I

---

21. Heschel, *Man Is Not Alone*, 91.

22. Of course, if the sole criterion of "speaking in tongues" is an encounter with the presence of God, then one could argue that everyday speech can also be a type of tongues-speech if it enables that encounter.

23. There is still room here to employ the term "sacramental language" by understanding language as a grace conferred by God that allows humanity the opportunity to be communicable before God.

24. Of course tongues-speech is not the exclusive domain of the religious. For aficionados of Pop Culture, tongues-speech makes an appearance in the oft-time irrever-

travel and worship in an assembly where tongues-speech as an ecstatic unknown language would seem like an intrusion. I do not think any less of these people and if it is a healthy congregation it does not take long before I pick up the communicable signals that the congregation uses that contribute a similar perlocutionary effect whereby the congregants come into contact with God as he passes by them.

Second, such a position necessitates rethinking the gift of interpretation in relation to tongues when used in a corporate setting as outlined in 1 Corinthians 12–14. In traditional Pentecostal theology the gift of interpretation is understood as just that, namely, a gift that enables someone to translate the audible sounds into a known discernable language for corporate edification.[25] If, however, as in a performative icon, the meaning is not found in the actual sounds, an interpretative act is still required to translate what God is doing and subsequently saying through this interruption in the liturgical order.

MARTIN BUBER

Martin Buber adds what could be another variable into this investigation. Buber has much to say about language and spirit. In fact, for Buber the spirit is found in language. For Buber the issue is not between

---

ent and always subversive DC comic series *The Invisibles*. See Morrison, Thompson, and Cramer, *The Invisibles*. In an email exchange with Nicholas Greco (a friend of mine), the author of *The Invisibles*, Grant Morrison, was asked why he introduced a "*glossolalic* speaking head" into the series. Morrison responded, "I was doing a lot of speaking in tongues experiments in the early 1990s and it occurred to me that the seemingly incoherent sounds of glossolalia could be seen as the voice of the "subconscious" body mind and could be interpreted by the unconscious minds of others—everyone hears different words in a string of glossolalia. Everyone makes their own interpretation of such "inspired" vocalizations, based on body language cues, intonation, and the mishearing of phonemes according to personal bias. We all hear what we need to hear in a glossolalic exchange, making it a truly international language. Or so it seemed to me at the time." While Morrison's intuitive connection between unconscious communication and glossolalia is interesting, his conclusion that we all "hear what we need to hear" fails to take into consideration context. I argue it is precisely the context behind the occasion of tongues-speech that potentially transforms the "incoherent sounds" into a transcendent spiritual event worth experiencing.

25. This can have interesting and dramatic results. In one church I attended, I remember when an English visitor in a French congregation sang an interpretation of what someone else had given through tongues-speech. As a result, the presiding pastor sang the interpretation of the interpretation in French for the benefit of the congregation. Presumably, if what was required was an exact translation of specific words, God could have gotten the receptor language the first time.

learned language or what we might call ecstatic language, a difference he does not seem to make, rather it is a question of posture or positioning. Where does one stand in relation to language? Does one stand in language or outside of language? For Buber, one stands in language in the measure one *receives* from God as in an I-Thou correspondence. One stands outside of language in the measure one *uses* language to objectify the other or carry out the stuff of daily life. In the former case, language/Spirit is the doer and we are the done unto; whereas in the latter case, we are the doer and language is the done unto. Writes Buber:

> Man speaks in many tongues of language, of art, of action—but the spirit is one; it is response to the You that appears from the mystery and addresses us from the mystery. Spirit is word. And even as verbal speech may first become word in the brain of man and then become sound in his throat, although both are merely refractions of the true event because in truth language does not reside in man but man stands in language and speaks out of it—so it is with all words, all spirit.... Spirit is not like the blood that circulates in you but like the air in which you breathe.... Man lives in the spirit when he is able to respond to his You.[26]

And here we take another cue from Buber, who suggests that whenever we find ourselves breathing the Spirit or living in the Spirit, and try to objectify the moment through words, the moment is largely lost, and God, who was our subject, becomes a he or a she or an it, in any case an object. Again, we might conclude that since all language is inherently sacred insomuch as it is a gift from God, even mundane language can transcend the ordinary and bring people into a special place of communion with God. But from a Pentecostal vantage, Buber's observation about the relation between spirit and language suggests that tongues-speech as an ecstatic post-language discourse has a potential perlocutionary effect on the speaker by avoiding any objectification of God and prolonging the audience with God.

To use a simple illustration, a couple under a starry sky may be lost in wonder of each other. They may respond in silence, an embrace, and they may even use words, but unless they have objectified the moment, I suspect that to anyone who overhears the words it will be as if they are speaking in tongues. And for onlookers, it may even create an additional perlocutionary spark as they remember times past and perhaps antici-

---

26. Buber, *I and Thou*, 89.

pate experiencing their own future I-Thou moments. In any event, the emphasis is not found in the words but in the motives and experience that lie beyond the words. However, it should also be noted that any derivative edification from the moment cannot replace the experience of the moment itself any more than a sentimental Hallmark card can accurately convey the experience of being in love.

In the end, we could conclude such speech is not rehearsed or learned speech, rather it is a suspension of rational discourse because the heart is limited and sometimes deceitful. It is limited in its capacity to find the right words to express the ineffable and it is sometimes deceitful in that, given a chance, it chooses words that reflect self-interests that invariably betray the moment.

TONGUES IN A POSTMODERN CONTEXT

Since my initial journey in this direction was inspired by James Smith, I was fortunate to have Smith graciously respond to my musings at the thirty-seventh Annual Meeting of the Society for Pentecostal Studies. He subsequently cranked the conversation up one more notch by presenting his own proposal, a "Naturalizing Glossolalia." In summary, and very much in the spirit of Heschel and Buber, he defended tongues-speech as a prayer language on the very edge of speech. To quote: "tongues-speech is a paradoxical linguistic expression of the failure of speech; it is also the sort of utterance that displaces one from the position of being a confident, articulate master of the situation. In short, it reduces one to a babbling idiot, but that is precisely the virtue of the practice: it is a mode of linguistic humility . . . a humbling, kenotic mode of prayer."[27] But, he quickly adds, he learned to do this. In a similar way, Smith pointed to other gifts of the Spirit such as teaching, where those so gifted submit their natural talents to the operation and ministrations of the Spirit. In effect, what happens is a meeting between human-inspired abilities and the ongoing incarnational work of God through the Spirit.

And in that spirit, I picked up another resource suggested, but not elaborated on by Smith. In this case, I refer to Peter Enns's provocative volume, *Incarnation and Inspiration*. In this book, Enns explores new models for thinking about the inspiration of Scripture. He proposes using the incarnation of Christ as the model par excellence to speak of

---

27. Smith, "A Modest Proposal."

biblical authority, where the biblical text is held in dialectical tension between its humanity and divinity.

Enns grounds the inspiration of Scripture in the Incarnation of Christ, whose divinity shone precisely because he was fully human. Now in the absence of Jesus in the flesh, the Bible as divine witness to Christ has taken up that role, but its composition and authority continue to share the same incarnational tension that defined Christ. While I find this a helpful analogy for understanding Scripture, it might be even more appropriate to apply the analogy to the work of the Holy Spirit. It was Jesus who assured his disciples that as the Father sent him so Jesus sends his disciples into the world, but now under the watchful presence of the Holy Spirit who was breathed on the disciples (John 20:21–22). The presence and work of the Spirit is no less incarnational than that of Jesus. And if this is the case, we must be careful not to isolate the spiritual gifts of 1 Corinthians 12–14 from the cultures in which they are practiced/experienced.

In the not-so-distant past our cultural context was defined by modernity. In spiritual terms, the language of worship was linear, systematic, and orderly. Even Pentecostals, with their occasional flights of disorder, distinguished themselves as following a structured pattern when it came to the operation of spiritual gifts and in particular of tongues-speech.[28] When the order was disrupted, it was either dismissed as a human display or a demonic interruption. Pentecostals were reminded, "God is not a God of disorder but of peace" (1 Cor 14:33). As such, even the relationship between God and his people is orderly and well managed. As believers we ask and God responds. And his response is interpreted as a supernatural visitation from the outside. And should God not respond, the situation is often internalized, laying the failure of God's acceptance to the invitation on the interceder who either lacks the necessary faith or knowledge to understand God's plan or simply has been open to some sin. There really is no middle option.

With post-modernity the rules have changed, and so have the possibilities. Post-modernity concludes that linearity and order are simply one narrative that is used by the Spirit. Echoing this idea, theologian Michael Welker adds:

---

28. Few things exercise a Pentecostal pastor more than a violation of Paul's admonition in 1 Cor 14:29 that cautions against letting more than two or three prophets speak in a congregational setting.

> A realistic theology gives up the illusion that a single system of reference could put God and God's power at our disposal ... God does not fit into metaphysical constructs that we have designed in harmony with important characteristics of our structural patterns of life. Rather God's vitality and God's freedom are expressed in a plurality of contexts and structural patterns of life, including ones that are not automatically compatible with each other.[29]

I confess that I began this journey several years ago with considerable fear and trepidation. I am Pentecostal in experience, history, and practice, and I worried what would happen if I reached the end and could not accommodate my conclusions. I am grateful for my modest and serendipitous collaboration with James Smith, which has perhaps helped both of us work through some of these issues, as they have been part of the histories of both of us.

I am further grateful that post-modernity is opening fresh ways of identifying and exploring truth. In the end, my fear has been realized. Applying an incarnational model, I am humanizing the Pentecostal charisma of speaking in tongues. But, at the same time, I have discovered a new door of infinite possibilities. By humanizing spiritual gifts in this way, we are at the same time sacralizing all space, time, and speech because God created them all. Authentic worship may then be a collaboration between the Spirit and the human that is evidenced at times symbolically, iconically, sacramentally, and physically. And it may further be that tongues-speech learned or unlearned may be a privileged doorway to allowing worshippers the grace to indulge in the incarnating work of the Holy Spirit in all avenues of life.

CONCLUSION

Not unlike their first-century Jewish counterparts the Pharisees, since the beginnings of the church, church leaders have persistently struggled to pare God's work into standardized models. Ironically, despite their attachment to the presence of the Spirit, classical Pentecostals have not been immune to this tendency. Pentecostals have been as diligent as other Christian movements in their efforts to return God's Spirit to the proverbial bottle where the Spirit can be managed in due course. These efforts, however, are not presented as an attempt to deny the working of the Spirit. Instead they are played out as a way of being faithful to

---

29. Welker, *God the Spirit*, 47.

Scripture, thereby maximizing the Spirit's resourcefulness. Nonetheless, as much as Pentecostals may pine for a homogenized experience of the Spirit, they cannot escape the clash of merging global theologies of the Spirit. And they cannot help but wonder if they too are guilty of handcuffing the work of the Spirit.

The reality of globalization has exacerbated these questions. Understandably it impacts every corner of Pentecostal theology, including but not limited to theological positions on tongues-speech. The traditional evidential construct as defined by Classical Pentecostals was significantly instrumental in the current Pentecostal revival. It helped codify and perpetuate an experience of the Spirit that many within the church found confusing and bewildering. Today that same construct is being challenged as being too limited. This essay is an attempt to explore further options in this regard. Perhaps at best we can conclude with the sage advice of the Pharisee Gamaliel. When confronted by the unconventional demonstration of the Spirit in Peter and John, he urged others, "Leave these men alone! Let them go! For if their purpose or activity is of human origin, it will fail. But if it is from God, you will not be able to stop these men; you will only find yourselves fighting against God" (Acts 5:38–39).

BIBLIOGRAPHY

Austin, J. L. *How to Do Things with Words*. Cambridge, MA: Harvard University Press, 1962.
Brumback, Carl. *What Meaneth This?* Springfield, MO: Gospel Publishing House, 1947.
Buber, Martin. *I and Thou*. New York: Scribner's, 1970.
Burgess, Stanley M., and Gary McGee, editors. *Dictionary of Pentecostal and Charismatic Movements*. Grand Rapids: Zondervan, 1988.
Enns, Peter. *Inspiration and Incarnation: Evangelicals and the Problem of the Old Testament*. Grand Rapids: Baker Academic, 2005.
Heschel, Abraham Joshua. *Man Is Not Alone: A Philosophy of Religion*. New York: Harper & Row, 1951.
———. *Quest for God: Studies in Prayer and Symbolism*. New York: Crossroad, 1984.
Macchia, Frank. "Sighs Too Deep for Words." *Journal of Pentecostal Theology* 1 (1992) 47–73.
Morrison, Grant, Jill Thompson, and Dennis Cramer. *The Invisibles: Arcadia Part IV*, no. 8. New York: DC Comics, April 1995.
Smith, James K. A. "A Modest Proposal." Paper response, 37th Annual Meeting of the Society for Pentecostal Studies, Duke University, March, 2008.
———. "Tongues and Philosophy of Language: Conceptual Production at the Limits of Speech." Lecture, 35th Annual Meeting of the Society for Pentecostal Studies, March, 2006.
Welker, Michael, *God the Spirit*. Minneapolis: Fortress, 1994.

PART THREE

Globalization and Pentecostal Ministry and Mission

6

Implications of Globalization for Pentecostal Leadership and Mission

BYRON D. KLAUS

SOME INITIAL THOUGHTS

THE ERA OF GLOBALIZATION is fast becoming a preferred term for describing the current times. Just as the Cold War Era or the Space Age might be used to describe particular periods of history, globalization describes the political, economic, and cultural atmosphere of today. People around the globe are more connected to each other than ever before. Information and money flow with great ease across the planet. Goods and services from one region of the world are increasingly available across the globe. International travel and, more importantly, communication are commonplace and have taken on the character of globalization. Limiting globalization to describing economics worldwide would certainly ignore the long reach of this phenomenon. As with many issues in the early twenty-first century, coming up with an agreed-upon definition for globalization is a challenge. However, the larger challenge is evaluating whether globalization is a good thing or actually a problem.[1]

Dr. Ivan Satyavrata observes that globalization is not some new economic theory discussed in developed nations, but a new form of culture that knows no boundaries and is spread throughout the world.

---

1. Porter, "Globalization: What Is It?" See also Berger, "Religion in a Globalizing World."

It involves multi-national interconnectedness in the transfer of ideas and products and includes the transnational corporations and Western governments that ride the economic globalization wave, as well as the global anti-capitalism movements that oppose it. Satyavrata says that when ideas get to their new destination they are not imbibed as they are; rather, they are adapted to fit the local situation. This interaction between global and local is sometimes referred to as *glocalization*. Thus, rather than eliminating cultural differences, globalization includes localization as an essential feature.[2]

In a very real sense, postmodernism and globalization are linked together. Western discussions of post-modern theory tend to reframe it for the safe domain of epistemology, when a more realistic understanding sees it as synonymous with the flattening of the world by globalization. This movement, by any description, is a global movement. The "globopomo" (global post-modern) turn is not about whether we will offer fair-trade coffee at our image-driven worship event aimed at the "creative" class of slick urbanites. It is not merely the domain of the educated "chattering class" adept at the intricacies of continental philosophy. It is a broader theme, encompassing global conflicts like the world of mass migration, persistent genocides, increased gaps in global wealth distribution, and the growth of global Islam.[3]

This twenty-first-century experience of emerging realities has created a growing challenge for Pentecostals. Our tradition has only one century of history. Inadequate historiography sometimes leaps over the 1900 years between the day of Pentecost and early twentieth-century Holy Spirit outpourings as if God did nothing in the intervening time. Moreover, contemporary Pentecostal-Charismatics often demonstrate a similar disconnect with the historicity of Christianity by acting as if their current "version" of Christianity has no antecedent; God has spoken directly to them and they have "mysteries" revealed akin to St. Paul's revelation of mysteries in his letter to the Ephesians (Eph 3:3–6).

Meanwhile, the last fifteen years have seen a growing awareness of what has been going on for several decades. In the era of globalization (however it is described and defined), Christianity has been growing vigorously. Fifteen years ago, Harvey Cox predicted the shape of Pentecostal

---

2. Satyavrata's remarks were delivered at the Oxford World Missions Briefing, May 2004, sponsored by the Oxford Centre for Mission Studies in Oxford, England.

3. Raschke, *GloboChrist*, 12.

spirituality fit for the twenty-first century. He foresaw that this "religion made to travel" would contextualize itself globally and be the primary texture of Christianity in this century.[4] Sociologists like David Martin and David Stoll began applying new lenses to the massive Pentecostal growth in Latin America, asking such unthinkable questions as: "Is Latin America turning Protestant?"[5] Liberation theologians adjusted their interpretive lenses and even dared to see Pentecostals as the future of the Christian church.[6] Philip Jenkins has confirmed what evangelical missiologists had been saying for years, namely, that Christianity has a new center and it is geographically in the southern hemisphere. Jenkins goes so far as to say that Pentecostals might be the most successful social movement of the twentieth century. We are only beginning to understand the significance of a single century of Pentecostal history on this planet.[7]

This significant growth and its global occurrence require reflection on how the current context, replete with globalized realities, affects the fabric of Pentecostalism worldwide. While acknowledging the particularity of local "Pentecostalisms"[8] and avoiding the temptation to generalize about Pentecostals based on personal experience, we must acknowledge that the historical holiness DNA of many Pentecostals has left us vulnerable to the serious and uncritiqued impact of culture on Pentecostals globally. We can laud our growth worldwide, but triumphalism is a haughty response to the grace of God. The incipient vitality experienced by a spiritual movement needs serious reflection to remain effective. Experience is not self-interpreting and globalization's insistence on reducing people to mere consumers impacted by a marketplace does separate us from a reflective nature as the addiction to consumption of goods and experiences creates an ahistorical "funk" that permeates our minds.

---

4. Cox, *Fire from Heaven*.

5. Stoll, *Is Latin America Turning Protestant?*; Martin, *Tongues of Fire*.

6. Shaull and Cesar, *Pentecostalism and the Future of the Christian Churches*.

7. Jenkins, *Next Christendom*, 8. Also see Jenkins, "Reading the Bible in the Global South."

8. Bonino, "Changing Paradigms."

INFLUENCES ON THE DAWN OF THE PENTECOSTAL CENTURY

Pentecostals initially framed their understanding of mission in a particular era. Regardless of where in the world the wellsprings of Pentecostalism expressed themselves, some dimensions of the following emphases were present. An understanding of this confluence of spiritual "winds" is necessary to see how the spirituality and theology of *Pentecostals* emerged at the beginning of the twentieth century. The several streams of influence would include the following:

- *The Wesleyan-Holiness influence* roots itself in the Christian perfection emphasis. In this particular stream of influence on the Pentecostal movement, *the power of the Holy Spirit takes control of a person's life to bring about entire sanctification: making him or her a vessel fit for God to use.*[9]

- *The Keswick influence*, with a root in J. N. Darby's emphasis on the second coming of Christ, provides a significant link between Spirit baptism and urgent evangelistic effort. This "baptism of the Holy Spirit" is a crisis experience not to sanctify, but *to empower people for service so that all may hear the gospel before Christ's return.*[10]

- *The Millennial influence* yielded a focus on the imminent return of Christ as the only solution to the world's dilemmas. It was those socially marginalized people of the day who understood clearly the call *for a people radically committed to the cause of Christ, where the eternal purposes of God have already defeated the powers of this world.*[11]

- *Restorationist primitivist influences* anticipated the emergence of a New Testament church—the true church restored. Expectancy was the watchword of a people who felt that their destiny was to

---

9. Faupel, *Everlasting Gospel*, 85–90, 96–114.

10. Petersen, *Not by Might*, 19–21.

11. R. S. Anderson provides an apologetic for the second coming of Christ being the most significant of Pentecostal themes in *Vision of the Disinherited*. See also Dayton, *Theological Roots of Pentecostalism*, and Faupel, *Everlasting Gospel*.

serve *the "restored" church during the final thrust in the harvest field before Christ's return.*[12]

- *The multi-cultural dimension* of Pentecostal beginnings critiques attempts to purport that the white Pentecostal movement is normative for incipient Pentecostalism. William Seymour preached a message that highlighted the empowerment of Spirit baptism as the necessary force for a new type of community where race, gender, and ethnicity would not be categories for division. This multicultural perspective can be summarized as *focusing on a new community of justice and equity, a foretaste of "glory divine" for ethnic minorities living in (racist) Jim Crow America.* This was the anticipation and experiencing of liberation by any definition.[13]

This very short summary of theological and social forces influencing the emergence of the Pentecostal movement provides an initial rationale for why early Pentecostals forged a very close relationship between the baptism of the Holy Spirit as *empowerment* for service (Acts 1:8), a keen *hope* in the soon return of Christ (1 Thess 4:1–16), and Christ's *command* to evangelize to the uttermost parts of the earth (Matt 28:19–20; Mark 16:15–20). Most significant to a consideration of Pentecostal missiology is the contribution that each of these streams of influence makes to a Pentecostal "pathos" of urgency, and emphasis on supernatural empowerment for world evangelization. The common thread in this stream of influence is the sovereign gift of power that God is using in a significant new chapter in this stage of redemptive history. A sense of participation in a story of eschatological significance, supported by supernatural Spirit empowerment(s), creates a strong sense of destiny in the Pentecostal identity. Only the divine intrusion of the Spirit of God is viewed as an adequate eternal resource for the end-time harvest (Zech 4:6).[14]

---

12. Wacker, "Playing for Keeps."

13. Daniels, "Dialogue between Black and Hispanic Pentecostal Scholars." A vigorous proponent of the African roots of Pentecost is Hollenweger, *Pentecostalism*, 46–48.

14. See a more complete description in Klaus, "Holy Spirit and Mission in Eschatological Perspective."

EARLY PENTECOSTAL REFLECTION ON MISSION

These descriptions are helpful to give texture to a theology of mission, which was certainly more acted out than codified. The conjunction of Holy Spirit empowerment for worldwide evangelism with eschatological urgency occurred at a unique juncture in mission history. The nineteenth century had just been completed, and it was being described as the "Great Century" for mission efforts. Early Pentecostal missionaries were those who, in many cases, had already served the *civilizing as Christianizing* mission strategy of the nineteenth century. The newfound urgency that came with Pentecostal experience caused many to question the necessity of the structures that had accompanied nineteenth-century mission efforts. The building of schools and hospitals did not seem prudent when Jesus' return was imminent.

Alice Luce, an early Pentecostal writer on mission strategy, summarized the perspective of many of these early missions participants when she said, "When we go forth to preach the Full Gospel, are we going to expect an experience like that of denominational missionaries or shall we look for signs to follow?"[15] Luce is quite succinct in her statement. The urgency of the hour requires nothing less than the preaching of the gospel and an accompanying belief in the necessity of signs and wonders along with that proclamation (another reason why the Mark 16:15–20 Great Commission passage is quoted as much as the Matt 28:19–20 passage, regardless of the critical issues surrounding verses 9–20 in the earliest of manuscripts).

Early Pentecostals did look for ways to conceptualize their experience surrounding mission. A critic of nineteenth-century mission theology and strategy, Roland Allen, became a guiding light of early Pentecostal mission efforts. Allen's emphasis on the Pauline pattern of church planting as seen in the book of Acts was a template for Pentecostal action. Allen's work was a welcome framework for these early Pentecostals who affirmed that God had restored signs and wonders for an end-time harvest worldwide.[16]

An exclusive focus on the *kerygmatic* dimension of the gospel became the centerpiece of Pentecostal mission priorities throughout most

---

15. McGee, "Surprises of the Holy Spirit," 61.

16. Allen's books that had significant impact on early Pentecostals included *Missionary Methods: St. Paul's or Ours?*, *Essential Missionary Principles*, and *Pentecost and the World*.

of the twentieth century. The most concise book written by a Pentecostal that brings together this particular pathos of urgent evangelistic effort empowered by the Holy Spirit and focus on the planting of churches as the central task of mission effort is the classic volume *The Indigenous Church* by Melvin Hodges, published in 1953. Taking the influence of Henry Venn, John Nevius, and particularly Roland Allen, Hodges clarifies why Pentecostals so intentionally embraced the priorities of planting churches and the establishment of the churches to be indigenous on the three-self model.[17] This characterization of Pentecostal missiology seen in Hodges's *Indigenous Church* was given further impetus in the 1985 publication of *The Third Force in Missions* by Paul Pomerville. Pomerville was quite direct in his affirmation that the historical lack of emphasis on the Holy Spirit in mission had necessitated Pentecostalism's emergence as a renewal movement that in contrast emphasized the Holy Spirit's work in missions.[18] Pomerville says, "As a renewal movement emphasizing a neglected dimension of the Holy Spirit's ministry, Pentecostals set the subtle influence of post-Reformation Protestant Scholastics in bold relief. It is at this point that Pentecostalism's 'God with us' experience makes its major contribution to contemporary mission."[19]

Gary McGee's work on the history of Pentecostal mission has posited a discontinuity between nineteenth-century mission strategy and the "radical strategy" espoused in early Pentecostal efforts focused on the *kerygmatic* aspect of mission. The nineteenth century was an era when the fullest implications of the Enlightenment and colonization were evident in mission strategy. For example, the renowned Scottish missionary to India, Alexander Duff, stated clearly in 1839 that the "missionaries of the Church of Scotland have been sent forth in the absence of miracles." The secretary of the Baptist Missionary Society from England declared in 1860, "Divest the apostles of miraculous power and you have the modern missionary, a true successor to the apostles."[20] Miraculous power was to be replaced by the blessing of higher civilization. The optimism of post-millennialism in the latter part of the nineteenth century nurtured the hope that conversion and civilizing worked in tandem would lead

17. For a more complete insight into the significance of Hodges as a Pentecostal missiologist, see McGee, "Legacy of Melvin Hodges."
18. Pomerville, *Third Force in Missions*, 63–78.
19. Ibid., 79.
20. McGee, "Radical Strategy." See also McGee, "Miracles and Mission Revisited."

the "heathen" out of darkness.[21] The "radical strategy" of Pentecostal mission was actually a critique of the missions of the nineteenth century that viewed the missionary as equal to the New Testament apostles, sans miracles. Voices like A. B. Simpson and A. J. Gordon emerged toward the end of the nineteenth century and decried the slow pace of missions. The alliance of spiritual empowerment and world evangelization was championed by Pentecostals who viewed this as a renewal of apostolic priorities dependent on the empowerment of the Holy Spirit.

We might summarize early twentieth-century Pentecostal reflection on a theology of mission as follows:

- Eschatological urgency about evangelism
- The *kerygmatic* dimension of the gospel as central to Pentecostal mission priorities
- An affirmation of the immediacy of the miraculous (a radical strategy)
- A propensity toward strategies with quick impact
- A suspicion about complex structures
- An unwillingness to evaluate long-term implications of strategies and structures.

A HAUNTING QUESTION

In 1998, missiologist Ralph Winter queried whether or not the Christian world was still taking seriously the maintenance of intentional evangelistic effort across geographical and cultural barriers.[22] A related question loomed on the horizon as to what eschatological motivation might be present in this continuing zealous cross-cultural witness. Will the "this worldly" empowerment of the Pentecostal identity actually disconnect the "eternal perspective" from eschatological rootings?[23]

As we enter the twenty-first century, globalization impacts all aspects of our planet. Robert Webber raises a haunting question in the title of his latest volume, *Who Gets to Narrate the World?* The world in which a theology of mission is developed must navigate a new set of realities

21. McGee, "Radical Strategy," 70.
22. Winter, "Meaning of Mission."
23. A most persuasive argument for the influence of eschatology on Pentecostal mission identity and strategy is made by Faupel, *Everlasting Gospel*.

while discerning what of its incipient character is truly transferable to this new century. The well of thematic resources from which to draw as we begin this new endeavor will contain:

- *Apostolicity*: Twenty-first century mission must still have at its core the proclamation of the gospel to places and people that are most resistant and have the least opportunity to hear it. Alan Johnson summarizes apostolic ministry well when he states that a new sense of missionary identity

   > should be formed around the notion of apostolic function. By this term, I mean that cross-cultural work should be framed around the understanding that apostles had of their work and the actual kind of work that they did. After reviewing the biblical material on apostleship, I argue that apostolic function must focus on the apostolic task of preaching the Gospel where it has not been heard, planting the church where it does not exist, and leading people to the obedience of faith so that they will express Jesus Christ in their social worlds and participate in God's global mission.[24]

- *Gospel and Culture*: The exclusive focus on the *kergymatic* dimension of mission may still be defended by some as foundational, but the reality of the majority world will certainly require fresh and critical theologizing on mission that takes the biblical theme of the kingdom of God with greater seriousness. Gordon Fee has long been the Pentecostal voice "preaching" the message of the kingdom.[25] It is our effective evangelism to date that will force us to enrich our understanding of the breadth of our theological mission.[26] The exploration of the kingdom motif will face fresh understanding of the *diakonic* and *koinoniac* dimen-

---

24. Johnson, *Apostolic Function*, 50–51.

25. The term "majority world" has replaced "third world," "the South," and "developing countries" as a way to refer to the majority of the world's population that lives outside of "the West," i.e., outside of countries such as Canada, France, Germany, Italy, Japan, Russia, the United Kingdom, and the United States, which comprise a minority of the world's human population, but exert significant influence over the majority of the world's population and natural and economic resources.

26. Fee, "Kingdom of God."

sions of kingdom life that are to be perpetuated in the planting of local church bodies.[27]

The success of our efforts in mission will also require Pentecostals to explore even further the tension-filled terrain of gospel and culture. While some might historically view Pentecostals as stuck in Niebuhr's category of "Christ against culture," it might be more truthful to say that much of Pentecostalism has been characterized as "Christ oblivious to culture." Whatever the past may be described as, the complexities of social change, the revival of historic world religions, and the desperation of national and state politics requires a new awareness of gospel and culture, if only to strengthen the growth of the church in those spots of the world where Christianity is least tolerated. While Western Pentecostals may be entering new understandings of the gospel and culture through innovative missiology that takes seriously the social sciences, it will be those followers of Christ in the oppressed places in the world who will read the book of Acts and identify with their brothers and sisters of the early church and obediently follow Jesus empowered by the Spirit and oblivious to the cost of trusting God in a faith-filled way.

- *Pentecost and eschatology*: The guarantee that God's redemptive mission, fully actualized and fulfilled in Jesus Christ, continues today intact, with urgency and destiny, is a motivational factor. Perhaps Walter Hollenweger's summary of the significance of Pentecostalism worldwide demonstrates succinctly a challenge both to non-Pentecostals and to Pentecostals, as the paradigm shift he describes emerges in the twenty-first century. Hollenweger suggests: (1) Pentecostalism is a church *of* the poor *for* the poor and is not (in the best examples) dependent on the power centers of the West; (2) It is a church/tradition that cannot be grasped through confessional evaluation; (3) It is a decidedly theological and social factor in the Third World; (4) It confronts the whole of Christianity with the basic question of what theology really is.[28]

---

27. Dempster, "Evangelism, Social Concern, and the Kingdom of God."
28. Hollenweger, "From Azusa Street to the Toronto Phenomenon," 12.

Within such a twenty-first-century reality, Puerto Rican Eldin Villafañe poignantly describes what will energize the continuing significance of Pentecostalism. He says:

> The baptism of the Spirit in Pentecostalism is rightfully seen as empowerment for service impacting the believer deeply by giving him/her a tremendous boldness, a heightened sense of personal holiness and a new sense of self worth and personal power. Yet, the narrow individualistic focus and purpose implies the dissipation ... of so much energy and spiritual power that can and should be "tapped" for the boarder missional objective of the church. The Hispanic Pentecostal church has the spiritual resources to face the spiritual power encounters of our social struggles. If the new object of the baptism of the Spirit is the ongoing mission of the Messiah ... it remains then for [Pentecostals to catch the vision] of the broader faithful fulfillment of the prophetic and vocational role of the baptism in the Spirit. [29]

Villafañe's challenge to a broader pneumatological vision will necessitate a renewed emphasis on community. The uniqueness of the day of Pentecost is that it serves as a guarantee that the mission of Jesus continues intact to this very day by the continuing presence of the Holy Spirit. The empowerment provided at Pentecost was not merely a story of individuals chosen and anointed with extraordinary capabilities for the purposes of Christian mission. What was created at Pentecost was a *community* that is described in its most incipient form in Acts 2:42–47. Even this earliest of pictures presents a glimpse of the church that focuses on the interdependence between people who were followers of Christ. The existence of this newly created "eschatological community" was centered in their reliance on the Spirit's empowerment to bear witness, in word, deed, and power that the reality of the kingdom of God was visible among them. Gordon Fee describes this Holy Spirit dynamic through Pauline eyes as the "experienced, empowering return of God's own personal presence in and among us, who enables us to live

---

29. Villafañe, *The Liberating Spirit*, 204.

as a radically eschatological people in the present world while we await the consummation."[30]

- *The Church as the Hermeneutic of the Gospel*: Lesslie Newbigin focuses on the congregation:

  > As hermeneutic of the gospel . . . how is it possible that the gospel should be credible, that people should come to believe that the power which has the last word in human affairs is represented by a man hanging on a cross? I am suggesting that the only answer, the only hermeneutic of the gospel, is a congregation of men and women who believe it and live by it.[31]

Newbigin's clear picture of the church as a functional hermeneutic is placed into an even larger framework by the haunting question of Lamin Sanneh, "Whose religion is Christianity?" Sanneh paints another horizon that Pentecostals in both the majority world and the Western world will have to face. My guess is that it will be handled with greater dexterity by the majority world simply because they intuitively understand the Good News in pre-modern terms and rejoice at the transformation of their lives by a Savior who has the power to abundantly pardon and save to the uttermost.[32] Yet as Amos Yong points out, Pentecostals of the twenty-first century can build on our current scholastic efforts, move ahead, and come of age by engaging the broad spectrum of dialogue partners. He views that the future is wide open for the development of a world Pentecostalism that is along the way: a pneumatological theology of gusto.[33]

THE IMPACT OF PENTECOSTAL THEOLOGY OF MISSION ON PENTECOSTAL LEADERSHIP

Leadership studies and the publications that ensue are a huge industry in North America. One only needs to access *amazon.com* to see that approximately 282,000 entries are available in a search for books under the keyword "leadership." Additionally, 800,000 more entries are offered

---

30. Fee, *Paul, the Spirit, and the People of God*, xv.
31. Newbigin, *Gospel in a Pluralist Society*, 227–32.
32. Sanneh, *Whose Religion Is Christianity?* See also Martin, *Pentecostalism*.
33. Yong, *Spirit Poured Out on All Flesh*, 30.

by *amazon.com* in a search under the keyword "management." Allowing for significant overlap does not diminish the fact that leadership related books and resources are readily available. As with much in North American life, topical fads are evident and church leaders strain to keep up with the latest angle on leadership so as to make sure they are deemed "current" and their effectiveness can be in tune with the latest measurements. Titles such as *The 21 Indispensable Qualities of a Leader, Leadership Jazz, Leadership Self-Deception: Getting Out of the Box, Monday Morning Leadership, Good to Great,* and *The Leadership Secrets of Santa Claus* all demonstrate the wide variety of resources available.

The propensity for the creation of popular culture and its accessories is thoroughly personified in the 2001 Public Broadcasting Service (PBS) investigation of the consumerist forces that shape the image consciousness and purchasing predispositions of teenagers in North America. Their significant study, entitled "The Merchants of Cool," posited that the current tendency to want to define generations in distinct groups such as Boomers, Busters, Gen-X, Millennials etc. was not so much the function of cutting edge social science research as it was sophisticated consumer branding. PBS argued that the "tribalization" that seemingly separated generations was merely a highly effective method of defining the market and maximizing the sales to that niche market. The reality is that popular leadership studies in North America have followed suit, and the massive availability of leadership/management resources at *amazon.com* testifies to a self-perpetuating attempt to respond to the cultural shifts so deeply impacted by the consumerist predisposition of an increasingly globalized world.

Filipino Pentecostal scholar Joseph Suico has observed a shift in Pentecostal leadership from a highly spiritual approach that favored souls over structures to an increasing adoption of a more corporate understanding of organizational life with Pentecostal church leaders increasingly comfortable with calling themselves Chief Executive Officers. Suico observes, at least in an Asian context, the following leadership climate in Pentecostal churches:

1. A corporate model of leadership as key to success.
2. The strong spiritual authority that emanates from the position of pastors tends to be "heroic," which focuses on a single magnetic leader at the top of a hierarchy who authoritatively sets policy.

3. Pentecostal leaders are increasingly more inaccessible as their church or denomination becomes large. Like the offices of a corporate CEO, the offices of church leaders are by design closed-off from workers.

4. Leaders' authority comes from status symbols like huge church buildings and large congregations, rather than spiritual and moral integrity.

5. Leadership models that are being "peddled" in seminars are mostly foreign to the local socio-economic and cultural context.

6. Transition in leadership is practiced in terms of popularity and patronage in leadership.[34]

IMPLICATIONS FOR THE MAJORITY WORLD

The connection between current events in a local culture and their impact on spiritual leadership is nothing new. The Bible is replete with examples of blindness about how current models of leadership, painfully dominated by contextual realities, cripple the potential of kingdom leadership. Jesus' dialogue with his disciples in Mark 10:35–45 is a glimpse into a startling level of cluelessness. When Jesus suggests that the disciples' perception of leadership models worth emulating is lacking, he offers them an alternative connected to his redemptive mission. The dialogue of the disciples in this passage gives clear indication that they are products of the models of leadership they have observed and that they are fully committed to actualizing these models in their own lives on behalf of the "cause." They are participants in a peasant culture that has experienced hundreds of years of conquest by different invaders. They long for freedom and believe that such freedom will be gained by a champion who will defeat an unjust system and the leaders who perpetuate it. Yet the models of leadership with which they have experience predispose them to believing that military might and positional dominance will serve them well. Jesus' simple statement, "Not so with you" (Mark 10:43a) must have seemed as if it was from another planet.

This brief glimpse into the understanding of Jesus' disciples regarding what it means to be a leader in the kingdom is a foretaste of what Christian leadership globally faces today. The Brazilian political and ed-

---

34. Suico, "Reflection."

ucational activist Paulo Friere further describes this dangerous dilemma when he says, "*to be* is *to be like,* and *to be is to be like* is *to be like the oppressor.*"[35] In other words, if you are limited to the models of leadership most observable in your context and uncritically believe them to be the standard worthy of your emulation, you are bound to replicate them in an increasingly counterproductive manner. The initial mental roadmaps of leadership are largely framed by cultural and ecclesial models for better or worse. The position or status we try to achieve, through aspiring to effective mastery of these models, may actually short-circuit our effectiveness from a kingdom perspective. Alternative leadership models that are formed in reaction to the liabilities found in current models have a long history of being short-sighted and self-serving. Here is where an uncritical absorption of North American church strategies and leadership priorities can be most debilitating for majority world leaders.

The posture that the church and culture in North America is discontinuous with the majority world is a position I would humbly ask you to reconsider. In addition, for the majority world to merely lament over our long history of Western exportation of church toxicity could be debilitating to the sovereign work of the Spirit of God globally. Philip Jenkins's work entitled *The Next Christendom: The Coming of Global Christianity* has confirmed to the academic and journalistic world what missiologists have been saying for a decade. The center of gravity in the church has moved from North to South. This new and exciting reality must be met by the emerging leadership of the global church with a proactive response to its emerging Spirit-bestowed responsibility.

CHALLENGES FOR THE MAJORITY WORLD TO NAVIGATE IN ITS NEW LEADING ROLE

A Global Youth Culture

MTV has played a huge role in creating a global village and an increasingly homogenous youth culture. Similar brand names are worn and coveted world wide. To view MTV as merely the purveyor of crass North American ideals would be to seriously underestimate the power of MTV. Media critic Mark Miller observes that the MTV machine listens to youth very carefully. When corporate revenues depend on being ahead of the curve, you have to listen; you have to know exactly what they want and

---

35. Freire, *Pedagogy of the Oppressed,* 48.

exactly what they are thinking so that you can give what you want them to have. The task is not to come up with new forms of music. The MTV machine tunes in so it can figure out how to pitch what Viacom (MTV's owner) has to sell to those kids. MTV studies the young and keeps them under very tight surveillance to figure out what will push their buttons. They take that and blare it back at them relentlessly and everywhere.[36]

Global urbanization only heightens the challenges that the church in the majority world will face. Rural village life is no longer a place to hide. Where there is a generator there will be electricity that will power a video player that will sell the child in the most rural setting the idea that the acquisition of a certain brand of clothing will bring them respectability and identity. The culprit is not merely the North American pop star's crass sexuality, but the reduction of every viewer into an object of focused marketing. The challenge in the majority world, as it has been in the minority world, is how the church's mission can be empowered by the Spirit to create the vibrant community where youth find purpose and destiny beyond the consumerist appeal of MTV's powerful and increasingly global influence. Do not take lightly this growing challenge. Community can no longer depend on tradition, ethnicity, nationality, gender, or age. The consumerist impulse, which media can so easily exploit, challenges the church to dig deep into spiritual resources previously unexplored.

Traditional Cultures Challenged

Much of the literature available about organizations and leadership is in English and no small part of that is North American. The translation of North American leadership books into other languages can be only minimally helpful. The primary contribution of such literature is to motivate readers to understand the nature of leadership and church-related leadership in particular. As North American church leadership has certainly been found struggling in its efforts to respond to twenty-first-century challenges, so will Christian leadership globally. Understanding organizational history and culture is necessary. Critiquing the limitations of preferred local models of leadership is crucial. The venerable Dutch scholar Geert Hofstede has provided seminal research by which common denominators of leadership across cultures can be the founda-

---

36. PBS, "Merchants of Cool."

tion for serious Christian critique of preferred local leadership models.[37] Lawrence Harrison and Samuel Huntington's *Culture Matters* provides a valuable international perspective on the inhibitors and provocateurs of effective leadership globally. Of particular usefulness is the work of Argentine economist Mariano Grandona, whose taxonomy of cultural factors shaping leadership is invaluable. While aimed at the business world, his insights are vital to understanding culture's tight connection to effective leadership.[38] We cannot legitimize church leadership by merely saying, "This is the way we do it" in Botswana, Malaysia, or Uruguay. The stakes are too high and the responsibility of our destiny as God's redemptive community is too crucial for the blunting of kingdom leadership by non-attention to the barnacles of culture's deterrents to fairly representing Christ.

Signs of Organizational Dilemma

Dilemmas reflective of organizational maturation inevitably impact our attempts to communicate the dynamic of the gospel across cultures and generations over a protracted period of time and through periods of social change. Sociologist Thomas O'Dea has provided a helpful taxonomy of five organizational dilemmas that are increasingly obvious as a church organization gets older. Such processes are more likely to occur more quickly in majority world contexts as sovereign works of the Spirit emerge quickly within contexts not given to self-critique and acknowledgment of destructive elements within incipient organizational life.

This is most notable in five specific organizational dilemmas that become increasingly obvious with the age of an organization:

- The dilemma of *mixed motivation*: As focus changes through the years, single-mindedness of purpose characteristic of early devotees is replaced by professionalism.

- The dilemma of *administrative order*: This is the tendency of a structure to over-elaborate itself and of the organization to become an unwieldy machine. Once-purposeful structures solidify and refuse to change.

---

37. Hofstede, *Cultures and Organizations*.
38. Harrison and Huntington, *Culture Matters*, 44–45.

- The dilemma of *power*: This is the struggle of religious leaders to avail themselves of close relation between religion and general cultural values in order to reinforce the position of religion itself.

- The dilemma of *delimitation*: This is the inevitability of growing older as a movement and running the gauntlet between "translating" the original message and holding a rigid position that kills the spirit of the movement.

- The dilemma of *symbolism*: This is the problem of trying to objectify the original charismatic moment in stable forms and procedures with routinization. How does spontaneity rule when we have moved beyond the incipient stage of first generation experience?[39]

CHARISMATIC LEADERSHIP: A PENTECOSTAL DEFAULT POSITION

A clue to understanding contemporary church leaders, including those in the Pentecostal/Charismatic tradition, is found in charismatic leadership theory, usually connected to German sociologist Max Weber and contemporary leadership theorists. *Charisma*, used in two letters of the apostle Paul (Rom 12 and 1 Cor 12) is a "gift of grace," a term used to describe the participation of people in the body of Christ. Such gifts were determined from God; they were not prescribed roles determined by other humans. Max Weber expanded this theological term into a leadership ability that derived its authority not from rules, traditions, or position, but from the extraordinary characteristics of an individual person. In 1947, Weber defined charisma as follows:

> [Charisma is a] certain quality of an individual personality by virtue of which he is considered extraordinary and treated as endowed with supernatural, superhuman, or at least specifically exceptional powers or qualities. These as such are not accessible to the ordinary person, but are regarded as of divine origin or as exemplary, and on the basis of them the individual concerned is treated as a leader.... What alone is important is how the individ-

---

39. O'Dea, "Five Dilemmas."

ual is actually regarded by those subject to charismatic authority, by his "followers" or "disciples."[40]

Historians have kept records of leaders in all sectors of society who, with committed followers at the fitting time, accomplished extraordinary feats. They communicated a compelling image of the future that tapped into rising hopes and dreams of followers in an existing social order, took risks at a severe cost of personal sacrifice and together with followers, pulled it off.[41] But what happens when such influence for mutual benefit goes bad—when the leader's power goes uncontrolled and values become skewed? The triumph of successful charismatic leaders is heady stuff, and the dangers and temptations that daily confront leaders are insidious and powerful. There is a potentially dark side to leaders who employ leadership charisma. Thomas Oden insightfully points out, "The leader whose mission and task is to care for others . . . must not be a slave to one's own unexamined passions. Otherwise the souls entrusted to one's care may be subject to manipulation by the supposed care-giver, whose passions are projected on to the relationship."[42]

Regardless of the context, an ideology that powerfully connects a liberating belief system and its practice for a people of destiny will be attractive to those who perceive themselves to be trapped. However liberating such an ideology might be, it also yields a potential opportunity for abusive leaders to thrive.

In other words, charismatic leadership is very likely to emerge as the model of choice in the context where a supernaturalistic religious ideology is present. That reality offers the powerful presence of a self-sacrificing, pioneering leadership that forges new frontiers under the "fire and cloud" of an eschatological identity. Simultaneously, it yields the possibility of non-accountable dynamic leaders who fashion a following with the "sound-bites" of God-like utterances in the context of manipulative phenomenology, thus creating an image of powerful ministry leadership. This scenario becomes increasingly possible globally with

---

40. Weber, *Theory of Social and Economic Organization*, 258–59.

41. Some have questioned the legitimacy of emphasis placed upon leadership to the neglect of the followers' role in significant change and accomplishments. For an insightful challenge to the exaggerated importance of leadership, see Kelley, *Power of Followership*. See also Klaus and Heuser, "Charismatic Leadership."

42. Oden, *Becoming a Minister*, 12.

the increased reliance upon mass media to further the cause of Christ evangelistically.

FINAL OBSERVATIONS

My observations have obvious limitations. I am the president of the only seminary the Assemblies of God has in the USA. The Assemblies of God is a 95-year-old organization that has growing edges (in the USA) primarily among immigrant communities. We are aging and leadership is facing significant challenges that are rooted in obviously different generational perspectives about church and mission and what models of leadership can keep us on mission in the twenty-first century.

The redemptive process that restores the life-giving nature to church organizations/structures gains empowerment through a full understanding of the power of Pentecost. Pentecost is central to the unfolding of the full revealing of the mission of God in Jesus Christ. It is at Pentecost that we are oriented to the inner logic of God's incarnational manifestation in the world through Jesus Christ. At Pentecost we experientially encounter the eschatological vision of redemption for the world through Christ's presence and coming. That indwelling power of the Spirit of Christ is the source of the church's life and ministry. The Holy Spirit reveals the full redemptive purpose of the mission of God by commissioning us into his ongoing redemptive ministry.[43]

Leadership and the structures through which they work may have a culturally informed fabric, but connectedness to Christ's redemptive mission must take prominence. The twenty-first century dawns with a significantly different world Christianity than the Christianity existing at the dawn of the twentieth century. To steward kingdom ministry for the twenty-first century, the new center of balance in the majority world will be faced with contemporary, but recurring challenges. Karl Barth suggested three guidelines by which leaders (in any culture) might evaluate the pathways/structure by which they facilitate ministry in Christ's name. Barth suggested that leaders need to be continually validating structures around three tests. Structures are valid so long as they (1) facilitate ministry based on divine gifts and endowments, not arbitrariness and self will, (2) build up, not disrupt, the work of the Holy Ghost to build community and (3) facilitate witness to the world in need

---

43. I first presented these ideas in Klaus, "Unless the Lord Build the House."

of redemptive mission. The continuing effectiveness of any church is only possible as we intentionally participate in the release of the gospel's fullest power.[44] In conclusion, I would suggest that twenty-first century Pentecostal leaders need to exhibit leadership qualities for effectiveness that minimally include the following:

- Knowing who we are and what factors shape us to be who we are
- Knowing the impact we have on others
- Knowing the values that we exhibit in ministry practice
- Valuing integrity and knowing what truly drives us to serve
- A commitment to the greater good/health of the communities we serve
- An ability to use power/influence constructively and ethically
- A deep commitment to growth toward Christ-likeness with that process merely being the cost we pay for recognition as a successful leader
- The growing capability to know the difference between humanly devised ministry strategies and divinely initiated redemptive mission.[45]

---

44. Guder, *Continuing Conversion of the Church*, 184. For Karl Barth's discussion of this material, see Barth, *Church Dogmatics*, 4:3/2, 856.

45. Cheung-Judge, "Primal Leadership."

BIBLIOGRAPHY

Allen, Roland. *Essential Missionary Principles*. London: Robert Scott, 1913.
———. *Missionary Methods: St. Paul's or Ours?* London: Robert Scott, 1912.
———. *Pentecost and the World: The Revelation of the Holy Spirit in the Acts of the Apostles*. London: Oxford University Press, 1917.
Anderson, Robert Mapes. *Vision of the Disinherited: The Making of American Pentecostalism*. New York: Oxford University Press, 1979.
Barth, Karl. *Church Dogmatics* 4:3/2, translated by G. W. Bromiley. Edinburgh: T. & T. Clark, 1962.
Berger, Peter. "Religion in a Globalizing World." Online: http://pewforum.org/events/?EventID=136.
Bonino, José Míguez. "Changing Paradigms: Response." In *Globalization of Pentecostalism: A Religion Made to Travel*, edited by Murray W. Dempster, Byron D. Klaus, and Douglas Petersen, 116–23. Oxford, UK and Irvine, CA: Regnum, 1999.
Cheung-Judge, L. Mee-Yan. "Primal Leadership: The Power of Positive Emotions in Shaping Optimal Organizational Functioning." Oxford Centre for Missions, May 2004.
Cox, Harvey. *Fire from Heaven: The Rise of Pentecostal Spirituality and the Reshaping of Religion in the Twenty-First Century*. Reading, MA: Addison Wesley, 1995.
Daniels, David. "Dialogue between Black and Hispanic Pentecostal Scholars: A Report and Some Personal Reflections." *Pneuma* 17 (1995) 219–28.
Dayton, Donald. *Theological Roots of Pentecostalism*. Grand Rapids: Francis Asbury, 1987.
Dempster, Murray. "Evangelism, Social Concern and the Kingdom of God." In *Called and Empowered, Global Mission in Pentecostal Perspective*, edited by Murray A. Dempster, Byron D. Klaus, and Douglas Petersen, 29–38. Peabody, MA: Hendrickson, 1991.
Faupel, William. *The Everlasting Gospel: The Significance of Eschatology in the Development of Pentecostal Theology*. Sheffield: Sheffield Academic Press, 1996.
Fee, Gordon. *Paul, the Spirit, and the People of God*. Peabody, MA: Hendrickson, 1994.
———. "The Kingdom of God and the Church's Global Mission." In *Called and Empowered: Global Mission in Pentecostal Perspective*, edited by Murray A. Dempster, Byron D. Klaus, and Douglas Petersen, 7–21. Peabody, MA: Hendrickson, 1991.
Freire, Paulo. *Pedagogy of the Oppressed*. Translated by Myra Bergman Ramos. New York: Continuum, 2006.
Guder, Darrel. *The Continuing Conversion of the Church*. Grand Rapids: Eerdmans, 2000.
Harrison, Lawrence, and Samuel Huntington, eds. *Culture Matters: How Values Shape Human Processes*. New York: Basic Books, 2000.
Hodges, Melvin. *The Indigenous Church*. Springfield, MO: Gospel Publishing House, 1953.
Hofstede, Geert. *Cultures and Organizations: Software of the Mind*. New York: McGraw-Hill, 1997.
Hollenweger, Walter. "From Azusa Street to the Toronto Phenomenon: Historical Roots of the Pentecostal Phenomenon." *Concilium* 3 (1996) 3–14.
———. *Pentecostalism: Origins and Developments Worldwide*. Peabody, MA: Hendrickson, 1997.
Jenkins, Philip. "Reading the Bible in the Global South." *International Bulletin of Missionary Research* 30.2 (2006) 67–73.

———. *The Next Christendom: The Coming of Global Christianity*. New York: Oxford University Press, 2007.
Johnson, Alan. *Apostolic Function in 21st Century Missions*. Assemblies of God Theological Seminary, J. Philip Hogan World Missions Series 2. Pasadena: William Carey Library, 2009.
Kelley, Robert. *The Power of Followership*. New York: Doubleday Currency, 1992.
Klaus, Byron. "The Holy Spirit and Mission in Eschatological Perspective: A Pentecostal Perspective" *Pneuma* 27 (2005) 325–28.
———. "Unless the Lord Build the House: Eschatology, Pentecostal Mission, and Life-Giving Organizations." Lecture, Lewis Wilson Institute for Pentecostal Studies at Vanguard University of Southern California, February 2001.
Klaus, Byron, and Roger Heuser. "Charismatic Leadership: A Shadow-Side Revealed." *Pneuma* 20 (1998) 161–74.
Martin, David. *Pentecostalism: The World Their Parish*. Oxford: Blackwell, 2002.
———. *Tongues of Fire: The Explosion of Protestantism in Latin America*. Oxford: Blackwell, 1990.
McGee, Gary. "Miracles and Mission Revisited." *International Bulletin of Missionary Research* 25 (2001) 146–49.
———. "The Legacy of Melvin Hodges." *International Bulletin of Missionary Research* 22 (1998) 20–24.
———. "The Radical Strategy in Modern Missions: The Linkage of Paranormal Phenomena with Evangelism." In *The Holy Spirit and Mission Dynamics*, edited by C. Douglas McConnell, 69–95. Pasadena: William Carey Library, 1997.
———. "Surprises of the Holy Spirit: How Pentecostalism Has Changed the Landscape of Modern Mission." In *Between Past and Future: Evangelical Mission Entering the Twenty-First Century*, edited by Jon Bonk, 51–65. Pasadena: William Carey Library, 2003.
Newbigin, J. E. Lesslie. *The Gospel in a Pluralist Society*. Grand Rapids: Eerdmans, 1989.
O'Dea, Thomas F. "Five Dilemmas of the Institutionalization of Religion." *Journal for the Scientific Study of Religion* 1 (1961) 30–41.
Oden, Thomas. *Becoming a Minister*. New York: Crossroad, 1987.
PBS. "The Merchants of Cool." Online: http://www.pbs.org/wgbh/pages/frontline/shows/cool.
Petersen, Douglas. *Not by Might nor by Power*. Irvine, CA: Regnum, 1996.
Pomerville, Paul. *The Third Force in Missions*. Peabody, MA: Hendrickson, 1985.
Porter, Keith. "Globalization: What Is It?" Online: http://usforeignpolicy.about.com/od/trade/a/whatisgz.htm?p=1.
Raschke, Carl. *GloboChrist: The Great Commission Takes a Post-modern Turn*. Grand Rapids: Baker Academic, 2008.
Sanneh, Lamin. *Whose Religion Is Christianity? The Gospel beyond the West*. Grand Rapids: Eerdmans, 2003.
Satyavrata, Ivan. Lecture. Oxford World Missions Briefing, May 2004 sponsored by the Oxford Centre for Mission Studies in Oxford, England.
Shaull, Richard, and Waldo Cesar. *Pentecostalism and the Future of the Christian Churches*. Grand Rapids: Eerdmans, 2000.
Stoll, David. *Is Latin America Turning Protestant?* Los Angeles: University of California Press, 1990.

Suico, Joseph. "A Reflection on Evolving Understandings of Christian Leadership: A Filipino Pentecostal Perspective." Lecture, Asia Pacific Theological Association Assembly, Kuala Lumpur, Malaysia, September 2005.

Villafañe, Eldin. *The Liberating Spirit: Toward an Hispanic American Pentecostal Social Ethic*. 1992. Reprint, Grand Rapids: Eerdmans, 1993.

Wacker, Grant. "Playing for Keeps: The Primitivist Impulse in Early Pentecostalism." In *The American Quest for the Primitive Church*, edited by R. T. Hughes, 196–219. Urbana: University of Illinois Press, 1988.

Webber, Robert. *Who Gets to Narrate the World? Contending for the Christian Story in an Age of Rivals*. Downers Grove, IL: InterVarsity, 2008.

Weber, Max. *The Theory of Social and Economic Organization*. Trans. Talcott Parsons. New York: Free Press, 1947.

Winter, Ralph. "The Meaning of Mission: Understanding This Term Is Crucial to Completion of the Missionary Task." *Mission Frontiers* 20, nos. 3–4 (March–April 1998) 15.

Yong, Amos. *The Spirit Poured Out on All Flesh: Pentecostals and the Possibility of Global Theology*. Grand Rapids: Baker Academic, 2005.

7

J. Philip Hogan's Spirit-Led Vision and the Globalization of Pentecostal Missions in the Twenty-First Century

IVAN SATYAVRATA

If a man knows not what harbor he seeks, any wind is the right wind.

—Seneca

A Leader is someone you choose to follow to a place you wouldn't go by yourself.

—Joel Barker

THE WIND AND THE WAVE...

IN AN ARTICLE THAT sets forth the critical issues facing Assemblies of God missions towards the turn of the century, J. Philip Hogan draws attention to the movement's greatest responsibility: "Perhaps the most important thing we must remember in addressing the future . . . our greatest responsibility . . . is to continue to seek God for discernment, that we might be aware of the times and listen to the wind which in a sovereign way 'bloweth where it listeth.'"[1] The most difficult task a leader has is to lead. If you are a leader, you have the formidable assignment of

---

1. Hogan, "Critical Issues," 88. His principal commentator notes: "Hogan knew that a leader must keep his eyes on the horizon to discern emerging and often fleeting opportunities" (Wilson, *Strategy of the Spirit*, 127).

asking people to follow you to places they have never been before. You may also ask them to follow you to a place that you yourself have never been before. That is why the kings of the Old Testament had prophets to help them. The prophets were people of the Spirit who could look into the dark and read the signs of the times and indicate the way ahead.

Great leaders are, however, not just kings or generals, they are prophets—people of exceptional vision who are able to look into the future and see dangers and opportunities long before others see them. J. Philip Hogan was just such a statesman leader with rare prophetic insight. The worldwide growth of the Assemblies of God and the global Pentecostal movement as a whole owes its existence in no small measure to J. Philip Hogan's far-reaching Spirit-led vision.

In considering the vision of J. Philip Hogan, I have been drawn to focus on a phenomenon that has begun to occupy center stage in much of both Christian and secular scholarship—the fascinating convergence of two global mega-trends. The movement of cultural, socio-political, and economic interconnectedness sweeping across the globe, and the exploding growth of the Pentecostal movement are two inescapable realities of the times in which we live. Harvard scholar Harvey Cox refers to them as "globalization and Pentecostalization."

The spectacular growth of the Pentecostal movement has captured the interest not just of missiologists and theologians, but of growing numbers of historians and social scientists as well.[2] We need hardly belabor the point, but a recent survey by the Pew Forum on Religion and Public Life estimates that the Pentecostal movement comprises one-quarter of the world's two billion Christians, making one out of every twelve people on planet earth Pentecostal-Charismatic.[3] This growth has made Pentecostalism the most dynamic and fastest growing segment of Christianity today. Pentecostalism is on its way to becoming the predominant global form of Christianity in the twenty-first century.[4]

---

2. Stalsett, *Spirits*, 1.

3 A decade and a half earlier, Peter Wagner had made this astute observation: "My research has led me to make this bold statement: In all human history, no other non-political, non-militaristic, voluntary human movement has grown as rapidly as the Pentecostal-Charismatic movement in the last 25 years" (Synan, *Spirit Said "Grow,"* ii). For the Pew survey, see http://pewforum.org/Christian/Evangelical-Protestant-Churches/Spirit-and-Power.aspx.

4. Joel Robbins provides an excellent summary review of the anthropological and other scholarly literature dealing with the global spread and impact of Pentecostalism (Robbins, "Globalization").

The phenomenal expansion of the Pentecostal movement coincided with momentous changes in the international political and economic order over the last half of the twentieth century, resulting in the emergence of a new international system called "globalization." The globalization wave represents a fundamental transformation of the world socio-economic and geopolitical order—a new reality that is here to stay and that has serious implications for our mission theology, strategy, and praxis. To quote just one informed opinion: "There is scarcely a Christian organization, alliance, or individual writer in the new millennium who discounts the reality of globalization. This applies to Catholics . . . , Protestants . . . , evangelicals . . . , and organizations such as the World Evangelical Alliance."[5]

While the significance of these two mega-trends for the future of global missions can hardly be overemphasized, the convergence of these two trends continues to intrigue scholars, especially since the Wave of globalization and the Wind of Pentecost both appear to be growing most rapidly in the same geographical areas—the global South and East.[6] Are these trends interconnected or is the overlap merely coincidental?[7] Recent studies have drawn attention to the inherently globalizing nature of Christianity, placing the modern missionary movement—of which Pentecostalism is a prominent part—in the forefront of the globalizing process.[8] Cox is one of those who, rather than seeing any political or economic cause-and-effect relationship, prefers to explore a subtler psycho-social affinity between the two. He arrives at the interesting conclusion that the Wind of Pentecost continues to gather momentum because it

---

5 Pocock, Van Rheenen, and McConnell, *Changing Face*, 24.

6 There appears to be no standard way of denoting this region of the world. Various terms used include: *third world, two-thirds world, majority world, non-Western world*, and so forth. While these can sometimes be confusing, all have a context for their emergence, and for the most part, are used interchangeably in the relevant literature. While my preference is for the geographical categories: *East–West, North–South, Western–non-Western*, I am not averse to using the others terms when contextually appropriate.

7 Among the explanations offered, some look for an underlying multinational-sponsored, market-driven, capitalist conspiracy in this convergence; others see a correlation with Max Weber's hypothesis linking the emergence of capitalism to the Protestant Ethic of Calvin following the Reformation (Stalsett, *Spirits*, 13–15).

8 R. V. Pierard perhaps shows this most lucidly in Pierard, "Viewing Denominational Histories," 140–43. See also Freston, "Evangelicalism and Globalization," 69–88; Freston, "Globalization, Religion, and Evangelical Christianity"; and Martin, "Evangelical Expansion."

enables millions of people to stay in touch with the "primal" experiential spirituality of their traditional cultures while coping with the pressures of modern life intensified by the rising Wave of globalization.[9]

Our interest in considering the convergence of the Wind and the Wave is, however, from a different direction. As those standing within the Hogan tradition of Pentecostal mission, we are less concerned with cause-effect theories than with trying to read the "signs of the times"— gauging how the forces of social and economic change will impact the future of Christ's mission in the world. We do not view social change in purely naturalistic terms. We see the hand of divine providence, as the sovereign Lord of history orchestrates the flow of world events in order to further his purpose for the universe. Our theology, thus, compels us to recognize that there is a sense in which the Wind and the Wave are both ordered by God: one is transcendent—having its source in the mighty rushing wind that comes directly from heaven, the other immanent— built into the complex interplay of political, social, and economic forces that control the movement of history. Responsible stewardship requires that we attend to both of these: we must follow the Wind and we must ride the Wave.

In taking time to explain the selection of this theme, I have a broader concern in view as well. Pentecostal pragmatists like me constantly struggle with the value of exercises in scholarship such as this. Why should we be devoting time, energy, and money to academic research and scholarship? Why not just get on with the job of reaching the lost, going to the unreached people groups, planting churches, feeding the poor—all of the things passionate Pentecostal activists love to do so well? For me personally, why am I presenting academic lectures and writing scholarly essays away for my home in Kolkata, where I could be reaching millions of unreached people in India?

The world of academic research and scholarship can often seem very remote from the hard realities of church life and the mission field. God forbid that we should ever let the cold armor of theological research and reflection crush the chest of fiery Pentecostal passion. But we tend to forget all the revival movements that were sidetracked or dissipated, and

---

9. Stalsett, *Spirits*, 1–22. Although we cannot concur with the naturalistic reductionism implicit in Cox's analysis, right-thinking Pentecostals can celebrate his implicit affirmation of the effectiveness of Pentecostal spirituality in meeting human needs at their deepest level, and its relevance to turbulent times in the twenty-first century.

those that died, because of bad theology or no theology. There is only one thing more important than saving lost souls today—that is, ensuring the enduring vitality of a missionary movement that will continue to carry the burden for lost souls and unreached people groups in future generations.

Stewarding our legacy is a responsibility that both the organizational and prophetic leadership of any movement must take to heart. This is why the mission and role of Pentecostal institutions of higher education are so critical. Even as we fan the flame of Pentecostal passion, we must continue to nurture a tradition of Pentecostal scholarship. Both are essential for the future of our movement. If Pentecostal mission is to survive and grow even more vibrant in the twenty-first century, Pentecostal scholarship of the knowledge on fire vintage must continue to be both guarded and grown. This is critical to shaping our ability to ride the Wave even as we continue to follow the Wind.

The principal assumptions undergirding our approach to this topic are twofold: (1) The formation of the Assemblies of God (AG) as a missionary movement in 1914 was a key factor in the globalization of the Pentecostal movement in the previous century; (2) During the thirty crucial years of his tenure as chief architect and administrator of the Assemblies of God World Missions program, J. Philip Hogan played a pivotal role in shaping missionary policy and practice that impacted the worldwide growth and expansion of the Pentecostal Movement. But an important clarification is in order here: this is not an attempt at another comprehensive assessment of Hogan's contribution.[10] Our concern rather is to examine how Hogan's far-reaching vision and Spirit-led insights can inform an approach to the unique challenges facing the Pentecostal missionary movement in the opening decades of the twenty-first century.

The main thesis of this essay is grounded in the conviction that the Hogan legacy gives Pentecostals a robust foundation and fresh impetus for Pentecostal mission in the twenty-first century. Hogan's Spirit-led vision provides the essential basis needed for a fresh, revitalized approach that is both consistent with the Pentecostal heritage and relevant to

---

10. Everett Wilson has already done this service for the Assemblies of God and the church at large (Wilson, *Strategy of the Spirit*). There will doubtless be subsequent in-depth studies in the future, necessary "alternative" readings that help us draw from the rich wisdom and seminal insights of Hogan. But this does not purport to be a study of that nature.

changing conditions in an era of rapid globalization. The globalization of Pentecostalism in the previous century could thus become an effective prelude and precursor to the globalization of Pentecostal missions in the second Pentecostal century. Thoughtful and discerning application of the Hogan legacy can help the Assemblies of God, remain at the forefront and cutting edge of Pentecostal missions in the twenty-first century, and it can help all Pentecostals remain at the forefront and cutting edge of missions generally in the twenty-first century.

Our treatment of this theme requires us first to focus on the globalization Wave, looking for some correlation, if any, with the Wind of Pentecostal Missions. We then go on briefly to consider Hogan's contribution, examining the underlying basis for his success in advancing the Pentecostal movement and confirming its potential for enhancing the future effectiveness of Pentecostal missions. We conclude by outlining some recommendations for strengthening and revitalizing Pentecostal global mission strategy. This essay will help set the stage for the response to the broader question: What should be the priorities for Pentecostal mission as we follow the Wind of Pentecost and ride the Wave of globalization to remain on the cutting edge of missions in the twenty-first century? My two subsequent essays in this book will expand in greater detail what this essay recommends in outline form, presenting further justification and spelling out the implications of what is being proposed.

A WORLD IN MOTION: THE WAVE OF GLOBALIZATION

Globalization[11] is without question the buzzword of the moment—some would say "the most talked-about and perhaps the least understood concept of this new millennium."[12] Globalization is historically complex, encompassing several large and multidimensional social processes.[13]

---

11 Although the term "global" is more than four hundred years old, the word "globalization" appears to have entered the English language only in the 1960s and came into common use only in the 1980s; see Hutchinson and Kalu, eds., *Global Faith*, 26. Richard Osmer notes that the term and its cognates became academically significant in sociology, political science, economics, and communication studies only in the mid-1980s, after which it has significantly influenced the fundamentals of many academic disciplines (Osmer, "Teaching Ministry," 37–38).

12. Ellwood, *No-Nonsense Guide*, 8.

13. How and where did globalization begin? There are various theories. Some see its advent at the dawn of history itself. Others see its beginning in the modern period with the emergence of capitalism, or more recently in the post-industrial era. All, however,

It refers broadly to the expansion of global linkages, the organization of social life on a global scale, and the growth of a global consciousness, leading to the consolidation of world society.[14] The literature on globalization is voluminous and descriptions of the phenomenon are so profuse that any attempt to define it here may seem superfluous. However, the term is not neutral; approaches to defining globalization are extremely diverse and variously nuanced depending on whether the author's slant is primarily economic, political, or sociological.[15] Hence, while a detailed analysis remains outside the scope of this paper, it is important to clarify the use of the term.

Although globalization is notoriously difficult to define, several widely accepted characteristics can be noted. First, Thomas Friedman's influential and popular definition (although it portrays globalization in terms of the spread of neo-liberal economics) highlights the most common feature associated with globalization—global interconnectedness:

> ... the inexorable integration of markets, nation-states, and technologies to a degree never witnessed before—in a way that is enabling individuals, corporations and nation-states to reach around the world farther, faster, deeper and cheaper than ever before.... Globalization means the spread of free-market capitalism to virtually every country in the world.[16]

In similar vein, Jonathan Inda and Renato Rosaldo view globalization in terms of transnational spatial-temporal processes, which are increasing the flow of capital, people, goods, images, and ideas across the world through heightened interconnectedness, resulting in "a world in motion . . . a shrinking world."[17] This global interconnectedness or interrelatedness that marks globalization manifests itself in different

---

agree that there has been a sudden acceleration in globalization in recent years due to opportunities created by advances in technology (Tiplady, *One World*, 2–3).

14. Paul Hiebert lists five main carriers of globalization: business and finance, global and regional governing bodies (e.g., UN, NATO, ASEAN), the academy, people movements, and popular culture (Hiebert, *Transforming World Views*, 243–46).

15. Steger, *Globalization*, 13. For instance, in Samuel Huntington's classic work, *Clash of Civilizations and the Remaking of World Order*, he seems to view globalization in primarily cultural terms: "culture and cultural identities, which at the broadest level are civilizational identities, are shaping the patterns of cohesion, disintegration, and conflict in the post-Cold War world. (Huntington, *Clash of Civilizations*, 20).

16. Friedman, *Lexus and the Olive Tree*, 8–9.

17. Inda and Rosaldo, *Anthropology of Globalization*, 9.

areas of human life, including economics, politics, and the media, and is transforming world affairs by linking capital, technology, and information across national borders.[18] Some people too easily identify globalization with Westernization, viewing it as the inevitable logical outcome of the impact of modernization. Globalization, however, is not exclusively about Western culture, but a new form of culture that knows no boundaries and is spreading from everywhere to everywhere. Its interconnectedness is multi-directional, and includes the transnational corporations and Western governments that ride the economic globalization wave as well as the global anti-capitalist movements that oppose it.

Second, globalization involves not only the fact of interconnectedness, but also a heightened awareness of global interconnectedness. This is highlighted in Roland Robertson's understanding, based on careful socio-cultural analysis: "The compression of the world and the intensification of consciousness of the world as a whole . . . concrete global interdependence and consciousness of the global whole."[19] Robertson insists that the relationship between the universal and the particular must be central to our understanding of the globalization process and its ramifications.[20] An important corollary of Robertson's conception is his belief that by bringing distant cultures into closer proximity, globalization inevitably generates a heightened awareness as a reflexive response, giving rise to a corresponding response of "localization" by which local cultural traditions are reinforced. Consequently, when ideas get to their new destination, they are not imbibed as they are—they are adapted to fit the local situation. Thus, rather than eliminating cultural differences, globalization includes localisation as an essential feature.[21]

At this point we are able to observe a fascinating correlation between these two essential impulses of globalization—universalization and localization—with corresponding features in the Pentecostal movement that have helped shape its unique appeal and widespread popular-

---

18. Tiplady, *One World*, 2.

19. Robertson, *Globalization*, 8.

20. Ibid., 97.

21. While suggesting that the term "glocalization" may describe the end result of the process more accurately, Robertson does not want it to replace globalization. For thoughts on unity, difference, and the Trinity see Osmer, "Teaching Ministry," 64. Hiebert does not hesitate to use the terms "glocal" and "glocalization" to describe the worldview emerging at the convergence of the globalization-localization movements (Hiebert, *Transforming World Views*, 241–55).

ity. While this has been pointed out by numerous analysts, Byron Klaus was among the earliest Pentecostal scholars to express this lucidly in a volume devoted to investigating Pentecostalism's nature as "a religion made to travel":

> Pentecostalism has been the quintessential indigenous religion, adapting readily to a variety of cultures. As a religious movement it has taken on the likeness of a particular culture of people. In one sense, Pentecostalism—with its autochthonous character—is a regionalized Christian movement.... In another sense, it can be argued that while regional differences are real, Pentecostalism has generated a global culture which shares a common spirituality.[22]

The seminal insights of Andrew Walls and Lamin Sanneh, two leading Christian historian-missiologists, are of crucial significance in this regard. For Walls, the universal relevance of the Christian faith is grounded in its central constitutive event—the Incarnation—and ensures its translatability. Christianity is, thus, essentially a vernacular faith, the most local of global faiths, and must always be rooted in the vernacular languages to be authentic.[23] Sanneh argues convincingly that in Christianity no individual culture or language has absolute normative status. Instead, diverse cultural forms are upheld in their plural diversity without being absolutized in their unique particularity.[24] Sociologist Paul Freston draws an important application of this idea to Pentecostalism from the Acts 2 narrative. He views this passage as the basis for Pentecostalism's "polycentric globalization," since it shows God reversing Babel by employing many languages, not by restoring a common language. Pentecostal Christianity is, thus, a universalism that affirms the particular, in contrast to modernity (a universalism that denies the particular) and post-modernity (particularisms that do not have universal application).[25]

---

22. Klaus, *Pentecostalism as a Global Culture*, 127.

23. Walls, *Missionary Movement*, 32.

24. Sanneh, *Translating the Message*, 117–51.

25. Freston, "Evangelicalism and Globalization," 72. Support for this observation can also be found in anthropological studies, such as Robbins's description of Pentecostalism as a homogenizing cultural force that is at the same time most susceptible to indigenous appropriation and localization, although his assumption that the homogenizing impulse is Western is open to debate (Robbins, "Globalization," 127–30).

This convergence of Robertson's socio-cultural analysis of globalization with Freston's description of Pentecostalism as "polycentric globalization" has momentous implications. Not only does it help explain why Pentecostalism is meeting with such spectacular success, it provides us with reasonable grounds for hope as we look into the future. It seems as though the Spirit of God who birthed the modern Pentecostal movement has been active both transcendently—blowing across the church, igniting revival fires, and raising up a massive missionary movement of the Spirit—and also immanently—in orchestrating world events and social processes that have given rise to the globalization phenomenon. We turn now to look more closely at the contribution of a key figure the Holy Spirit used in the Pentecostal missionary movement of the previous century, J. Philip Hogan.

J. PHILIP HOGAN'S VISION: "ANCHORED TO THE ROCK, BUT GEARED TO THE TIMES"

In his foreword to Hogan's missionary biography, Eastern European Pentecostal leader Peter Kuzmic quotes Hogan in offering this summary of Hogan's mission philosophy: "Hogan was not afraid to face new challenges and to adapt to change. 'The world has changed and so must we—anchored to the rock, but geared to the times.'"[26] Hogan was rock-hard in his commitment to what he believed was the source of Pentecostal missionary passion, a stewardship received from the founding fathers of the movement. Pentecost and mission are inseparably related, and mission is dependent on the Holy Spirit from start to finish:

> Make no mistake, the missionary venture of the Church, no matter how well planned, how finely administrated, or how fully supported, would fail like any other vast human enterprise, were it not where human instrumentality leaves off, a blessed ally takes over. It is the Holy Spirit that calls, it is the Holy Spirit that inspires, it is the Holy Spirit that reveals, and it is the Holy Spirit that administers.[27]

Hogan was also a strategic thinker who constantly sought out the power of creative and innovative ideas. His principal biographer notes: "Beyond

---

26. Wilson, *Strategy of the Spirit*, x.
27. Hogan, "Holy Spirit and the Great Commission," 32.

simply affirming a tradition . . . he demonstrated the relevance, adequacy, and universality of Pentecostal convictions."[28]

As a visionary leader whose eyes were always scanning the horizon, as far back as 1963 Hogan was making statements such as: "We cannot evangelize the world until we are willing to appraise the current world situation and fit our methods and message to these times. . . . We cannot evangelize this world until we are ready to adapt and be mobile."[29] His singular gift, as a Pentecostal missionary statesman, lay in his ability to hold in constant tension the need for strategic planning and absolute dependence on the Holy Spirit. There are many ways we could approach an assessment of Hogan's contribution to Pentecostal missions, but the genius of his mission legacy is best revealed when evaluated against the transmission of faith framework developed by Andrew Walls.

In his classic, widely-cited treatment of the issue, Walls takes us on an imaginary journey through time from the perspective of an extra-terrestrial visitor conducting an empirical study of Christianity. Walls's construct includes vivid descriptions of this visitor's observations of Christianity in Jerusalem in AD 37, Nicaea in AD 325, AD 650 in Ireland, London in the 1840s and Lagos, Nigeria in 1980. The observer from outer space is understandably perplexed by the contrasting features of these different communities, all of which claim to be Christian. If he were to look closely, however, the visitor would observe significant continuities as well: convictions regarding the centrality of Jesus and the Scriptures, the ritual use of bread, wine, and water, and consciousness about a historical connection with ancient Israel and other Christian faith communities world-wide and down through the ages.

Walls employs this illustration in a penetrating theological analysis of the missionary task of gospel transmission. He shows that it involves holding together in tension two opposing tendencies—the "indigenizing" principle and the "pilgrim" principle. The "indigenizing" principle, rooted in the fact of the Incarnation, keeps converts connected with the particulars of their local culture, so that Christ and Christianity are at home in any culture. The "pilgrim" principle, also grounded in the gospel, is the universalizing factor, which critiques the convert's local culture and unites him or her with the universal faith community, all the

---

28. Wilson, *Strategy of the Spirit*, 128.
29. Hogan, "Can the World Really Be Evangelized," 66.

people of God at all times everywhere.³⁰ As we have observed earlier, this relationship between the universal and the particular is central to our understanding of the globalization process, and a prominent feature of Pentecostalism as well. To what extent do we observe these two tendencies—the "indigenizing" principle and the "pilgrim" principle—in Hogan's missiology?

Although Hogan was a strategic thinker with a brilliant mind, he was primarily a mission statesman-practitioner, not an academic theologian. He did not have access to the conceptual framework of Professor Walls, and hence this important caveat: in what follows, I do not suggest that Hogan's approach concurs precisely with Walls's framework or that it anticipates its finer points. However, I do believe that evidence exists to indicate that the Spirit-led essential impulses of Hogan's mission philosophy, policy, and practice, resonate deeply with Walls's main thesis.

J. Roswell Flower and Noel Perkin, Hogan's predecessors in the executive office of AG Missions, strongly advocated the policy of indigenous missions and national autonomy. Melvin Hodge's book, *The Indigenous Church*, published in mid-century, reinforced the movement's commitment to raising national churches under national leadership. Hogan, however, pursued this ideal with passion and tenacity. In a March 1974 issue of Advance, after repeating the standard "three-self" formula, he establishes, or maybe emphasizes, the goal of the Foreign Missions department as follows: ". . . to evangelize the world, establish churches after the New Testament pattern, and to train national believers to preach the gospel both to their own people and in a continuing mission to other nations."³¹ He then goes on to give illustrations of how this policy has been effectively implemented in several regions of the world while asserting: "This means we have handed the torch of evangelism, training, and administration to nationals—where it belongs! There will never be enough American dollars or American missionaries to complete the job of evangelizing the world and discipling the nations. God never intended it to be done that way."³²

Hogan clearly went beyond some of his predecessors and peers in his vision of the local church overseas. Where many others saw poor, shallow, powerless, and unattractive congregations of native Christians,

30. Walls, *Missionary Movement*, 3–9.
31. Hogan, "Great Commission," 114.
32. Ibid.

Hogan's confidence in the power of the gospel helped him to see enthusiastic believers, rooted in their own culture, with a capacity for self-renewal and growth: "The church so born may not have a building; it may meet under the trees. It may have only the weakest of leadership; it may know nothing of Western forms of worship. But if it is a community-identified testimony of Jesus Christ, it is worth everything."[33] There is distinct resonance here with the "indigenous" principle of Walls's framework.

Hogan's strong emphasis on the indigenous national church was, however, balanced by a clear vision of the global church. As the Pentecostal movement began to grow exponentially in different regions of the world, Hogan began to fulfill the role of mission executive, religious diplomat, and mentor-encourager to national leaders all over the world. Much of his time and energy during this period was invested in trying to connect national Pentecostal tributary-movements with the ever-widening river of the emerging global Pentecostal movement.

The massive convocation at the Seoul meeting of the World Assemblies of God Fellowship in October 1994 represented the climax and fulfillment of Hogan's global missionary vision. In less than a century, Assemblies of God missions had facilitated the emergence of a truly global movement, which, as Wilson notes, was largely due to Hogan's vision. Many of the national leaders present were friends whom Hogan knew, loved, and had worked with for over thirty years, some of them leaders of powerful movements larger than the American Assemblies of God.[34]

Hogan's instinctive appropriation of the "pilgrim" principle is also evident in his active movement towards fellowship links with other Pentecostal and evangelical organizations from across the spectrum of biblical Christianity. He was concerned that the AG missionary movement remain connected to the wider church, so he often drew on expertise inter-denominationally and coordinated activities with other evangelical church and mission agencies when appropriate.[35]

Walls's framework sets forth a robust theological basis for the missionary transmission of faith, and the striking resonance of Hogan's mission philosophy with this framework is clearly a key factor that explains

33. Wilson, *Strategy of the Spirit*, 65.
34. Ibid., 179–83.
35. Ibid., 127–35.

the widespread success of Pentecostalism as "a religion made to travel." Consequently, today Pentecostalism has become both an "indigenous" movement, embedded in local cultures, as well as a "pilgrim" faith that is interconnected globally. Hogan's earnest and reflective dependence on the Holy Spirit guided the Pentecostal movement to a place of strategic influence, in step with the essential impulses of globalization and well positioned to respond effectively to the emerging missionary challenges of the twenty-first century.

PRIORITIES FOR PENTECOSTAL GLOBAL MISSIONS IN THE TWENTY-FIRST CENTURY

If the Wind of Pentecostalism and the Wave of globalization appear to be divinely synchronized as the discussion here suggests (a point developed further in chapter 8), and if the march of Pentecostal missions is in step with the drum beat of contemporary missions scholarship, have we not arrived? Why not just get on with the job—continue to do missions the same way as we have done before? God forbid! To lazily maintain the status quo, to continue business as usual, is to betray our legacy. For inherent in our legacy is a commitment to Follow the Wind, scanning the horizons, reading the signs of the times, listening to the voice of the Spirit even as we continue to be nourished deeply by the Word.

Following the Wind in this second Pentecostal century means that we seriously evaluate the potential impact of "globalization" upon the twenty-first century Pentecostal mission enterprise and strengthen our strategy accordingly. This concluding section of this paper will delineate briefly some priorities for Pentecostal missions emerging from necessary strategic responses to significant globalization trends.[36]

Massive Human Migration: Focus on Urban Centers

Migration is an irrepressible human urge, but people movements since the 1960s have been so extensive that the present period has been characterized as "the age of migration."[37] Large-scale migration is the most identifiable feature of contemporary globalization—people everywhere are on the move. While large-scale migration impacts several other

---

36. These will be elaborated on in greater detail and argued more closely in my subsequent essays.

37. Hanciles, "Migration and Mission: Religious Significance," 118.

trends of globalization, which affect the missionary task in ways we will consider separately, urbanization is a critical consequence of migration.

In 1700, 2 percent of the world's population lived in the cities. This figure grew to 9 percent in 1900, but since that time has grown to over 50 percent today. The United Nations, which offers the most conservative growth estimate, projects that by 2025 over 60 percent of the world's estimated 8.3 billion people will live in urban areas. By 2020 the urban population of Asia alone will be around 2.5 billion, having doubled in twenty-five years. Hogan observed this trend four decades ago. In a passionate plea to focus on the cities, in keeping with Pauline strategy, he writes: "we must not neglect the teeming, seemingly impenetrable metropolises from which the truth of the gospel can radiate into all corners of the nation."[38]

The "Deterritorialization" of Culture: Radically Rethink our Understanding of "Indigenous" Culture

Mission theology in the twentieth century paid much attention to the idea of "culture," employing concepts such as indigenization, inculturation, and contextualization to distinguish between the eternal truth of the gospel and its temporal expression in human culture. This understanding has helped clarify the task of missions and has undergirded the assumptions in much contemporary missiology and missions strategy. In their anthropological critique of globalization, Inda and Rosaldo have shown that in a globalizing world, the notion of culture itself needs to be revisited. They point out that anthropology ordinarily associates "culture" with a group of people (a nation, tribe, or ethnic group) and the idea of a fixed geographical territory. Thus, we see culture as rooted in the soil and take for granted that each nation-state embodies its own distinctive culture and society.[39]

Today, however, it seems almost anachronistic to think of culture in such localized terms. Globalization has pulled culture apart from place; culture has been deterritorialized, and we now live in a world of "culture in motion." Take the notion of "Indian" culture. Indian Tamils have more cultural commonalities with Tamils in Malaysia or Sri Lanka than they do with other Indians who live in adjoining Indian states. Bengali

---

38. Hogan, "Bush or the Boulevard," 77.
39. Inda and Rosaldo, *Anthropology of Globalization*, 10–14.

Indians have more in common with Bangla Deshis than other Indians. Young Indians in Mumbai or Kolkata have more in common with youth in Hong Kong or New York than they do with their peers who live fifty miles away out in the village. Our traditional framework and categories for cultural analysis are no longer relevant and need radical revision. Some sociologists are convinced that political globalization is taking us toward a borderless world in the twenty-first century in which the modern concept of nation may become redundant.[40]

Culture Shock and Religionquake: Respond Responsibly to Multiculturalism and Religious Plurality

The plurality of religions and cultures has always been an integral feature of the human race, but the shrinking world of globalization has forced a new experience of cultural and religious pluralism upon people everywhere. The massive migration of peoples that has accompanied globalization has brought about a degree of cultural diversity in societies today without parallel in the history of civilization. This situation has resulted in what Stackhouse calls "the shock of deprovincialization"—a sudden introduction to world religions and cosmopolitan cultures through the media and social engagement, which makes traditional certainties less stable.[41]

This unprecedented proximity to different religions and cultures can sometimes produce a strong, sometimes violent rejection of the alien "other." Or it can lead to a loss of confidence in one's faith, when growing familiarity leads to acceptance, even embrace of the cultural "other." Both responses are woefully inadequate. The greatest test facing the Christian global witness in the twenty-first century has to do with its ability to cope with the fact of cultural and religious plurality. What do we do with the "other"? Do we have only two ways to deal with difference: to either eliminate it coercively or to cave in to it tamely and uncritically?

The Shifting Center of Christianity: Work towards Partnership/ Covenant Relationship in Mission

The most significant demographic phenomenon in twentieth and twenty-first century Christianity is the southward shift in the center of

---

40. Steger, *Globalization*, 56–68; also see Kenichi, "End of the Nation State."
41. Stackhouse, "Theological Challenge of Globalization."

gravity of global Christianity. This southward shift has been thoroughly documented, statistically validated, and carefully analyzed by Philip Jenkins, Walls, and Sanneh, among others.[42] In 1800, 90 percent of the world's Christians were in Europe or North America. Today, northern Christians are in the minority for the first time in more than a thousand years. Sixty percent of the world's two billion Christians now live in the global South, and that proportion is rising.

We will side-step the huge theological and cultural implications for now and focus on the possible impact on mission strategy. In a careful study, Larry Pate and Lawrence Keyes observe that the mission movement emerging from the non-Western world, growing at a rate more than five times that of Western missions, will inevitably change the nature of the world missionary enterprise.[43] They convincingly conclude their assessment by arguing that the most mature response is that of partnership expressed in international networks devoted to interconnectedness and cooperation in evangelistic efforts, research, formulating strategy, training, and developing support structures.

Global networks and fellowship structures, which emerged during the Hogan era of missions, still continue to reflect New Testament patterns of covenant relationship and friendship in many areas of our movement. The Pentecostal movement will need to weigh thoroughly the implications of a firm commitment to this notion philosophically, and find ways to express this strategically. The potential benefits of such a South-North partnership are incalculable as we together face the twin challenges of "a post-Christian West and a post-Western Christianity" resulting from the southern shift of Christianity.[44]

The Rise of Global Poverty and Threat to Human Life: Develop a Theology of Integral Mission and Interdependence

Huge technological advances that accompanied globalization in the twentieth century have facilitated the emergence of a truly global economy. On the one hand, free market capitalism and the spread of

---

42. Barrett, "A.D. 2000," 39–54; Barrett, Kurian, and Johnson, *World Christian Encyclopedia*; Jenkins, *Next Christendom*; Walls, *Missionary Movement*; Walls, *Cross-Cultural Process*; Sanneh, *Translating the Message*; and Laing, "Changing Face of Mission."

43. Pate and Keyes, "Emerging Missions."

44. Walls, *Cross-Cultural Process*, 65.

multinational corporations have had an enormous positive impact on the global economy, providing employment to millions and creating significant middle class populations in some regions of the world.[45] On the other hand, economic globalization has also accentuated social disparities, widening the gap between the rich and the poor and driving a significant proportion of the world's population into extreme forms of poverty.[46]

A few painful globalization realities: (1) one out of five people in the world today does not have access to basic human needs of safe drinking water, adequate nutrition, health care, and basic education; (2) 1.3 billion people live in grinding poverty (less than one dollar per day) and 25 percent of them are Christians; (3) the total assets of the world's 225 richest people (one trillion dollars) equals the combined wealth of the three billion who comprise the poorer half of the world's population; and (4) a Nike quilted jacket costs $150 in a London shop, but less than 75 cents of that goes to the Bangladeshi women who make it.[47]

In addition to poverty, globalization has also brought with it various other threats to human life. It has increased the risk of infectious illnesses and epidemics, HIV-AIDS, and other sexually transmitted diseases. Human life is also endangered by human trafficking, cross-border terrorism, and environmental disasters due to humanly-engineered ecological imbalance. Latin American evangelical leader Samuel Escobar draws attention to the growing recognition among responsible evangelicals of the importance of the social component in mission before declaring, "in the coming century, Christian compassion will be the only hope of survival for victims of the global economic process."[48]

A strong case can be made for Pentecostalism's close alignment with the poor from its earliest inception.[49] Pentecostals who constantly

---

45. Osmer, "Teaching Ministry," 40–41; and Pocock, Van Rheenen, and McConnell, *Changing Face*.

46. Escobar, "Global Scenario," 32; Netland, "Introduction," 20–21. For a brief analysis of why and specific illustrations of how economic globalization is widening the gap between the rich and the poor, see Ellwood, *No-Nonsense Guide*, 90–106.

47. Valerio, "Globalisation and Economics," 21; Pocock, Van Rheenen, and McConnell, *Changing Face*, 48.

48. Escobar, "Global Scenario," 33.

49. Freston is one of those who sees its success as largely due to its essential quality as a counter-establishment movement that thrived among the poor and marginalized,

live in the world of the Bible have always instinctively practiced what we today refer to as "integral" mission—that the proclamation and demonstration of the gospel should go together. However, a clearer articulation of and commitment to this theology of "integral" mission is needed. The problems of global poverty and threats to human life are formidable, but the global presence of Pentecostalism—North and South; rich and poor; an incredible diversity of race and ethnicity—provides a unique opportunity of a truly global movement of witness against these forces of evil in our world. The key to success is to live out the New Testament ethical model of interdependence.

Political Resistance to Traditional Missionary Activity:
Pursue Creative Avenues of Access

In many regions of the world today, globalization finds a mixed response. While many welcome economic benefits, there also exists a resentment towards globalization with the view that it has a powerful tendency to homogenize cultures, akin to the cultural imperialism of the colonial era. In many parts of the world, earlier missionary efforts were frequently regarded as "religious" imperialism and closely associated with the colonial enterprise.[50] Consequently, the closing years of the twentieth century saw many nation-states closing their doors to vocational missionaries. The rise of religious fundamentalism in many Muslim, Hindu, and Buddhist majority countries has resulted in frequent hostility, even violent opposition, to the missionary presence in these countries.

In response to this challenge, Pentecostal missions will have to seriously consider redefining the function of missionaries and creative diversification of their role. Should all missionaries have to be theologically trained and ordained vocational ministers? Can we have missionaries whose primary vocations are doctors, university professors, professional consultants, or business entrepreneurs, enabling more free and privileged access to "closed" countries on the communication highways globalization provides?

---

by-passing the usual channels of wealth and power—a movement of "globalization from below" (Freston, "Evangelicalism and Globalization," 72–74).

50. For a glimpse into the ambiguities of the relationship between the missions and colonial powers, especially examples of collusion, see Robert, "Shifting Southward," 50–53.

The Explosion in Information-Communication Technology: Innovate Creatively

A prominent feature of globalization is the explosion of travel and communication. Human beings have maximized growing advances in technology in expressing the inexorable urge to communicate. The interconnectedness that the steam engine, telegraph, telephone, radio, automobile, and television provided for the previous generation has been heightened with the introduction of the computer, cell phone, internet, cable TV, and jet travel. The only difference is the multiplied speed and efficiency of these vehicles of communication.

The Christian global mission enterprise has always benefited from enhanced communication and transportation systems, but many of the tools of information technology and the media are a double-edged sword with huge risks as well as advantages. We must be boldly creative in innovations that can enhance the Pentecostal missionary enterprise without compromising our cherished values.

FOLLOWING THE WIND AND RIDING THE WAVE...

Pentecostal Missions is poised at a critical kairos[51] moment. This extraordinary convergence between the Wind and the Wave that we have observed in this essay is no accident of history. Christianity is inherently a globalizing movement and the Christian missionary movement is at the forefront of the globalizing process. The twentieth century saw the Pentecostal movement emerge as a powerful catalyst and facilitator of globalization. In Gal 4:4 we read: "But when the time had fully come, God sent his Son, born of a woman, born under law . . ." Scholars are in general agreement that the fullness of time referred to here points to the ideal cultural conditions provided by the rise of Greek civilization, the pax Romana, and the ethical monotheism disseminated by the Jewish Diaspora that helped promote the spread of the gospel in the first century.

Are we living in a similar time today? Does the rise of the globalization wave suggest that heaven is gearing up for the final push to reach the world before the return of Christ? I am convinced this is so, and if we respond as we should to the leading of the Spirit, we will see a

---

51. A Greek word for "time," but denoting a decisive—often divinely ordained—moment in history.

fresh surge of global Pentecostal missionary passion and power that will take the gospel to every person in the farthest, unreached corners of our world. The Christian globalizing movement will only reach its consummation with the fulfillment of the Christian kingdom vision of all things in heaven and on earth coming together under Christ:

> After this I looked and there before me was a great multitude that no one could count, from every nation, tribe, people and language, standing before the throne and in front of the Lamb. ... The kingdom of the world has become the kingdom of our Lord and of his Christ, and he will reign forever and ever. (Rev 7:9a and 11:15b)

Will globalization prove to be a friend or foe in this great venture? I believe the answer depends upon our response. We need both the courage and the discernment that the Spirit alone can give. In other words, we must be passionately Pentecostal! If we pursue the Spirit-led vision of J. Philip Hogan, we must be *anchored to the rock*—careful to eschew features of globalization that are at cross purposes with kingdom principles and values. But we will also be *geared to the times*—fearless in exploring where God is at work in globalization and maximizing the opportunities it offers to advance Christ's kingdom mission. For a movement of the Spirit, following the Wind and riding the Wave is not an option but a necessity—critical to our future, essential for our survival!

BIBLIOGRAPHY

Barrett, David B. "A.D. 2000: 350 Million Christians in Africa." *International Review of Mission* 59 (1970) 39–54.

Barrett, David B., G. T. Kurian, and Todd M. Johnson, eds. *World Christian Encyclopedia: A Comparative Survey of Churches and Religions in the Modern World, AD 1900–2000*. New York: Oxford University Press, 2001.

Ellwood, Wayne. *The No-Nonsense Guide to Globalization*. London: Verso, 2003.

Escobar, Samuel. "The Global Scenario at the Turn of the Century." In *Global Missiology for the Twenty-First Century: The Iguassu Dialogue*, edited by William D. Taylor, 25–46. Grand Rapids: Baker, 2000.

Freston, Paul. "Evangelicalism and Globalization: General Observations and Some Latin American Dimensions." In *A Global Faith: Essays on Evangelicalism and Globalization*, edited by Mark Hutchinson and Ogbu Kalu, 69–88. Sydney: Centre for the Study of Australian Christianity, 1998.

———. "Globalization, Religion, and Evangelical Christianity: A Sociological Mediation from the Third World." In *Interpreting Contemporary Christianity: Global Processes and Local Identities*, edited by Ogbu Kalu, 24–51. Studies in the History of Christian Missions. Grand Rapids: Eerdmans, 2008.

Friedman, Thomas L. *The Lexus and the Olive Tree.* New York: Farrar, Straus & Giroux, 1999.

Hanciles, Jehu J. "Migration and Mission: The Religious Significance of the North-South Divide." In *Mission in the Twenty-First Century: Exploring the Five Marks of Global Mission*, edited by Andrew Walls and Cathy Ross, 118–29. Maryknoll, NY: Orbis, 2008.

Hiebert, Paul G. *Transforming World Views: An Anthropological Understanding of How People Change.* Grand Rapids: Baker Academic, 2008.

Hogan, J. Philip. "The Bush or the Boulevard?" In *The Essential J. Philip Hogan*, edited by Byron D. Klaus and Douglas P. Petersen, 76–79. Springfield, MO: Assemblies of God Theological Seminary, 2006.

———. "Can the World Really Be Evangelized?" In *The Essential J. Philip Hogan*, edited by Byron D. Klaus and Douglas P. Petersen, 66–70. Springfield, MO: Assemblies of God Theological Seminary, 2006.

———. "Critical Issues." In *The Essential J. Philip Hogan*, edited by Byron D. Klaus and Douglas P. Petersen, 86-89. Springfield, MO: Assemblies of God Theological Seminary, 2006.

———. "The Great Commission: A Continuing Mission." In *The Essential J. Philip Hogan*, edited by Byron D. Klaus and Douglas P. Petersen, 113–16. Springfield, MO: Assemblies of God Theological Seminary, 2006.

———. "The Holy Spirit and the Great Commission." In *The Essential J. Philip Hogan*, edited by Byron D. Klaus and Douglas P. Petersen, 31–35. Springfield, MO: Assemblies of God Theological Seminary, 2006.

Huntington, Samuel P. *The Clash of Civilizations and the Remaking of World Order.* New York: Simon & Schuster, 1996.

Hutchinson, Mark, and Ogbu Kalu, eds. *A Global Faith: Essays on Evangelicalism and Globalisation.* Sydney: Centre for the Study of Australian Christianity, 1998.

Inda, Jonathan X., and Renato Rosaldo. *The Anthropology of Globalization: A Reader.* Oxford: Blackwell, 2003.

Jenkins, Philip. *The Next Christendom: The Coming of Global Christianity.* New York: Oxford University Press, 2002.

Kenichi, Ohmae. "The End of the Nation State." In *The Globalization Reader*, edited by Frank J. Lechner and John Boli, 214–18. 2nd ed. Oxford: Blackwell, 2004.

Klaus, Byron D. "Pentecostalism as a Global Culture: An Introductory Overview." In *The Globalization of Pentecostalism: A Religion Made to Travel*, edited by Murray Dempster, Byron D. Klaus, and Douglas P. Petersen, 127–30. Oxford: Regnum, 1999.

Laing, Mark. "The Changing Face of Mission: Implications for the Southern Shift in Christianity." *Missiology* 34 (2006) 165–77.

Martin, David. "Evangelical Expansion in Global Society." In *Christianity Reborn: The Global Expansion of Evangelicalism in the Twentieth Century*, edited by Donald M. Lewis, 273–94. Grand Rapids: Eerdmans, 2004.

Netland, Harold A. "Introduction: Globalization and Theology Today." In *Globalizing Theology: Belief and Practice in an Era of World Christianity*, edited by Craig Ott and Harold A. Netland, 14–34. Grand Rapids: Baker Academic, 2006.

Osmer, Richard. "The Teaching Ministry in a Multicultural World." In *God and Globalization. II. The Spirit and the Modern Authorities*, edited by Max L. Stackhouse and Don S. Browning, 37–75. Harrisburg, PA: Trinity Press, 2001.

Pate, Larry D., and Lawrence E. Keyes. "Emerging Missions in a Global Church." *International Bulletin of Missionary Research* 10, no. 4 (1986) 156–61.
Pierard, R. V. "Viewing Denominational Histories in Global Terms." In *A Global Faith: Essays on Evangelicalism and Globalization*, edited by Mark Hutchinson and Ogbu Kalu, 140–55. Sydney: Centre for the Study of Australian Christianity, 1998.
Pocock, Michael, Gailyn Van Rheenen, and Douglas McConnell. *The Changing Face of World Missions: Engaging Contemporary Issues and Trends*. Grand Rapids: Baker Academic, 2005.
Robbins, Joel. "The Globalization of Pentecostal and Charismatic Christianity." *Annual Review of Anthropology* 33 (October 2004) 117–43.
Robert, Dana L. "Shifting Southward: Global Christianity since 1945." *International Bulletin of Missionary Research* 24 (April 2000) 50–58.
Robertson, Roland. *Globalization: Social Theory and Global Culture*. London: Sage, 1992.
Sanneh, Lamin. *Translating the Message: The Missionary Impact on Culture*. Maryknoll, NY: Orbis, 1989.
Stackhouse, Max L. "The Theological Challenge of Globalization." Religion Online. http://www.religion-online.org/cgi-bin/relsearchd.dll/showarticle?item_id=60 (accessed September 7, 2003; webpage now discontinued).
Stalsett, Sturla J., editor. *Spirits of Globalization: The Growth of Pentecostalism and Experiential Spiritualities in a Global Age*. London: SCM, 2007.
Steger, Manfred B. *Globalization: A Very Short Introduction*. Oxford: Oxford University Press, 2003.
Synan, Vinson. *The Spirit Said "Grow."* Innovations in Mission 4. Monrovia, CA: MARC, 1992.
Tiplady, Richard, editor. *One World or Many? The Impact of Globalisation on Mission*. Globalization of Mission Series. Pasadena, CA: William Carey Library, 2003.
Valerio, Ruth. "Globalisation and Economics: A World Gone Bananas." In *One World or Many? The Impact of Globalisation on Mission*, edited by Richard Tiplady, 13–32. Pasadena, CA: William Carey Library, 2003.
Walls, Andrew F. *The Missionary Movement in Christian History: Studies in the Transmission and Appropriation of Faith*. Maryknoll, NY: Orbis, 1996.
———. *The Cross-Cultural Process in Christian History: Studies in the Transmission and Appropriation of Faith*. Maryknoll, NY: Orbis, 2002.
Wilson, Everett A. *Strategy of the Spirit: J. Philip Hogan and the Growth of the Assemblies of God Worldwide 1960–1990*. Carlisle, UK: Paternoster Press, 1997.

8

Mission "Made to Travel" in a World without Borders

Ivan Satyavrata

INTRODUCTION

MY FIRST ESSAY IN this book drew attention to the remarkable convergence of the *Wind* and the *Wave*—the two global mega-trends, Pentecostalization and globalization. The summary assessment of the Hogan legacy was directed towards indicating how the Pentecostal mission movement is suitably poised to effectively ride the globalization wave. I observed especially how Pentecostalism's success in holding together the *universal* and the *particular* resonates with globalization's essential impulses of *universalization* and *localization*. A reasonable theological inference drawn from this discovery is that God is at work in advancing the inherently globalizing Christian missionary movement both *transcendently*, in igniting the revival fires of Pentecost resulting in the spectacular spread of the gospel across the globe, and *immanently*, in orchestrating world events and social processes giving rise to globalization.

There is, however, no room for complacency as Pentecostal missions enters the second Pentecostal century. Movement into the next phase—from the globalization of *Pentecostalism* to the globalization of *Pentecostal mission*—calls for a revitalization of Pentecostalism's global mission strategy in step with the wave of globalization. *What should be* the priorities for Pentecostal mission as we follow the Wind of Pentecost and ride the wave of globalization to remain on the cutting edge of mission in the twenty-first century? The previous essay provided the first phase of the answer to this central question by identifying some key trends with recommended responses. This essay and my subsequent one explores these trends in closer detail, corresponding to two crucial shifts that need to take place in Pentecostal mission strategy. As a prelude to that task, however, we need to attend to an important preliminary concern. How do Pentecostals understand mission today? While my primary consideration in these essays is with mission strategy, the biblical and theological understanding of mission undergirding our discussion needs to be made explicit.

PENTECOSTAL MISSION AND MISSION IN THE TWENTY-FIRST CENTURY

Where does a Pentecostal theologian begin when trying to understand a concept as essential to biblical faith as mission? The first place to begin is the Bible of course! The obvious difficulty, however, is that neither the term "mission(s)" nor "missionary" is to be found in our English Bible. For the first fifteen centuries of its history, the church used the Latin term *missio* in theology to refer to the "sending" of the Son by the Father, and the "sending" of the Holy Spirit by the Father and the Son. What we today refer to as "mission(s)" was referred to by phrases such as "preaching of the gospel," "propagation of the faith," "extending the reign of Christ," or "planting the church." It was only during the colonial era that the Jesuits began to employ the term "mission(s)" to denote the spread of the Christian faith among those outside the church. From then on "mission(s)" has come to be used to refer to the means by which the church fulfils Christ's mission in our world.[1]

If the term "mission(s)" is not to be found in the Bible, how may we arrive at a biblically sound understanding of the concept? The difficulty with definition arises not from the lack of adequate biblical terminology as much as the richness and breadth of biblical teaching on the subject, which Christians today have tried to capture in the all-encompassing term "mission(s)." As David Bosch observes, while no single overarching term for mission exists in the New Testament, the New Testament uses

---

1. Bosch, *Transforming Mission*, 1.

close to one hundred Greek expressions that have a direct bearing on a biblical understanding of mission.[2] The Bible is thus the *original* handbook on mission, and any attempt to derive a definition of "mission(s)" exclusively from a few select terms, or from one or two preferred scriptural texts, is bound to lead us to a truncated and deficient understanding of mission. The theme is too critical, too central to the purpose of God, for us to limit the fullness of its biblical scope and vision.

How may we take Bosch's caution to heart in trying to arrive at a truly biblical understanding of mission? A safe starting point would appear to be the life and ministry of Jesus, assuming that the church's mission in the world is to be a continuation of the mission of Jesus. The basis for this is clearly set forth in the Fourth Gospel in at least two places: "As you sent me into the world, I have sent them into the world," and, again, "As the Father has sent me, I am sending you" (John 17:18 and 20:21).[3] The word "as" here has crucial significance, since it suggests that the manner in which the Father sent the Son determines the manner in which the church is sent by Jesus.[4] Thus, our understanding of "being sent" should be modeled after Jesus' manner of "being sent"—his way of mission should determine the way we understand and carry out mission. Jesus, in turn, sends his disciples "as the Father sent him."

The Gospels clearly indicate that Jesus' mission on earth was inseparably connected to the kingdom of God. Jesus' mission thus consisted essentially in making known and manifesting the reality of the kingdom of God, and the words and works of Jesus were directed towards a clear end and purpose: extending the kingdom-rule of God in the hearts of people.[5] The concept of the kingdom is central to a biblical understanding of mission, and the church's mission can only be rightly understood in the light of the kingdom of God. Mission is then simply *God extending his kingdom-rule through the church by calling all people everywhere to submit their lives to the Lordship of Christ.* Two important implications

---

2. Ibid., 16.

3. Leslie Newbigin follows John Stott here in gravitating towards the Johannine version of the Great Commission; Stott's preference is based on its distinct servanthood and incarnational implications. Newbigin, *Mission*, 23; cf. Stott, *Christian Mission*, 23.

4. Newbigin, *Mission*, 23; cf. Kraus, *Authentic Witness*, 20: "We must affirm . . . despite a prevalent and influential dispensationalist interpretation to the contrary, that the witness of the church is in direct continuity with the witness of the Christ."

5. Padilla, *Mission*, 186–89.

of this understanding need to be highlighted before we proceed any further.

To begin with, mission is properly *Missio Dei*—regardless of how this is interpreted—mission is about God and God's kingdom. God is bringing his kingdom in, and we are invited to participate in the process. Chris Wright, whose careful application of a *missional* hermeneutic to the message of the Bible as a whole has given us a truly comprehensive *missional* biblical theology, argues strongly for the theological priority of *God's* mission: "Fundamentally, our mission (if it is biblically informed and validated) means our committed participation as God's people, at God's invitation and command, in God's own mission within the history of God's world for the redemption of God's creation."[6] Wright argues that it is misleading to take our missiological starting point only from the human activities of mission, however biblical, Spirit-directed, and important they may be. *God* is on mission, and all humanly-initiated mission or missions flow from the prior and larger priority of the mission of God.[7]

Mission is thus not primarily a human enterprise; it is the outworking of God's sovereign, eternal purpose and plan for God's world. It is important to emphasize this especially in a day and age when technology, education, media, funding strategy, and marketing seem to have become indispensable to the work of missions.[8] God's mission must never degenerate into a humanly-engineered, corporate marketing enterprise. From start to finish it must always remain a God-dependent, Spirit-empowered, Christ-glorifying endeavor.

Second, since mission is centered on God's kingdom, and because the church, the community of God's people, is the *locus* of God's kingdom on earth, mission must be *church-centered*. In mission, God works

---

6. Wright, *Mission of God*, 23.

7. Most Bible-believing Christians would agree that the Bible provides a basis for mission. Chris Wright believes that there is actually a missional basis for the whole Bible—it is generated by, and is all about, God's mission (ibid., 531).

8. Alan Johnson cites evangelical sociologist John Seel's scathing critique of Evangelicalism's uncritical accommodation, before adding his own solemn word of caution: "When we scratch beneath the surface of our rhetoric about the leading of the Spirit and spiritual dynamics we find ourselves to be part of a system. . . .Thus, we believe that more money and better technology will solve our problems. . . . As we pursue the efficient production of results based on our market driven indicators of success our agendas supersede all else, while those we purportedly come to serve become the tools that we utilize to achieve our ends (Johnson, *Apostolic Function*, 221).

to expand his kingdom, to extend his rule in the hearts of men and women, but God seeks to do this through the church. Christ entrusted the completion of God's mission and the commission to make disciples of all nations to his faith-community of followers (the church), and equipped them for this purpose with the supernatural endowment of the Holy Spirit on the day of Pentecost (Matt 28:18–20 and Acts 1:8). Pentecostal mission has, since its earliest stages, always viewed the church as being at the center of God's missionary purpose. For instance, this is both reflected in the title, structure, logic, and content of Melvin Hodges's Pentecostal theology of missions, and also explicitly stated in his introduction:

> *Missions* refers to the carrying out of the redemptive purpose of God for mankind through human instrumentality . . . missions does not begin with the missionary or evangelist. The missionary is only the instrument. Moreover, he does not stand alone—he is a member of the Church and its representative. Hence, the importance of the study of ecclesiology in the study of missions. . . . The study of missions then becomes the study of the Church. *A weak theology of the Church will produce a weak sense of mission.*[9]

A third crucial element in the above conception of mission is its understanding of kingdom-rule extension. God's kingdom-rule is extended every time an unbeliever repents and accepts Christ as Lord. But what does this involve? How does God extend his kingdom-rule? A series of processes are involved in taking the gospel of the kingdom to the various peoples of the world, enabling them to understand it and respond to it meaningfully. The actual task of mission today entails: recruitment and training of workers; their administrative, financial, and pastoral support; research into unreached people groups/mission fields; language acquisition and translation work; evangelistic activity; compassionate ministry/ development work that authenticates verbal witness; discipling and nurturing; church-planting; and training of workers/ ministerial education.

Disagreement and debate sometimes arises over whether "mission(s)" should properly be restricted to all or only some of those aspects referred to above.[10] Thus, in contemporary usage, a distinction

---

9. Hodges, *Theology*, 10.

10. The term "mission(s)" today is thus used in a wide variety of ways. In the opening page of Bosch's classic work on mission, he lists no less than twelve conventional uses, and in the course of his extended treatment introduces a wide range of contemporary

has sometimes been made between "mission"—its broader biblical and theological sense, and "missions"—a more restricted reference to the more "apostolic" functions or specifically cross-cultural missionary ventures.[11] In addressing this dilemma, Bosch, on the one hand, recalls Stephen Neill's famous words, "If everything is mission, nothing is mission," in cautioning against the tendency to define mission too broadly. On the other hand, he warns against "straight-jacketing" what is in reality "a multifaceted ministry" by "any attempt at delineating mission too sharply."[12] Bosch's wise conclusion reminds us again that the truth in this case, as in many other aspects of biblical precept and practice, lies in the balance between two extremes.

The issue is less about terminology than about biblical integrity and theological consistency. For drawing such a distinction between "mission" and "missions" runs the risk of distancing the church from mission—of separating, and in some cases "legitimizing" the church's "non-missional" activities from its "missional" activities, including its cross-cultural mission mandate. A truly Pentecostal ecclesiology, however, always views the church as the church-in-mission, and a truly Pentecostal missiology refuses to see the mission apart from the life of the church. The church and mission are thus organically related as root to the fruit, and any understanding of one that does not include the other will result in an inadequate view of both.[13] Hence, all that the church does—its worship, discipleship and church growth, salt and light living, evangelism, church planting, and cross-cultural mission—should be intentionally directed towards extending the kingdom of God on the earth.[14]

Two important clarifications are necessary. First is the concern that a broader definition of mission runs the risk of the term losing its cutting edge when it is inflated to include everything that the church does. When the church *is* the church as Jesus intended it to be, it should be a church-in-mission, and must not engage in any activity that does not

---

applications of the term, especially focused in his discussion of thirteen paradigms in chapter 12 (Bosch, *Transforming Mission*, 1, 368–510).

11. There is no real biblical or theological warrant for such a distinction, and hence we do not make such a differentiation in our use of the terms "mission" and "missions."

12. Bosch, *Transforming Mission*, 511–12.

13. A point stressed in Emil Brunner's famous saying: "The Church exists by mission as a fire exists by burning," quoted in Shenk, *Write the Vision*, 87.

14. Moreau, Corwin, and McGee, *Introducing World Missions*, 77–79.

in some way further God's kingdom-mission. The counter argument is that, in actual fact, the church often does not do what it should, and hence every activity it engages in cannot be called mission. The difficulty with this objection is that it derives legitimacy implicitly from deviant contemporary social expressions and practices of the church rather than from the biblical vision. A constricted understanding thus poses an even greater danger to "apostolic" mission in that, by distancing church from mission, it deepens and legitimizes the divide between the church's routine non-missional activity and the specialist "mission" activity.

Second, a broader understanding of mission in no way undermines the strategic priority of cross-cultural mission and church planting among unreached people groups. Rather it seeks to provide theological legitimacy and motivation for broader participation in the church's cross-cultural missionary enterprise. Hence, rather than seeing mission as the responsibility of a privileged few with an apostolic calling and gifting, it envisions mission as an enterprise in which the whole body of Christ is actively involved: the researcher whose work assists the church planter; the health or development worker whose motivation is to authenticate the gospel message so that unbelievers will be drawn to Christ; the educator who helps equip missionaries for the mission field; the pastor who nurtures a mission-giving and mission-sending church; and the mission official who administers, mentors, and cares for the needs of missionaries.

To use a military metaphor, the various functions of the church are to cross-cultural or frontier "missions" what the armament factory, corps of engineers, military training camps, and supply lines are to the front-line of the battle. Each have a different function, but all are equally soldiers in the same army, fighting for the same cause, at war with the same enemy. Mission is likewise an enterprise in which the whole church should be engaged intentionally and instrumentally, and should be the filter that orients and directs every activity of the church towards the extension of God's kingdom. The present reflection is thus based on the conviction that mission is *God extending his kingdom-rule to people of all nations as the Holy Spirit empowers the whole church to take the whole gospel to the whole world.*

With this clarification of an important guiding premise, I return then to the main flow of the discussion and evaluate the impact of globalization on the nature and task of mission in the twenty-first century, beginning with a closer examination of the first three globalization trends and the corresponding responses to each identified in my previous essay.

MASSIVE HUMAN MIGRATION: FOCUS ON URBAN CENTRES

Large-scale migration is the most identifiable feature of contemporary globalization—people everywhere are on the move. Migration movements give rise to "cultures in motion," for as people move, they carry their ideas, beliefs, and religious practices with them.[15] Migration remains a prime factor in the global expansion of religions and will continue to have an even greater impact in the twenty-first century.[16]

In his analysis of the migrant movements of the modern period, Jehu J. Hanciles observes that from about 1500 to 1950 international migration was largely dictated by the needs and designs of European colonial expansion and the flow of missionary activity. During the 125 years between 1800 and 1925, an estimated fifty to sixty million Europeans moved overseas, effectively occupying or settling in over one-third of the inhabited world. From the 1960s, however, the tide has been reversed with the vast majority of migrants coming from the non-Western world to Europe and North America. By 2000, Europe and North America received close to 60 percent of the 175 million international migrants. Reasons for the rising tide of South-North migration include demographic imbalances, the growing economic divide, refugee crises, and increasing global connectivity.[17]

The number of international migrants across the globe has increased by over 150 percent in the last four decades and more than doubled between 1975 and 2005.[18] The largest *diaspora* is Chinese, with an estimated fifty-five million living outside mainland China, followed by twenty-two million Indians who live outside India.[19] According to United Nations estimates, in 2010 the total number of international migrants in the world is expected to reach 214 million, a projected 10 per-

---

15. Stearns, *Cultures in Motion*, 69–72.
16. Hanciles, "Migration and Mission: Some Implications," 146.
17. Hanciles, "Migration and Mission: Religious Significance," 119–24.
18. Ibid., 118–19.
19. McConnell, "Changing Demographics," 48.

cent increase since 2005. The more developed regions will be impacted the most, as they are expected to gain forty-five million international migrants between 1990 and 2010, a 55 percent increase. As a result, international migrants will account for 10 percent of the total population in the more developed regions by 2010.[20]

Large-scale migration flows into other trends of globalization in several significant ways, but one of its critical effects impacting the missionary task is the urban explosion. The movement of more than a billion people to the cities during the last two decades of the twentieth century is the largest population movement in history.[21] In the last two hundred years, the number of cities (over 100,000 people) in the world has grown one hundred times, from forty in 1800 to about four thousand in 2000.[22]

This massive shift towards urban cultures and civilizations is without precedent in history. Between 1950 and 1980, the urban population in third world mega-cities grew from 275 million to almost one billion.[23] At the beginning of the twentieth century, about 14 percent of the world's population lived in cities. Today, the figure has grown to over 50 percent—and this movement has occurred entirely in one century during which time the total population of the world has quadrupled.[24] The United Nations, which offers the most conservative growth estimate, projects that by 2025 over 60 percent of the world's estimated 8.3 billion people will live in urban areas. The growth of urbanization presents both formidable challenges and huge opportunities for mission. Urbanization has produced several giant shifts resulting in profound and permanent changes in many societies. Since it is a global phenomenon, many of the same manifestations are evident around the world, regardless of culture or society.

The greatest disparity between the wealthy and poor, as well as extreme cultural and religious diversity, is found in the cities. Urban poverty around the world shares similar problems of lack of adequate housing, limited access to health care, lack of job opportunities, family breakdown, and loss of traditional socio-cultural identity. The majority of migrants to the mega-cities live in slums or squatter areas in abso-

20. United Nations, *Trends in International Migrant Stock*.
21. Greenway, "Challenge of the Cities," 553.
22. Barrett, Johnson, and Crossing, "Christian World Communions," 25–32.
23. Grigg, "Urban Poor," 582.
24. Barrett, Johnson, and Crossing, "Christian World Communions," 32.

lute poverty, and are generally unable to meet their basic needs of food, clothing, and housing. The number of slum dwellers and urban squatters in the world's major cities doubles every decade.[25] The family unit has also come under severe assault in the city, resulting in a marked increase in divorces, separations, and a general lack of healthy family life. Many cultures that once had a healthy, solid family structure have witnessed serious and rapid erosion of traditional family values in the city. Yet at the same time, urban dwellers are generally very open and responsive to the gospel due to rapid change, social dislocation, and alienation. Cities offer tremendous opportunity since they are centers of communication from which ideas spread effectively to rural areas. In today's cities, culturally distant peoples frequently live right next door to each other and are easily accessible to the gospel.

Timothy Keller, who has experienced remarkable success in urban mission as pastor of Redeemer Presbyterian Church in Manhattan, New York, makes a strong case for more *Christians to locate long-term in cities for strategic and more effective Christian witness*. Marshalling convincing historical evidence, he points out that by AD 300, the urban populations of the Roman Empire were largely Christian, while the countryside was pagan (the word *pagan* originally meant someone from the countryside). Likewise during the first millennium AD in Europe, the cities were Christian, but the broad population across the countryside was pagan. He concludes: "The lesson from both eras is that when cities are Christian, even if the majority of the population is pagan, society is headed on a Christian trajectory. Why? As the city goes, so goes the culture. Cultural trends tend to be generated in the city and flow outward to the rest of society."[26]

In contrast, today, while the general global urban population grows, the percentage of Christians in urban areas has been steadily declining, from 69 percent in 1900 to 46 percent in 1985, and is projected to shrink further to less than 40 percent by the middle of the century. Keller issues a twofold challenge to Evangelicals:

> Reach the city to reach the culture. Protestant (evangelical) Christians are the least urban religious group and thus have the

25. Grigg, "Urban Poor," 581–82.

26. Keller, "Urban Christian," 38. According to Paul Hiebert, "One reason for the rapid spread of early Christianity was its movement through the cities" (Hiebert, "Social Structure," 428).

least impact culturally. Three kinds of people here affect the future: a) elites, b) new immigrants, c) the poor. The single most effective way for Christians to "reach" the US would be for 25% of them to move to two or three of the largest cities and stay there for three generations. Reach the city to reach your region and the world.... You can't reach the city from the suburbs, but can reach all the metro area from the city.... The cities of the world are now linked more to one another than to their own states and countries. Each major city is a "portal" to the other major cities of the world.[27]

How should Pentecostal mission respond to the challenges of urbanization? Augustus Cerillo has listed several strengths that Pentecostals are able to bring to the challenge of urban mission.[28] He points out that Pentecostalism has had a significant urban heritage and has been immensely successful in cities all over the world, prompting the comment that "Pentecostal growth and urbanization seem to go together."[29] Cerillo's assessment of available data leads him to conclude that "a majority of the world's Pentecostals and charismatics are urban dwellers."[30] Their supernatural worldview enables Pentecostals to reach out aggressively in helping meet felt needs of people in cities.

Pentecostal mission in the twenty-first century needs to develop a strategic focus on the cities and urban centers. The fact that many cities of the world face similar social and spiritual challenges presents us with an opportunity and obligation to work in close global partnership for efficient sharing of information and of human and material resources.

THE "DETERRITORIALIZATION" OF CULTURE: RADICALLY RETHINK OUR UNDERSTANDING OF "INDIGENOUS" CULTURE

> Jesus shall reign where'er the sun, does his successive journeys run;
> His kingdom spread from shore to shore, till moon shall wax
>   and wane no more.
> From north to south the princes meet, to pay their homage at His feet;
> While *Western empires* own their Lord, and *savage tribes*
>   attend His word.

27. Keller, "Biblical Theology."
28. Cerillo, "Pentecostals and the City," 98–104.
29. Quoted in ibid., 99.
30. Ibid., 100.

In his discussion of the great missionary expansion of the eighteenth and nineteenth centuries, Jaroslav Pelikan refers to this hymn as a symbol of Christian growth.[31] This great hymn of Isaac Watts, based on Psalm 72, is deeply cherished as one of the earliest missionary hymns, but sometimes seen by people of the erstwhile "savage tribes" as merging God's purpose and Great Britain's ecclesiastical, political, and economic destiny. Given that Watts was known to have substituted "Britain" for "Israel" in some of the psalms, it is possible that in the heyday of the colonial era, some British parishioners subconsciously sang: "[Britain] shall reign where'er the sun does its successive journeys run; [Her] kingdom stretches from shore to shore, till moon shall wax and wane no more."

The text of "Jesus Shall Reign" clearly reflects the culture of its time and a period when the Protestant and Catholic missionary movements that flooded countries like India and China and the African continent aligned with and often supported the goals of imperialism.[32] The Western missionary enterprise in the post-Enlightenment period was clearly tainted by cultural imperialism. Several Western nations assumed not only the intrinsic superiority of their national cultures over all other cultures, but viewed themselves as God's instruments for the Christianization of the colonized territories, a conviction variously referred to as "the white man's burden" or "manifest destiny."[33]

The twentieth century saw a growing awareness of the naiveté and arrogance implicit in this widespread cultural nationalism, although a full realization of the vital theological distinction between the gospel and culture came only in the wake of the world wars. The rise of the social sciences helped with the analysis and understanding of human behavior, and the notion of culture has been central to the framework of analysis. Mission theology has benefited immensely from the social sciences and found a particularly helpful friend in cultural anthropology. Concepts such as indigenization, inculturation, and contextualization have been introduced into mission discourse to distinguish between the eternal truth of the gospel and its temporal expression in human culture. The impetus for indigenous churches and contextualized expressions of

---

31. Pelikan, *Jesus through the Centuries*, 221.

32. While this is now a common theme in missiological discussion, for a concise but thorough, and honest yet balanced treatment, see Bosch, *Transforming Mission*, 291–313.

33. Ibid., 298–302.

the Christian faith was derived from this discourse and based on a certain notion of culture.

The powerful spatial-temporal processes of globalization have, however, caused many to feel that the notion of culture has been undermined to the point that it needs to be radically revised. For instance, anthropologists Jonathan Inda and Renato Rosaldo point out that culture is ordinarily associated with a group of people (a nation, tribe, or ethnic group) and is closely linked to the particularities of place. The idea of culture traditionally carries with it expectation of roots in the soil and a fixed geographical territory.[34] In their exploration of how space and place impact culture and cultural difference, Akhil Gupta and James Ferguson explicate this further:

> The distinctiveness of societies, nations, and cultures is predicated on a seemingly unproblematic division of space, on the fact that they occupy "naturally" discontinuous spaces. . . . For example, the representation of the world as a collection of "countries," as on most world maps, sees it as an inherently fragmented space, divided by different colours into diverse national societies, each "rooted" in its proper place. . . . It is so taken for granted that each country embodies its own distinctive culture and society that the terms "society" and "culture" are routinely simply appended to the names of nation-states, as when a tourist visits India to understand "Indian culture" and "Indian society" or Thailand to experience "Thai culture" or the United States to get a whiff of "American culture."[35]

We have thus taken for granted in the past that each nation-state embodies its own distinctive culture and society. Today, however, it seems almost anachronistic to think of culture in such localized terms. In support of this argument, Gupta and Ferguson point to several illustrations of how the traditional notion of culture is no longer helpful as it applies to those who inhabit the border regions of nation states, also immigrants, refugees, exiles and expatriates, and its inadequacy in relation to the phenomena of "multiculturalism" within a locality and the hybrid cultures of postcoloniality. The category also fails to do justice to social and cultural

---

34. Inda and Rosaldo, Anthropology of Globalization, 10–14.
35. Gupta and Ferguson, "Beyond 'Culture,'" 65–66.

change proceeding freely across hitherto autonomous spaces today due to the interconnectedness we have in a globalized world.[36]

Globalization has pulled culture apart from place; culture has been uprooted from particular localities, and we now live in a world of "culture in motion." Anthropologists refer to this weakening of the ties between culture and place as the deterritorialization of culture. This does not thereby imply that culture is free-floating. Rather culture no longer necessarily belongs in or to a particular place—it is always "reterritorialized" in another place or places. The processes that shape it thus simultaneously transcend territorial boundaries and continue to have territorial significance.[37] What is of crucial importance to note is that the traditional notion of culture as predicated on geographical boundaries or national borders is a thing of the past.

This anthropological commentary on the impact of globalization on the deterritorialization of culture resonates remarkably with the observations of those who see the powerful transnational currents of economic globalization progressively weakening traditional cultural and national identities. In an article somewhat provocatively entitled "The End of the Nation State," Kenichi Ohmae points out that nation states which were at one time "independent, powerfully efficient engines of wealth creation" have now become "little more than bit actors . . . remarkably inefficient engines of wealth distribution."[38] Basing his political verdict on incisive, if at times disconcerting, economic analysis, he observes:

> So powerful have these currents [of economic globalization] become that they have carved out entirely new channels for themselves—channels that owe nothing to the lines of demarcation on traditional political maps. Put simply, in terms of real flows of economic activity, nation states have already lost their role as meaningful units of participation in the global economy of today's borderless world.[39]

According to Ohmae, to speak of a nation state like Russia or China as a single economic unit is "nostalgic fiction." It is also impossible to attach an accurate national label to goods and services produced and traded in today's economically globalized world when the components

36. Ibid., 66–67.
37. Inda and Rosaldo, *Anthropology of Globalization*, 11–12.
38. Ohmae, "End of the Nation State," 207; see also Steger, *Globalization*, 56–68.
39. Ohmae, "End of the Nation State," 207.

assembled in one country may actually be manufactured and sent from various corners of the globe. This "borderless economy" has resulted in the decline of nation states as units of economic activity and may result in cultural, religious, ethnic, and tribal affiliations replacing anemic notions of nationhood as more stable sources of group identity. According to Ohmae, the controlling feature of the global culture of the future is the web of shared interest marked by "information-driven participation in the global economy."[40]

Our traditional categories of cultural analysis are thus no longer relevant. For instance, how are we to apply concepts such as "indigenous" or "cultural context" to the Tamil diaspora scattered throughout Europe, Malaysia, Sri Lanka, North America, and different parts of India? Is the Chinese American who speaks both Mandarin and English more Chinese or American? Is her cultural affiliation closer to her African-American colleague at work or Cantonese Chinese in Hong Kong or Taiwan? Hanciles uses the term "transmigrants" to describe such individuals who reflect multiple cultural affinities. Transmigrants are typically at least bilingual, can lead dual lives, move comfortably between cultures, may maintain homes in two countries, and are active social players in both.[41]

Wilbert Shenk believes that these changing socio-political realities call for a complete revisioning of how mission is to be carried forward.[42] He describes the present movement as an "era of polycentric history" when the centers of power will likely be increasingly dispersed, posing important questions for missiological theory. According to Shenk, the theory of the indigenous church emerged to explain and make more efficient a unidirectional movement from West to non-West. Today, however, the locus of power has shifted irreversibly away from its traditional

40. Ibid., 208–10. The diminishing role of the nation state is a contested claim in globalization discourse. For example, in the wake of the recent economic crisis during which global financial corporations were powerless and on the verge of collapse (e.g., AIG), it was the central banks and governments of nation states that stepped in to stop the bleeding–whether or not their action was correct, it was to the nation state that people looked to wield power to control a global economic crisis.

41. Although the traditional Western missionary was the "classical" transmigrant who lived simultaneously in two societies, the intensification of global interaction and connectedness in the present era has made the transmigrant lifestyle accessible to a wider spectrum of the world's population; see Hanciles, "Migration and Mission: Some Implications," 148.

42. Shenk, *Changing Frontiers*, 174–76.

Western base to multiple new centers across the world, where church structures are being developed, local theologies formulated, and mission programs launched. Shenk concludes optimistically: "Viewing the world as consisting of multiple centres of resource and initiative will force us to think in new ways about the shape of Christian mission in the twenty-first century."[43]

We have yet to see how the notion of "indigenous culture" will be redefined in a polycentric world of "cultures in motion." Culture is a complex entity comprising not only language, dress, food habits, and social mores, but deeper, subliminal elements—attitudes and values regarding race, gender, ethnic identity, and national allegiance—all of which shape our basic identity. However the notion of "indigenous" is redefined in future discourse on culture, culture can never be an obstacle to mission. Christ is never the guest of culture; he is always the Lord over culture!

CULTURE SHOCK AND RELIGIONQUAKE: RESPOND RESPONSIBLY TO MULTICULTURALISM AND RELIGIOUS PLURALITY

The rise of globalization at the dawn of the new millennium attended by massive migrations of people and unprecedented global interconnectedness has forced a new experience of cultural and religious pluralism upon people everywhere without parallel in the history of civilization. Our planet has become a web of criss-crossing influences. Air travel, the internet, information technology, television, and the media have brought about a mingling of peoples and cultures that our parents could not have imagined, giving rise to the twin phenomena of multiculturalism and religious plurality.[44]

While multiculturalism is sometimes understood as "a deliberate fashioning of society so as to make it culturally/ethnically heterogeneous,"[45] its use here is in its more passive connotation to refer simply to the fact of plurality, the multicultural environment that characterizes life in the twenty-first century in most developed regions of the world. The religious landscape, especially of Europe and North America, has

---

43. Ibid., 175.

44. Lundy, "Multiculturalism and Pluralization," 71–76; and Netland, *Religious Pluralism*, 9–15.

45. Lundy, "Multiculturalism and Pluralization," 71.

undergone rapid and profound changes over the past half century.[46] The USA will have a population with more than 50 percent non-white by 2050; New York city has more than 350,000 Dominicans, the capital of the Dominican Republic has only 225,000 people; Paris has more North Africans than most cities in North Africa; Los Angeles is home to over one hundred spoken languages, Toronto has almost two hundred languages; two thousand mosques and Islamic centers exist across the USA, eight million Muslims currently live in the USA and that number is increasing at a rate of 200,000 per year.

The encounter between cultures can be exhilarating, but also fraught with tension and even violence. For instance, globalization has brought closer the sharp disparities and uneven distribution of economic resources: Nine out of ten people have never made a phone call; ninety-nine out of one hundred people do not have access to the internet; Tokyo, with twenty-three million people, has three times as many telephone lines as Africa with 580 million people. The most serious tensions, however, are manifested in the area of religious conflict, intensified by widespread religious revival and global expansion of most of the world religions, including Islam, Hinduism, Buddhism, and other eastern religions, as well as Christianity. Hanciles indicates this in his study of the impact of human migrations on mission: "It is gradually becoming obvious that the process(es) of globalization . . . is potentially transforming several major faiths into truly global religions, present in nearly every country, even if in culturally distinctive forms."[47]

This clash of religious cultures produces what Gailyn Van Rheenan describes as a "Religionquake"[48] and Max Stackhouse calls "the shock of deprovincialization"[49]—anxiety and insecurity in relation to traditional certainties. This can sometimes lead to a strong, sometimes violent rejection of the alien "other," of which 9/11 was an extreme manifestation of the worst kind—this is why post-9/11, religion is seen as the most powerful source of conflict, and conservative wings of most religions are viewed askance as hate-generating fundamentalisms. Some who document the rise of religious terrorism point out the close connection

---

46. Most of these illustrative statistics have been gleaned from ibid., 72–74 and Netland, *Religious Pluralism*, 9–10.

47. Hanciles, "Migration and Mission: Some Implications," 146.

48. Van Rheenen, "Religionquake," 79.

49. Stackhouse, "Theological Challenge of Globalization."

between religious fundamentalism and terrorist violence, providing chilling insight into the world of fanatics in most of the world's major religious traditions, including Christianity, Islam, Hinduism, Judaism, Buddhism, and Sikhism.[50]

The only reasonable alternative appears to be to nurture a culture of tolerance. For most people, however, this tolerance is shaped by the controlling pluralistic ethos that marks our culture, and is viewed as implying the relativization of everything through pluralization. The pressure is then to celebrate diversity or differences in their own right, whether they are cultural or moral or religious. The only absolute is the conviction that there are no absolutes. Every culture and religion is to be respected as equally legitimate and valid. Perhaps the best popular expression of this is in the words of Rabbi David Hartman, whom Thomas Friedman quotes in an article written shortly after 9/11:

> All faiths that come out of the biblical tradition—Judaism, Christianity and Islam—have the tendency to believe that they have the exclusive truth.... The opposite of [this] religious totalitarianism is an ideology of pluralism—an ideology that embraces religious diversity and the idea that my faith can be nurtured without claiming exclusive truth.... Can Islam, Christianity and Judaism know that God speaks Arabic on Fridays, Hebrew on Saturdays and Latin on Sundays, and that he welcomes different human beings approaching him through their own history, out of their language and cultural heritage? ... can we have a multilingual view of God—a notion that God is not exhausted by just one religious path?[51]

Are these then our only two choices when it comes to coping with the other—uncompromising hostility or pluralistic compromise? I believe there is a better way, and the greatest test facing the Christian global witness in the twenty-first century is our ability to discover and pursue it.[52] We can respond to the fact of religious plurality with uncompromising allegiance to the truth of God's Word and an unyielding commitment to love people of other faiths. The claims of Christ's unique and universal

---

50. See Juergensmeyer, *Terror in the Mind of God*.

51. Friedman, "Real War."

52. Van Rheenen expresses the conviction of a wide spectrum of scholars when he says: "In the new climate of the twenty-first century the most significant theological issue is the relationship between Christianity and the other world religions" ("Religionquake," 81).

lordship are not something Christians have invented—we have received the facts of the gospel as a stewardship, and we are obligated to share it. But we are called to share the truth in love, with gentleness and respect (Eph 4:15; 1 Pet 3:15).

Paul's address at Athens (Acts 17:22–31) provides us with some helpful guidelines for sharing the gospel with people of other faiths. We need to listen before we speak, display sensitivity and confidence, and seek to build bridges rather than walls in communicating with people of other faiths. Paul did not see only the error and darkness in pagan religion, he also discerned within it an expression of a thirst for God that only Christ could satisfy (Acts 17:23). We need to do likewise, and then freely share our experience of Christ with others as fellow travelers on a common journey rather than as saints who have already arrived at a state of moral or spiritual perfection.

Our stewardship of the gospel and faithfulness to Christ require that we affirm the decisiveness of God's word and action in the historic Christ-event. However, being a follower of Jesus is no reason to have feelings of religious arrogance or cultural pretentiousness. Our mission is to share the story of the saving love of God in Christ—a story that has transformed millions of lives down through the centuries. We share this story with confidence and enthusiasm, but also with sensitivity and respect for the other person's faith and experience.

MEGASHIFT ONE: MISSION FROM EVERYWHERE TO EVERYWHERE

Globalization has given us a world characterized by massive people movements and cultures in motion resulting in a borderless world. What will this mean for Pentecostal missions in the twenty-first century? Our examination of three trends stemming from the globalization wave has helped us to see an interesting convergence of features that indicate the need for a crucial megashift in the way we do missions in the days ahead. Massive migrations of people are making traditional borders of geography and nationality increasingly redundant. Neat categories of cultural identity delineated by space and locality are likewise becoming irrelevant, having to give way to the inexorable movement of trans-local and transnational currents of change. The mission frontiers marked by national and cultural difference, which were hitherto geographically distant, are suddenly appearing next door. We now live in a new world—a world without borders.

These observations obviously have massive socio-political implications, but may seem remote to the more pressing immediate concerns that some of us face. It is hard for some of us to conceive of a "world without borders" today. But is it really such a fanciful notion? Perhaps it is easier for me to see it as a Christian minority citizen in a majority Hindu nation, with the added privileged perspective of having observed life in the West. But I think the indicators have been with us for a while.

Cricket is India's national game and Pakistan is India's traditional rival. Since my early childhood I have known that every time India loses to Pakistan, fireworks go off in celebration in Muslim areas everywhere in India. What about affluent Hindu American citizens who are more passionate about funding and driving the fundamentalist Hindu agenda back in India than they are about exploring their American identity? Are French Canadians really French or Canadian? There are American Muslims in the United States who enjoy Disneyland and KFC, yet hate their fellow Americans who are Jews and would die for their Muslim brothers and sisters in Egypt or Saudi Arabia.

Let me highlight what I believe is the crucial issue by means of a personal illustration. A few years ago, I was privileged to be part of a panel of two-thirds world Christian leaders at Oxford, being interviewed by representatives of the British Christian Press. At a certain point in our interview, a Malaysian member of the panel asked one of the interviewers why he seemed so reluctant to report cases of persecution against Christians in the developing world. The Christian journalist's candid response was that he was afraid of antagonizing people of other faiths and disrupting communal harmony in the UK. My question slipped out as a reflex response: "Then what makes your paper Christian?" I did not intend to embarrass him but the audience exploded with laughter at the incongruity of his position. He was more concerned about not antagonizing people of other faiths in the UK than identifying with suffering Christian brothers and sisters in our part of the world.

A renewed emphasis on the imminent eschatology of the early Pentecostal revival is perhaps what is needed to help us balance even our "this-worldly" dual identities. For we are called to be loyal citizens of both realms, holding active local cultural and national allegiances, while remaining vibrant participants in the forward sweep of a pilgrim faith tradition as members of a global community of Jesus followers. But traditional borders of culture, ethnicity, and nationhood are becoming increasingly fuzzy with the passage of time. This is a great moment for Christians to reassert their true identity as those whose only real, enduring citizenship is in heaven (Phil 3:20), to which all earthly identities are subservient and of lesser significance. Such a mindset will go a long way in preparing us to engage more meaningfully in "mission from everywhere to everywhere." What, then, is the future course of mission in the twenty-first century?

At the beginning of the twentieth century, Christianity was essentially a Western religion, with 90 percent of the world's Christians living in Europe, North America, Australia, and New Zealand. Today, 70 percent of the world's Christians are to be found in the non-Western world. This movement of the center of gravity of Christianity from the North to the South and East is viewed by some as the transformation of Christianity from a territorial (European) faith to a global faith.[53] In Andrew Walls's oft-quoted study of the expansion of the Christian movement, he is careful to emphasize that Christianity has never had a permanent territorial center. While the missionary movement of the previous era was closely tied to the notion of Christendom, with the growing decline of Christianity in the West, he regards the idea of territorial Christianity as now "irretrievably broken."[54] In summarizing the impact of this development upon the future course of Christian missions, Walls makes the following perceptive observations, germane to our concluding assessment:

> Christian faith is now more diffused than at any previous time in its history; not only in the sense that it is more geographically, ethnically, and culturally widespread than ever before, but in the sense that it is diffused *within* more communities. The territorial "from-to" idea that underlay the older missionary movement has to give way to a concept more like that of Christians within

---

53. Pierard, "Viewing Denominational Histories," 143. This is a phenomenon I will be looking at more closely in the final essay in the continued assessment of the impact of globalization trends on future mission.

54. Walls, *Missionary Movement*, 258. Shenk registers a similar assessment, albeit in slightly different language: "Today we can speak only nostalgically about the geographical frontiers. We now require new metaphors to describe the missiological frontier in this space age. We stand at the junction between two eras.... The new era will be shaped by the vitality of the faith in the newly established centers in the non-Western world and sociopolitical forces quite different from the period dominated by Pax Britannica and Pax Americana" (Shenk, *Changing Frontiers*, 187).

the Roman Empire in the second and third centuries: parallel presences in different circles and at different levels, each seeking to penetrate within and beyond its circle. This does not prevent movement and interchange and enterprise ... but it forces revision of concepts, images, attitudes, and methods that arose from the presence of a Christendom that no longer exists.[55]

It is hard to add to these wise words of one of the most respected missiologists of our time, especially as his thesis finds strong affirmation among the finest minds in contemporary scholarship.[56] The emergence of a world without borders and the rise of a truly global church in this generation mean that mission today must become multidirectional. The real mission boundary is no longer between East and West, between Western empires and savage tribes, or between "Christian" countries and the mission field, but between faith and unbelief—that is a boundary that runs through every nation and culture, every local community, every street. Mission today is from everywhere to everywhere.[57] Perhaps no expression of contemporary Christianity is better positioned or prepared to *ride the Wave* of mission "made to travel" in a world without borders than Pentecostalism—a religion "made to travel" that passionately seeks to *follow the Wind!*

---

55. Walls, *Missionary Movement*, 258–59.
56. Newbigin, Sanneh, Escobar, and Wright, to mention a few.
57. Wright, "An Upside-Down World."

BIBLIOGRAPHY

Barrett, David B., Todd M. Johnson, and Peter F. Crossing. "Christian World Communions: Five Overviews of Global Christianity, AD 1800–2025." *International Bulletin of Missionary Research* 33.1 (January 2009) 25–32.

Bosch, David J. *Transforming Mission: Paradigm Shifts in Theology of Mission.* Maryknoll, NY: Orbis, 1991.

Cerillo, Augustus. "Pentecostals and the City." In *Called and Empowered: Global Mission in Pentecostal Perspective,* edited by Murray Dempster, Byron Klaus, and Douglas Petersen, 98–119. Peabody, MA: Hendrickson, 1991.

Friedman, Thomas. "The Real War." *The New York Times.* Tuesday, November 27, 2001.

Greenway, Roger S. "The Challenge of the Cities." In *Perspectives on the World Christian Movement: A Reader,* edited by Ralph D. Winter and Steven C. Hawthorne, 553–58. 3rd ed. Pasadena, CA: William Carey Library, 1999.

Grigg, Viv. "The Urban Poor: Who Are We?" In *Perspectives on the World Christian Movement: A Reader,* edited by Ralph D. Winter and Steven C. Hawthorne, 581–85. 3rd ed. Pasadena, CA: William Carey Library, 1999.

Gupta, Akhil, and James Ferguson. "Beyond 'Culture': Space, Identity, and the Politics of Difference." In The Anthropology of Globalization: A Reader, edited by Jonathan X. Inda and Renato Rosald, 65–80. Oxford: Blackwell, 2003.

Hanciles, Jehu J. "Migration and Mission: Some Implications for the Twenty-First Century Church." *International Bulletin of Missionary Research* 27.4 (2003) 146–53.

———. "Migration and Mission: The Religious Significance of the North-South Divide." In *Mission in the Twenty-First Century: Exploring the Five Marks of Global Mission,* edited by Andrew Walls and Cathy Ross, 118–29. Maryknoll, NY: Orbis, 2008.

Hiebert, Paul G. "Social Structure and Church Growth." In *Perspectives on the World Christian Movement: A Reader,* edited by Ralph D. Winter and Steven C. Hawthorne, 422–28. 3rd ed. Pasadena, CA: William Carey Library, 1999.

Hodges, Melvin. *A Theology of the Church and Its Mission.* Springfield, MO: Gospel Publishing House, 1977.

Inda, Jonathan X., and Renato Rosaldo, editors. The Anthropology of Globalization: A Reader. Oxford: Blackwell, 2003.

Johnson, Alan. *Apostolic Function in 21st Century Missions.* Pasadena, CA: William Carey Library, 2009.

Juergensmeyer, Mark. *Terror in the Mind of God.* Berkeley: University of California Press, 2003.

Keller, Timothy. "A New Kind of Urban Christian." *Christianity Today* 50, no. 5 (May 2006) 36–39.

———. "A Biblical Theology of the City." *Evangelicals Now.* http://www.e-n.org.uk/p-1869-A-biblical-theology-of-the-city.htm (accessed October 2, 2009).

Kraus, Norman. *The Authentic Witness.* Grand Rapids: Eerdmans, 1979.

Lundy, David. "Multiculturalism and Pluralization: Kissing Cousins of Globalization." In *One World or Many? The Impact of Globalization on Mission,* edited by Richard Tiplady, 71–84. Pasadena, CA: William Carey Library, 2003.

McConnell, Douglas. "Changing Demographics: The Impact of Migration, HIV/AIDS, and Children at Risk." In *The Changing Face of World Missions: Engaging Contemporary Issues and Trends,* edited by Michael Pocock, Gailyn Van Rheenen, and Douglas McConnell, 45–78. Grand Rapids: Baker Academic, 2005.

Moreau, A. Scott, Gary R. Corwin, and Gary B. McGee. *Introducing World Missions: A Biblical, Historical, and Practical Survey.* Grand Rapids: Baker, 2004.
Netland, Harold. *Encountering Religious Pluralism.* Downers Grove, IL: InterVarsity, 2001.
Newbigin, Leslie. *Mission in Christ's Way.* Geneva: WCC Publication, 1987.
Ohmae, Kenichi. "The End of the Nation State." In *The Globalization Reader*, edited by Frank J. Lechner and John Boli, 207–11. Oxford: Blackwell, 2000.
Padilla, C. Rene. *Mission between the Times.* Grand Rapids: Eerdmans, 1985.
Pelikan, Jaroslav. *Jesus through the Centuries: His Place in the History of Culture.* New York: Harper & Row, 1985.
Pierard, R. V. "Viewing Denominational Histories in Global Terms." In *A Global Faith: Essays on Evangelicalism and Globalization*, edited by Mark Hutchinson and Ogbu Kalu, 140–55. Sydney: Centre for the Study of Australian Christianity, 1998.
Shenk, Wilbert R. *Write the Vision.* Harrisburg, PA: Trinity Press, 1995.
———. *Changing Frontiers of Mission.* Maryknoll, NY: Orbis, 1999.
Stackhouse, Max L. "The Theological Challenge of Globalization." Religion Online. http://www.religion-online.org/cgi-bin/relsearchd.dll/showarticle?item_id=60 (accessed September 7, 2003; webpage now discontinued).
Steger, Manfred B. *Globalization: A Very Short Introduction.* Oxford: Oxford University Press, 2003.
Stearns, Peter N. *Cultures in Motion: Mapping Key Contacts and Their Imprints in World History.* New Haven: Yale University Press, 2001.
Stott, John. *Christian Mission and the Modern World.* London: Falcon, 1975.
United Nations, Department of Economic and Social Affairs, Population Division. *Trends in International Migrant Stock: The 2008 Revision.* http://www.un.org/esa/population/migration/UN_MigStock_2008.pdf (accessed October 1, 2009).
Van Rheenen, Gailyn. "Religionquake: From World Religions to Multiple Spiritualities." In *The Changing Face of World Missions: Engaging Contemporary Issues and Trends*, edited by Michael Pocock, Gailyn Van Rheenen, and Douglas McConnell, 79–104. Grand Rapids: Baker Academic, 2005.
Walls, Andrew. *The Missionary Movement in Christian History: Studies in the Transmission and Appropriation of Faith.* Maryknoll, NY: Orbis, 1996.
Wright, Christopher J. H. *The Mission of God: Unlocking the Bible's Grand Narrative.* Downers Grove, IL: InterVarsity, 2006.
———. "An Upside-Down World." *Christianity Today* 50, no.1 (January 2007) 42–46.

9

Friends in Mission

Following the Wind and Riding the Wave

IVAN SATYAVRATA

THE PREVIOUS TWO ESSAYS have been an attempt to evaluate how the Pentecostal mission movement, which exploded onto the global stage with spectacular momentum and vitality in the previous century, is poised to face the challenges of the twenty-first century. Our focus has been on the extraordinary convergence of two global mega-trends—the *Wind* of the Pentecostal movement and the *Wave* of globalization. The first essay made what is at the least a *prima facie* case for believing that as the quintessential "religion made to travel," the Pentecostal movement thrives in a "world in motion" created by the social processes of globalization. In evaluating the first set of globalization trends, the second essay discussed how massive people movements have given rise to a world of "cultures in motion," marked by multiculturalism and religious plurality. This new "world without borders" requires a paradigmatic megashift in mission thinking, so that missions today can no longer be viewed only in terms of a movement from Western Christendom to Eastern pagan tribes. Christian missions of the future will have to be multidirectional—from everywhere to everywhere.

In my final essay in this volume, I begin with a brief theological critique of the globalization phenomenon before looking more closely at the four remaining globalization trends and mission priorities outlined in the first essay. This evaluation leads to a concluding description of the second crucial megashift that needs to take place in missions in the second Pentecostal century.

GLOBALIZATION AND GOD'S KINGDOM MISSION

Through the first two essays I have evaluated the impact of globalization upon Christian mission as a largely neutral sociological phenomenon. Apart from the broad theological inference drawn from the remarkable convergence between the movement of the Wind of Pentecost across the globe and the Wave of globalization, suggesting coordinated orchestration by a divine conductor, I have studiously avoided any theological critique or ethical evaluation. Globalization is, however, a hotly debated issue among Christians today, with advocates and critics both drawing support from different biblical themes.[1]

On the one hand, proponents defend globalization by arguing that the integration of markets that it facilitates is the only hope for overcoming world poverty. They see it as facilitating human development at every level, enabling substantial gains in the fields of science, technology, transport, and communication to be shared with the rest of the world. They point out that economic liberalization and the free market have facilitated prosperity and boosted the standard of living in significant sections of society, that growing global consciousness has promoted greater ecological awareness, and that globalization technologies have improved means to control our world and monitor environmental change.[2]

On the other hand, opponents of globalization maintain that globalization is increasingly the cause of political oppression and social injustice. They see it as widening the chasm between the rich and the poor, as global giants relentlessly further their economic prospects by co-opting the support of institutions like the World Bank, World Trade Organization, IMF, and the United Nations, leaving behind significant sections of humanity on the margins of disempowerment and misery. They regard globalization's homogenization of cultures through the imposition of a "world market culture" as dealing a deadly blow to indigenous cultural identities, and view its inherently secular and materi-

---

1. Tiplady, *One World*, 6–7.
2. Pocock, Van Rheenen, and McConnell, *Changing Face*, 22–30.

alistic values as fundamentally incompatible with a Christian worldview, in that they foster greed and an enticing new form of idolatry.³

Max Stackhouse traces the influence of Christian faith upon the emergence of some aspects of globalization by drawing upon Arend van Leeuwen's work Christianity in World History.⁴ The central thesis of this work is that the sociohistorical forces of modern technology, urbanization, democracy, and human rights were in fact grounded in Christian theological presuppositions and carried deep implications for social transformation. The spread of these "spiritual forces in secular garb" could both open the way to world evangelization and further the development of a global community.⁵ This adds credence to one of the key concluding observations in my first essay that Christianity is inherently a globalizing movement and the Christian missionary movement is at the forefront of the globalizing process.

As those attentive to the signs of the time, Christians recognize that globalization is a social reality that cannot be wished away. It is inherently neither good nor evil. It has outcomes that are simultaneously good and bad. Its complexity reflects the nature of twenty-first century human society, and it is here to stay. Although its dynamic nature leaves us uncertain about the kind of world contemporary globalization is creating,⁶ what we do know is that contemporary globalization creates conditions that can facilitate Christian witness, and discerning identification and application of its helpful impulses can greatly advance the cause of Christian mission.

3. Araujo, "Globalization," 64–67; and Wilson, "Globalisation," 181–83.

4. Stackhouse, "Theological Challenge of Globalization." Cf. Stackhouse and Paris, *God and Globalization*, 26–27.

5. Stackhouse's thesis is closely linked to his conviction that, as a leading player in globalization, the USA has been thrust into the leadership of a global civilization, a civilization that will not survive if it is built only on technological advancement, economic expertise, political power, and military might, without a deeper foundation in faith and a normative vision of eternal truth, justice, and goodness. The Christian faith has been a critical catalyst and facilitator of the globalization movement and the normative vision that has shaped most of the institutions of American civilization. The United States thus has a crucial role to play in furthering the global Christian witness in the twenty-first century (Stackhouse, "Theological Challenge of Globalization"). This case is argued from a different direction in D'Souza, *What's So Great about America?* If this is true, the economic power and the political influence the USA wields in our world should help promote world peace and create the right conditions for the furtherance of Christian mission.

6. Claydon, "Globalization," 24; and Ort, "Christian Response."

Tiplady points out that prior theological perspectives condition our response to globalization. Human beings made in the image of God are capable of good cultural innovations, but due to their fallenness, sin taints every human enterprise. Those concentrating on human fallenness tend to adopt a "Christ against culture" viewpoint, focus on the negative aspects of globalization, and see it as something to be resisted. Others with a more positive attitude to culture tend towards an unqualified appreciation of globalization, readily focusing only on its prospects for civilization's progress. A balanced assessment sees human cultures as reflecting simultaneously both God's image and human sinfulness, and globalization as neutral in and of itself, with the potential to advance God's design for world evangelization.[7]

This positive assertion must be qualified with two important riders. First, we must be careful not to confuse modernization or globalization with evangelization. It is possible to ride the forces of modernity without acknowledging Christ's lordship or being aware of the Christian sources that may have nurtured these forces. In fact, given the distance and detachment from their original roots, these forces easily become idols of modernity, which frequently work at cross purposes with the rule of God in Christ. Second, we dare not suggest that everything that takes place under the broad rubric of globalization is directly ordained by God. For instance, greed and love of mammon drives much of economic globalization, and thus accentuates social disparities, driving a significant proportion of the world's population into extreme forms of poverty, all of which is at cross-purposes with kingdom values and the church's mission.

Christian mission's appropriation of globalization is thus not indiscriminate or undiscerning. The church is rather called to apply its resources in a redemptive interpretation and employment of globalization so that the Wind of Christian mission can effectively ride the Wave without compromising essential kingdom commitments to peace, justice, and compassion.

With the above riders, however, we are able to celebrate the convergence between the globalization movement and the Christian kingdom vision of all things in heaven and on earth coming together under one head, Christ. Having provided this brief theological critique of a concept germane to the discussion, I continue the analysis of the impact

7. Tiplady, *One World*, 6–7.

of globalization on Christian mission in relation to the four remaining globalization trends identified in the first essay.

THE EXPLOSION IN INFORMATION-COMMUNICATION TECHNOLOGY: INNOVATE CREATIVELY

Life in the twenty-first century is marked by rapid and relentless technological change. Not only does its influence seem all-pervasive, its pace continues to accelerate. The components of the contemporary globalization engine are thus the "wonder" devices of modern technology like the personal computer, Internet, cell/i-phone, fax machine, digital technology, satellite, cable television, and jet travel. Technological advances in travel, communication, and media have traditionally always facilitated the efficiency of the global missionary enterprise. There is, however, a growing realization that technology is not always a neutral medium, but that some aspects of modern technology carry innate problems and concerns as well.[8] The strides in technology today not only impact our use of equipment and methodology in mission, but potentially have a bearing on our understanding of mission itself.[9]

The most significant impact of technology upon modern life is in the area of enhanced connectivity through reduced telephone rates, the Internet, cell phones, email, satellite television, DVDs, and other forms of global communication. This has amazing and positive benefits for missionary communication and sharing of worship experiences across the globe. The Internet has made a mind-boggling amount of information and mission resources available to anyone who can access the worldwide web.[10] It further enables convenient transfer of funds internationally and

---

8. See especially Postman, *Technopoly*. As a professor of Media Ecology and cultural critic, Neil Postman is well positioned to comment on the relation of technology to culture. Postman's pessimistic critique sees culture as subservient to and controlled by both invisible (I.Q. scores, statistics, polling techniques) and visible (television, computers, automobiles) technologies. His scathing verdict concedes few benefits of technology, regarding it as essentially an intrusive and dangerous enemy of culture. He describes *technopoly* as "the deification of technology, which means that the culture seeks its authorization in technology, finds its satisfaction in technology, and takes its orders from technology" (ibid., 71).

9. Pocock, Van Rheenen, and McConnell, *Changing Face*, 301.

10. Internet connectivity is shaping a new discourse of interpersonal relationships called social networking, which has begun to rewire the way people meet, interact, and stay connected. In the past, missionaries would return from the field to give their supporters a report every three to four years. Today, supporters want to do more than give

enables missionary families to communicate regularly with loved ones in distant countries. Internet technology also facilitates efficient and cost-effective delivery of online education through e-learning courses into even restricted-access nations.

Technology has helped reduce the emotional pain and trauma of missionary families relocating to a foreign country. Through e-mail, social networking sites, and other online technologies such as Skype, missionaries can be half a world away and still be in regular and close touch with family and friends. Some have serious objections to this phenomenon, since it seems to relieve missionaries of the pressure to enter a new culture deeply, and instead encourages them to have a foot in each culture.[11] This multi-place identification is, however, the more natural and necessary direction of the future missionary identity, in step with changing global realities.[12]

Employment of new technologies also raises a staggering range of ethical issues since technological solutions are often more task-efficient than people-friendly. The escalation of the pace of life precipitated by technological efficiency seems to be at the cost of relationships, in-depth reflection, and face-to-face interaction and learning. There is also the problem of the "digital divide" between the techno-savvy, who are frequently privileged due to more effective communication, and those who are disadvantaged by lack of access to sophisticated technology. A serious problem generated by enhanced technological connectivity is that of security, as public access to cyberspace makes confidentiality of information and communication increasingly difficult, placing missionary personnel at risk in restricted entry countries.[13]

---

regularly, they also want to stay connected with the missionary, and modern internet technology facilitates not only constant exchange of information, but also increased global awareness. See World Gospel Mission, "Future of Missions."

11. Pocock, Van Rheenen, and McConnell, *Changing Face*, 303.

12. Cf. Jehu Hanciles's description of the missionary as the "classical" transmigrant (Hanciles, "Migration and Mission: Some Implications," 148).

13. A recent *New York Times* article, "Surveillance of Skype Messages Found in China," noted that "Researchers in China have estimated that 30,000 or more "internet police" monitor online traffic, Web sites, and blogs for political and other offending content in what is called the Golden Shield Project or the Great Firewall of China." For missionaries in that country and those like it, using Skype or other online communication tools increases their personal security risk (Markoff, "Surveillance").

Many of the pitfalls of technology can be avoided through discerning and creative innovation. For instance, the "high touch–high tech" approach recognizes that technological solutions never exist in isolation, but must be complemented by greater face-to-face human interaction. The key is to see technology as facilitating greater intimacy in relationships rather than controlling them.

The use of technology in mission raises a number of questions, some of which have no easy answers.[14] To what extent have modern advances in technology actually enhanced mission efforts around the world? Have technological advances impacted missions more radically and at a deeper level perhaps than we envisage? For instance, missionaries are now able to use the internet and computer courses to train nationals in countries not open to Christian missionaries. Is this the future of missions? Why send individuals overseas to conduct training that could be completed over the Internet? Is there still benefit in sending missionaries to foreign fields for extended periods of time? Have technological advances changed the face of missions forever or are we in danger of losing elements of what was once an efficient and effective tradition?[15]

THE RISE OF GLOBAL POVERTY AND THREAT TO HUMAN LIFE: DEVELOP A THEOLOGY OF INTEGRAL MISSION AND INTERDEPENDENCE

In delineating this trend in the first essay, I pointed out that the positive impact of globalization on the global economy and the rise of free market capitalism has also driven a significant proportion of the world's population into extreme forms of poverty and given rise to a number of other threats to human life.[16] The poor and socially marginalized are especially vulnerable to infectious illnesses and epidemics, HIV-AIDS and other sexually transmitted diseases, the scourge of human trafficking, cross-border terrorism, and environmental disasters.

---

14. World Gospel Mission, "Future of Missions."

15. Some mission organizations even have manuals for people wanting to get involved in becoming a virtual missionary. I try to respond to these questions provisionally in the conclusion of this paper, but the purpose is not always to provide pat answers, but rather to stimulate awareness on certain issues with serious long-term implications, requiring careful ongoing study and honest critical reflection.

16. For a concise but fair analysis of the causes and consequences of this trend, see Ellwood, *No-Nonsense Guide*, 90–106; for an evangelical Christian summary perspective, see Escobar, "Global Scenario," 32.

The Lausanne Grand Rapids report of 1982 on "Evangelism and Social Responsibility" brought considerable clarity and resolution to the ongoing evangelical debate on the issue. Some expression of social concern is thus today an indispensable component of evangelical mission.[17] The Grand Rapids document sets out clearly the integral link between evangelism and social responsibility. First, social concern is viewed as a consequence of evangelism—the means by which God brings people to new birth, and their new life manifests itself in the service of others (Gal 5:6; James 2:18; and 1 John 3:16–18). Second, social engagement can be a bridge to evangelism. It can break down prejudice and suspicion, open closed doors, and gain a hearing for the gospel. Third, social action is a partner to evangelism. Jesus' words explained his works, and his works illustrated his words: both were expressions of his compassion for people. Evangelism and social responsibility are thus integrally related in our proclamation of and obedience to the gospel.

Pentecostals were not totally insulated from the ongoing evangelism–social action controversy, but Pentecostalism has always been essentially a religion of the poor. Its origins in North America were among the poor and socially marginalized, contributing to its distinctive appeal among the poor in South America, Africa, and Asia.[18] But while the Pentecostal praxis was marked by an intuitive engagement with the actual felt needs of the poor and dispossessed, it was not until the closing decades of the twentieth century that a robust Pentecostal theology of holistic mission began to emerge. In one of the finest early illustrations of such a well-articulated and Pentecostal holistic mission theology, Murray Dempster affirmed the vital organic link between kingdom social ethics and the mission of the church:

> [W]here God reigns, a new redemptive society is formed in which brothers and sisters enjoy an affirmative community; strangers are incorporated into the circle of neighbour love; peace is made with enemies; injustices are rectified; the poor experience solidarity with the human family and the creation; generous sharing results in the just satisfaction of human needs in which no one suffers deprivation; and all persons are entitled to respect, are to

---

17. Stott, "Evangelism and Social Responsibility"; cf. Escobar, *New Global Mission*, 152–54.

18. Anderson, *Vision of the Disinherited*; Martin, *Pentecostalism*, 4; and Freston, "Evangelicalism and Globalization," 72–74.

be treated with dignity, and are deserving of justice because they share the status of God's image-bearers.[19]

Grounding his construct in a sound kingdom theology framework, Dempster outlines an integrated Pentecostal theology of mission that includes the church's kerygmatic ministry of evangelism, koinoniac ministry of social witness, and diakonic ministry of social service. He insists that all of these are essential for the integrity of the church's mission of proclaiming the gospel of the kingdom in word, life, and deed.[20]

A recent study by two sociologists of religion has furnished convincing confirmation of Pentecostalism's strong orientation towards engagement of social issues. At the conclusion of a four-year extensive grassroots research journey, covering various expressions of Pentecostalism in twenty different countries in Africa, Asia, Latin America, and Eastern Europe, Donald Miller and Tetsunao Yamamori conclude that:

> [T]here is an emergent movement within Pentecostal churches worldwide that embraces a holistic understanding of the Christian faith. Unlike the Social Gospel tradition of the mainline churches, this movement seeks a balanced approach to evangelism and social action that is modeled after Jesus' example of not only preaching about the coming kingdom of God but also ministering to the physical needs of the people he encountered.[21]

Miller and Yamamori observe that Pentecostal social engagement encompasses a wide range of issues, extending from emergency humanitarian responses to natural calamities such as drought, floods, and earthquakes to medical work, counseling, education, and community development. Their essentially positive assessment is, however, tempered by the following telling observation: "Many churches are still putting bandages on problems and only recently have begun to think structurally about social issues."[22]

So, in the midst of a world of dire need, armed with a resolute commitment to biblical faith and convinced that the Spirit's empowerment can enable them to overcome all odds, Pentecostals are making a difference. They are healing the sick, uplifting the powerless, rescuing

---

19. Dempster, "Evangelism," 24.
20. Ibid., 38–39.
21. Miller and Yamamori, *Global Pentecostalism*, 212.
22. Ibid., 213.

children at risk, fighting against AIDS and other deadly diseases, serving the needs of the poorest of the poor, but they are also preaching the good news of Jesus, delivering the demonized, making disciples of Jesus, planting new churches, taking the gospel to unreached people groups, and offering hope to the hopeless.[23]

Although the mounting problems of global poverty and threats to human life are formidable, as Miller and Yamamori's study clearly illustrate, the Pentecostal movement has the theological resources and missionary passion for credible ongoing engagement with the global need. The global presence of Pentecostalism provides a unique opportunity of a truly global movement of witness against these forces of evil in our world. However, crucial to the effectiveness of this endeavor is the emergence of a model of missionary engagement that links various segments of global Pentecostalism together in a relationship of mutual interdependence.

POLITICAL RESISTANCE TO TRADITIONAL MISSIONARY ACTIVITY: PURSUE CREATIVE AVENUES OF ACCESS

In defining the concept of globalization in the first essay, I noted that globalization not only brings a heightened awareness of global interconnectedness by bringing distant cultures into closer proximity, it also gives rise to a corresponding response of "localization" by which local cultural traditions are reinforced. This assertion of local identity frequently takes the form of nationalist reactionary movements that zealously seek to shield the local cultures from foreign intrusions. Missionary efforts are accordingly regarded as a carry-over from the cultural imperialism of the colonial era, to be staunchly resisted. Consequently, today many nation-states have closed their doors to foreign missionaries. The challenge

---

23. A crucial question that frequently comes up in this regard is the question of priority: which should take precedence, evangelism or social responsibility? In terms of logical priority, there can be no doubt that since social concern presupposes a Christian social conscience and discipleship, and is a consequence and aim of evangelism, evangelism must take priority. Evangelism must take priority also because it relates to the supreme and ultimate need of all humankind for the saving grace of Jesus Christ, acceptance of which will determine a person's eternal destiny. We should, however, never have to choose between satisfying physical hunger and spiritual hunger, or between healing bodies and saving souls, since an authentic love for our neighbor will lead us to serve him or her as a whole person. In practice, as in the public ministry of Jesus, the two are inseparable, and can mutually support and strengthen each other; see Stott, "Evangelism and Social Responsibility."

facing the Christian missionary enterprise is: How do we evangelize and establish faith communities in restricted-access countries of the world where vocational missionaries are not permitted to enter?

The issue has come into prominence since the last quarter of the twentieth century, as following the end of the colonial era of missions, vocational missionaries were no longer welcomed in many parts of the world and missionary visas were simply not available. In response to this new reality, several missionary agencies came up with the concept of creative access platforms as a practical means for providing missionaries the opportunity and relational basis for entering and working in restricted-access regions of the world.[24] Creative access avenues of mission include bi-vocational or "tent-making" networks and kingdom business platforms, which add value to a community and help build bridges for witness and making disciples.

Although the creative access idea is gaining widespread acceptance today among evangelicals in general, Pentecostals have been relatively slow to adopt this strategy. This is largely due to the high degree of professionalization of ministry and mission, and the distance we have created between the specialist ordained clergy and the non-professional laity in our theology of ministry and mission. Paul, the greatest missionary of all time, was a philosopher, tentmaker, lecturer, and fund-raiser, and at the same time, a preacher, pastor, teacher, and church-planter. The early spread of the gospel in the post-apostolic period was spearheaded by merchant missionaries. The Moravian Brethren represent an entire mission movement of tentmakers who went to some of the most unreached regions of the world, even reaching the remote mountain kingdom of Tibet. William Carey, perhaps the most well-known missionary in modern times, was a bi-vocational cobbler-pastor.[25]

Seventy percent—a vast majority—of the world's unreached people groups live in restricted access countries, representing 55 percent of the world's population. At present only about 6 percent of the Christian missionary force serve in these "closed" countries, and only one dollar of every ten thousand dollars of the money spent on missions is invested in

---

24. Pocock, Van Rheenen, and McConnell, *Changing Face*, 211.

25. Carey entered India as an illegal missionary immigrant, and in the course of his thirty-two year missionary tenure, worked variously as a translator, university professor, factory manager, agriculturalist, social activist, scientist, medical worker, and author; see Pocock, Van Rheenen, and McConnell, *Changing Face*, 229–34.

these regions. In light of this massive need, should Pentecostal missions give serious attention to redefining the function of missionaries and creative diversification of their role? Should all missionaries always have to be theologically trained and ordained vocational ministers? Could missionaries in the twenty-first century be not only full-time vocational missionaries—evangelists, pastors, teachers, and cross-cultural church planters, but also missionaries who are doctors, nurses, university professors, development workers, and business-entrepreneurs, with more free and privileged access to "closed" countries along the communication highways globalization provides?

THE SHIFTING CENTER OF CHRISTIANITY: WORK TOWARDS PARTNERSHIP/COVENANT RELATIONSHIP IN MISSION

A little over three decades ago, the Swiss missiologist, Walbert Bühlmann, hailed "the coming of the Third Church" as an "epoch-making event of current church history."[26] Bühlmann used "Third Church" to signify the emerging church in the South, the first millennium of Christianity having been dominated by the church in the eastern half of the Roman Empire, and the second millennium by the Western church. A decade later Bühlmann made the following far-reaching observation: "Now the Third Millennium will evidently stand under the leadership of the Third Church, the Southern Church. I am convinced that the most important drives and inspirations for the whole church in the future will come from the Third Church."[27]

The most important development in Christianity during the late twentieth and early twenty-first centuries is, undoubtedly, the dramatic shift of global Christianity's demographic center to the southern hemisphere and parts of Asia.[28] For the first time in more than a thousand years, Western Christianity is in the minority: 60 percent of the world's two billion Christians now live in the global South, and that proportion is rising. Andrew Walls thus observes that although the church historian Kenneth Scott Latourette described the nineteenth century as the "great

26. Bühlmann, *Third Church*, 131.
27. Ibid., 6.
28. This southward shift has been thoroughly documented, statistically validated, and carefully analyzed; see Barrett, Kurian, and Johnson, *World Christian Encyclopedia*; Jenkins, *Next Christendom*; and Laing, "Changing Face of Mission," 165–77.

century of missions," according to Walls, "the most remarkable century in the history of the expansion of Christianity has been the twentieth."[29]

A recent work by the evangelical historian Mark Noll draws from Walls's seminal work in analyzing the contribution of American missions in shaping the new world Christianity. While Noll does not see American missions trying to control the shape of world Christianity, he does observe significant American influence in bringing the gospel to indigenous peoples who, in turn, shape Christian faith and practice into culturally relevant forms. He also sees newer expressions of Christianity around the world, despite many differences, sharing many characteristics of Christianity in the United States, because of a shared historical experience.[30]

This assessment concurs essentially with that of Walls who, while conceding the complementary roles of both Western and indigenous mission agencies, regards the missionary movement as "the detonator of the vast explosion" that brought about the demographic transformation of the Christian church, and thus "one of the most important developments in the entire history of western Christianity."[31] Walls traces the growth of the Christian movement in six sequential phases. Each phase is marked by the translation of the Christian faith into a major culture, during which it takes on the distinctive features of the culture. Walls shows how Christianity seems to spread serially by a process of expansion and concurrent recession, so that remarkably, at every stage, "a threatened eclipse of Christianity was averted by its cross-cultural diffusion."[32] Cross-cultural diffusion has been necessary to Christianity: it has been its life's blood, without which—in human terms—it seems as though the Christian faith could not have survived.[33]

The missionary movement from the West during the past century is the most recent instance of cross-cultural diffusion in which the Christian faith crossed cultural frontiers into African and Asian communities. However, during the period that the Western missionary acted as a connecting terminal for this cross-cultural diffusion process, Christianity

29. Walls, *Cross-Cultural Process*, 64.
30. Noll, *World Christianity*.
31. Walls, *Cross-Cultural Process*, 65.
32. Ibid., 32.
33. Ibid., 67.

lost its hold on much of the West.[34] The recession of Christianity in the West was thus accompanied by a strong resurgence in the South:

> [W]e seem to stand at the threshold of a new age of Christianity, one in which its main base will be in the Southern continents, and where its dominant expressions will be filtered through the culture of those countries. Once again, Christianity has been saved for the world by its diffusion across cultural lines.[35]

According to Walls, this demographic shift to the South, resulting from the modern missionary movement, presents us with twin challenges: a post-Christian West and a post-Western Christianity.[36] He predicts that Christianity in the third millennium will be more culturally diverse than all its earlier expressions, even as Africa, Latin America, and Asia become the defining hub of mainstream, normative Christianity. More than ever before, Christianity will need to be understood as a multi-cultural and global movement, an enduring tradition that has found new life in the lived realities of Africa, Asia, and Latin America. Walls cites Newbigin to support his conviction that within this changed scenario Western Christians will need the assistance of Christians from the non-Western world, but goes on to sound a note of warning:

> The demographic transformation of the church brought about by the missionary movement opens the possibility of testing our Christian witness by that of others, of experiencing one another's gifts and sharing our combined resources. Equally, it opens the prospect of a score of local Christianities operating independently without interest or concern in one another. Either of these processes is possible; only one of them reflects the New Testament view of the church or the Spirit of Christ.[37]

In pointing out the impact of the southern shift in Christianity upon the future course of the global mission movement, Mark Laing observes that the growing mission movement emerging from the non-Western world will inevitably change the nature of the world missionary enterprise. He points out the adverse consequences of Western and non-

---

34. Ibid., 66.
35. Walls, *Missionary Movement*, 22.
36. Walls, *Cross-Cultural Process*, 65.
37. Ibid., 69; cf. Hogan's warning against the danger of an overemphasis on nationalistic feelings in indigenization leading to Christian commitment and identity being undermined (Wilson, *Strategy of the Spirit*, 34).

Western missionary efforts developing independently of each other, and either essentially attempting to maintain the status quo of Western domination, or becoming "like ships in the night unaware that we are passing each other by," in needless competition or duplication of efforts.[38] The potential benefits of a South–North partnership are incalculable, but what should be the shape of such a partnership? Our concluding section is devoted to exploring a solution to this question and suggesting what the contours of future South–North partnership should look like.

MEGASHIFT TWO: FROM PATERNALISM AND PARTNERSHIP TO "FRIENDS IN MISSION"

The relentless advance of the juggernaut of globalization is bringing about socio-political, economic, and cultural changes of momentous proportions that will have a deep and inexorable impact on Christian missions in the twenty-first century. I concluded the evaluation of three globalization trends in the previous essay with a proposal for a radical megashift in the traditional paradigm of Christian mission. In the context of a world without borders and an emerging church that is truly global, mission must be multidirectional—from everywhere to everywhere. The analysis of the four remaining globalization trends in this essay leads to a proposal of a second megashift: from neo-colonial paternalism and foreign–indigenous partnership in mission, to serving as friends together in mission.

The Western missionary posture during the "great century" of missions and the early decades of the twentieth century was largely marked by what Andrew Walls describes as a spirit of "imperial religion." "The White Man's Burden,"[39] on which this posture was based, viewed the culture of Britain and the West as a whole as intrinsically superior to those of the newly-discovered and colonized territories, and missionaries believed that they had been entrusted with a God-given civilizing mission

---

38. Laing recommends Pate and Keyes's model of task-oriented partnership involving increasing cooperation and interconnectedness, quoting Paul Hiebert in support: "the future of mission is based in the formation of international networks ... which will exhibit a willingness to share resources of people and intellectual property rather than to compete" (Laing, "Changing Face of Mission," 174; cf. Pate and Keyes, "Emerging Missions," 156–61).

39. Derived from Rudyard Kipling's famous poem of that name, which—along with other Kipling poetry—captured the prevailing ethos of that time; see Walls, *Cross-Cultural Process*, 177–93.

to the pagan cultures of the East and South. This posture was what eventually gave rise to a condescending attitude and paternalistic relationship with the native Christian converts and churches. Paternalism assumes the lack of ability and knowledge of the people of the receptor cultures, requiring the perpetual dominance of the sending culture over the mission process.[40] The missionary–native Christian relationship during that era was thus marked by Western control and dominance on one hand, and subservient dependence on the other.

Meanwhile, an awareness emerged by the middle of the nineteenth century that saw this "colonial captivity" of mission methodology as detrimental to the enduring legacy of the Christian church and mission. Henry Venn and Rufus Anderson were the earliest proponents of a missiology that opposed long-term foreign control and advocated empowerment of indigenous leadership and local support of national churches. The indigenous church formula of self-government, self-support, and self-propagation, developed by Venn and Anderson, was adopted and developed further by John Nevius towards the end of the twentieth century. In the twentieth century, under the influence of Roland Allen, Melvin Hodges, and others, indigenous church principles gained widespread popularity and acceptance, almost acquiring the status of a doctrine in some circles.[41]

These indigenous church principles have helped further the Christian global mission in many significant ways. They have helped loose the church from indefinite overseas missionary control, instilled a sense of worth and dignity among the national leadership, facilitated the emergence of strong and vibrant national churches, and enabled them to move from an unhealthy dependence on foreign support and expertise to administrative autonomy and financial independence. There is, however, a growing feeling in mission circles that a paradigm forged essentially as a corrective reaction to deficient colonial missionary practice needs to be updated and morphed into a model that addresses more closely the needs of a rapidly globalizing twenty-first century world. The following is a summary proposal, not a blueprint as much as a sketch or map, submitted as a basis for further discussion.

---

40. Pocock, Van Rheenen, and McConnell, *Changing Face*, 285.

41. Rowell, *To Give or Not To Give*, 27–35; and Pocock, Van Rheenen, and McConnell, *Changing Face*, 285–86.

From Self to Servanthood

The term "indigenous" literally means "born from within"—what is local or native to a culture in contrast to what is foreign or alien. All cultures are fallen, and an overemphasis of the indigenous perspective can sometimes compromise the church's call to distinctiveness and countercultural living in pagan settings. Furthermore, some view the three "self" model as reflecting the reality of Western individualistic cultures more than group-oriented cultures of the majority world. Western individualism breeds an ideal of self-reliance not as highly valued in more closely-bonded and community-oriented African, Asian, and Latin American cultures.[42]

The rich West can learn the occasional lesson from the poorer nations. I personally witnessed an occasion when Bible students in India heard about the food crisis in a Bible College in an Eastern European country. In response they fasted one day, collected the money, took up an offering and mobilized support for a week's food bill for fellow students in Eastern Europe. God loves to take the weak, the little, the poor, and multiply the impact of sacrifices made by the poor. Widow's mites, little jars of oil, and five loaves and two fish are the most prized currency in the kingdom of God.

The emphasis on "self," self-sufficiency, and autonomy also seems to militate against Jesus' call to self-denial in the service of the other. Jesus began his closing discourse to his disciples prior to his passion with an acted out parable on servanthood, a prophetic prefigurement of his death on the cross by which he modelled servanthood as an irrevocable pattern for ministry (John 13). Jesus' explicit teaching rather seems to place a high premium on the kingdom value of servanthood, giving, sharing, and laying down one's life in costly service of the other.

From Competitive National Agencies to Collaborative Global Networks

In the times in which we live, ethnic identities are becoming increasingly fluid and national allegiances will become less and less relevant when it comes to responsible missionary stewardship. Western and majority world mission agencies will thus need to learn from each other. Agencies

---

42. Pocock, Van Rheenen, and McConnell, *Changing Face*, 287–89.

from different countries sometimes target the same areas and fail to coordinate their activities.[43]

We need to learn from the increasingly well-coordinated Islamic and Hindu plans for expanding their global presence. While the indigenous emphasis has pushed our churches to stronger nationalization and isolation, the pan-Islamic axis continues to grow and the Hindu global movement is getting more organized. There is a movement toward greater collaboration among agencies and churches within the global Christian community, but our cooperative efforts will have to be supported by stronger resolve, closer networking, and more coordinated strategy in the days ahead.

From "Mission to All the World" to "Mission from All the Church"

A strong motivation and impetus to reach every tribe, nation, and people group with the gospel marked the previous era of missions. But to date, missionary work remains largely a specialist enterprise, to be engaged in by only those who have been trained and ordained to the task. Preparation and training are always of critical importance, but the world of the twenty-first century presents us with challenges and opportunities that are beyond the scope of any full-time professional missionary force. Commenting on this, Marty Shaw notes:

> Every aspect of globalization offers an opportunity for Christians to share and demonstrate the Gospel. There are non-Western businessmen who are starting factories as an intentional and effective means of doing missions. There are artists and educators who do not see themselves as missionaries, but rather as Christians who are living out their faith and influencing the thinking of their discipline and thus a society.... Globalization is affecting all aspects of societies today. Missions in this reality must seek to intentionally model the Gospel in all areas, not just the religious. The idea of the Gospel going from everywhere to everywhere should not be just a geographical issue, but one that involves all aspects of culture and society, that is a holistic gospel for a holistic mission.[44]

---

43. This was to a great extent what exacerbated the problem of persecution in Kandhamal district of Orissa in India in 2008.

44. Shaw, "Future of Kingdom Work," 49.

We need missionary doctors who will help fight deadly epidemics, bi-vocational missionaries who will be able to enter restricted access countries as teachers, development workers, corporate executives, government officials on temporary assignment, and business entrepreneurs who will help create wealth and jobs and be seen as adding value to various overseas communities. The challenge is to mobilize awareness and training for all of these. The whole church must be co-opted to reach the whole world with the whole gospel.

From Independence to Interdependence

The rise of the indigenous church movement effectively arrested the paternalistic dependency that marked native–missionary relationships in an earlier era of missions. The unhealthy reliance on outside resources, accompanied by colonial control and missionary dominance has rightly given way to autonomy and independence, but is ethnic or national insularity and entropic independence the New Testament ideal? Paul's clear teaching on the church as the body of Christ (1 Cor 12:14–26 and Eph 4:16) clearly emphasizes interdependence rather than dependence or independence.[45] The church in our times should be encouraged to move closer to the New Testament ideal, from dependence to independence, from independence to interdependence.

From Foreign Partnerships in Mission to Friends and Family in Mission

The concept of partnership between the sending mission and receiving church is a great advance over the paternalism that treats natives as though they are at best children or at worst a deficient or inferior race. Commenting on the importance of the Assemblies of God missions philosophy,[46] John York makes the following crucial observation concerning partnership: "[P]artnership rests upon a foundation of mutual respect and warm personal relationships. There must be ongoing love, prayer, and fellowship. In short, unless genuine and abiding friendship develops between the partners, their relationship cannot hope to achieve the goals for which it was formed."[47]

---

45. Rowell, *To Give or Not To Give*, 46.

46. A key contribution in this regard is a work of much historical significance by Williams, *Partnership in Mission*, 160–246.

47. York, *Missions*, 158.

In explaining the meaning of true partnership, York introduces the phrase "genuine and abiding friendship," suggesting perhaps that the language of partnership may fall short of the biblical ideals of family and friendship so integral to the church's body-life. For partnership still implies the existence of racial, ethnic, or national distance between partners. In John 15:13–15, Jesus invites us to share in an intimate, loving, family relationship and friendship with him. Friends share what they learn; friends open their hearts and minds to each other without secrecy. True friends allow the other to see right in and know them as they really are. True friends are eager to help and to spend themselves for the other without counting the cost.

The Edinburgh World Missionary Conference in 1910 is regarded as a watershed event in Christian history. Bishop V. S. Azariah was one of the seventeen non-Western representatives out of a total of 1200 participants. Azariah is not a name many Pentecostal ministry leaders would recognize, but he is widely regarded as one of the most successful modern Christian leaders ever to emerge from the non-Western world.[48] What Gandhi was to the nation of India, Azariah has been to the church in India. Azariah was invited to speak at Edinburgh 1910 on the problem of cooperation between foreign and native workers. His closing words have become the most famous spoken at the historic conference:

> I do . . . plead for . . . the foreign missionary to show that he is in the midst of the people to be to them not a lord and master but a brother and a friend . . . Through all the ages to come the Indian Church will rise up in gratitude to attest the heroism and self denying labours of the missionary body. You have given your goods to feed the poor. You have given your bodies to be burned. We also ask for love. Give us FRIENDS![49]

CONCLUSION

The Christian missionary enterprise may be facing the most formidable challenge of its history in the twenty-first century as it encounters the aggressive religious resurgence that globalization is spreading all across the world. The questions that presently threaten the jugular of the Christian faith are essentially twofold. First, how can we keep from trib-

---

48. Harper, *Shadow of the Mahatma*, 236.
49. Stanley, *World Missionary Conference*, 125.

alizing the gospel by demonizing the "other" and alienating the Christian church from other religions and cultures? Second, how do we reach out to them with a loving and tolerant witness and yet resist their deadly embrace? Liberal pluralism has demonstrated its bankruptcy as it invites the Christian church to suicide by recommending that we abandon the distinctiveness of Jesus. Fundamentalist evangelicalism is likewise found wanting as it circles the wagons and beckons us to follow a constricted notion of Christ into a theological and ecclesiastical ghetto.

The Pentecostal movement has been blessed with the resources needed to face the missionary challenge that awaits us in the twenty-first century. God is at work in globalization and we must exploit the opportunities it offers for furthering Christ's kingdom mission, while eschewing points at which it is at cross purposes with kingdom principles and values. If we steward our legacy wisely and follow the Wind and ride the Wave responsibly, we will see a religion made to travel in the previous century become mission made to travel in the power of the Spirit in this century. While some may baulk at the triumphalism implicit in this vision, the triumphalist note in Scripture can hardly be missed by anyone who takes the biblical witness seriously: The kingdom of the world has become the kingdom of our Lord and of his Christ, and he will reign forever and ever (Rev 11:15b).

The paradox of the cross reminds us that while Christian triumph is inevitable, it is a triumph centered in death and servanthood. We thus need not recoil from a triumphalism that is rooted in the self-giving love of God as revealed in Christ crucified, which seeks to advance the kingdom mission of God in humble dependence on God's Spirit. Friendship in mission begins with friendship with God. When we are truly friends of God, what is of importance and value to him becomes significant and precious to us. God's heart reaches out to those in our world who are lost and alienated from him, and if we are his friends we must likewise be passionate about the lost.

If Pentecostal mission in the twenty-first century is to fulfill its stewardship, it is essential that we live out this reality at the heart of the gospel, critical to the credibility of our mission. Jesus calls us his friends; Azariah cried out for friends. An authentic witness to Christ is one that flows out of a friendship based on intimacy with God and grounded in community, reflected in radiant faith and genuine relational interconnectedness. Pentecostal mission in the twenty-first century must then be a journey in which we travel together as servants of Christ and of one another as friends in Mission.

BIBLIOGRAPHY

Anderson, Robert M. *Vision of the Disinherited: The Making of American Pentecostalism.* Peabody, MA: Hendrickson, 1992.

Araujo, Alex. "Globalization and World Evangelism." In *Global Missiology for the Twenty-First Century: The Iguassu Dialogue*, edited by William D. Taylor, 57–70. Grand Rapids: Baker, 2000.

Barrett, David B., G. T. Kurian, and Todd M. Johnson, editors. *World Christian Encyclopedia: A Comparative Survey of Churches and Religions in the Modern World, AD 1900–2000.* New York: Oxford University Press, 2001.

Bühlmann, Walbert. *The Coming of the Third Church.* Maryknoll, NY: Orbis, 1977.

Claydon, David, ed. *Globalization and the Gospel: Rethinking Mission in the Contemporary World.* Lausanne Occasional Paper No. 30. Lausanne Committee for World Evangelization, 2005.

Dempster, Murray W. "Evangelism, Social Concern, and the Kingdom of God." In *Called and Empowered: Global Mission in Pentecostal Perspective*, edited by Murray W. Dempster, Byron Klaus, and Douglas Petersen, 22–43. Peabody, MA: Hendrickson, 1991.

D'Souza, Dinesh. *What's So Great about America?* Washington: Regnery, 2002.

Ellwood, Wayne. *The No-Nonsense Guide to Globalization.* London: Verso, 2003.

Escobar, Samuel. "The Global Scenario at the Turn of the Century." In *Global Missiology for the Twenty-First Century: The Iguassu Dialogue*, edited by William D. Taylor, 25–46. Grand Rapids: Baker, 2000.

———. *The New Global Mission: The Gospel from Everywhere to Everyone.* Christian Doctrine in Global Perspective Series. Downers Grove, IL: InterVarsity, 2003.

Freston, Paul. "Evangelicalism and Globalization: General Observations and Some Latin American Dimensions." In *A Global Faith: Essays on Evangelicalism and Globalization*, edited by Mark Hutchinson and Ogbu Kalu, 69–88. Sydney: Centre for the Study of Australian Christianity, 1998.

Hanciles, Jehu J. "Migration and Mission: Some Implications for the Twenty-First Century Church." *International Bulletin of Missionary Research* 27, no. 4 (2003) 146–53.

Harper, Susan Billington. *In the Shadow of the Mahatma.* Grand Rapids: Eerdmans, 2000.

Jenkins, Philip. *The Next Christendom: The Coming of Global Christianity.* New York: Oxford University Press, 2002.

Laing, Mark. "The Changing Face of Mission: Implications for the Southern Shift in Christianity." *Missiology: An International Review* 34 (2006) 165–77.

Markoff, John. "Surveillance of Skype Messages Found in China." *New York Times.* http://www.nytimes.com/2008/10/02/technology/internet/02skype.html?fta=y (accessed October 28, 2009).

Martin, David. *Pentecostalism: The World Their Parish.* Oxford: Blackwell, 2002.

Miller, Donald E., and Tetsunao Yamamori. *Global Pentecostalism: The New Face of Christian Social Engagement.* Berkeley: University of California Press, 2007.

Noll, Mark. *The New Shape of World Christianity: How American Experience Reflects Global Faith.* Downers Grove, IL: InterVarsity Academic, 2009.

Ort, Larry V. "A Christian Response to Globalization." http://www.racu.org/archive/faculty/articles/Ort_globalization.html (accessed on October 27, 2009).

Pate, Larry D., and Lawrence E. Keyes. "Emerging Missions in a Global Church." *International Bulletin of Missionary Research* 10, no. 4 (1986) 156–61.

Pocock, Michael, Gailyn Van Rheenen, and Douglas McConnell. *The Changing Face of World Missions: Engaging Contemporary Issues and Trends*. Grand Rapids: Baker Academic, 2005.

Postman, Neil. *Technopoly: The Surrender of Culture to Technology*. New York: Knopf, 1992.

Rowell, John. *To Give or Not To Give?* Atlanta: Authentic, 2006.

Shaw, Marty. "The Future of Kingdom Work in a Globalizing World." In *Globalization and the Gospel: Rethinking Mission in the Contemporary World*, edited by David Claydon, 47–49. Lausanne Committee for World Evangelization, 2005.

Stackhouse, Max L. "The Theological Challenge of Globalization." Religion Online. http://www.religion-online.org/cgi-bin/relsearchd.dll/showarticle?item_id=60 (accessed September 7, 2003; webpage now discontinued).

Stackhouse, Max L., and Peter J. Paris, editors. *God and Globalization*. Vol. 1. *Religion and the Powers of the Common Life*. Harrisburg, PA: Trinity Press, 2000.

Stanley, Brian. *The World Missionary Conference, Edinburgh 1910*. Studies in the History of Christian Missions. Grand Rapids: Eerdmans, 2009.

Stott, John, ed. *Evangelism and Social Responsibility: An Evangelical Commitment*. Lausanne Occasional Paper No. 21. Lausanne Committee for World Evangelization, 1982. http://www.lausanne.org/all-documents/lop-21.html (accessed October 29, 2009).

Tiplady, Richard, ed. *One World or Many? The Impact of Globalization on Mission*. Globalization of Mission Series. Pasadena, CA: William Carey Library, 2003.

Walls, Andrew F. *The Missionary Movement in Christian History: Studies in the Transmission and Appropriation of Faith*. Maryknoll, NY: Orbis, 1996.

———. *The Cross-Cultural Process in Christian History: Studies in the Transmission and Appropriation of Faith*. Maryknoll, NY: Orbis, 2002.

Williams, Morris O. *Partnership in Mission: A Study of Theology and Method in Mission*. Springfield, MO: Gospel, 1986.

Wilson, Everett A. *Strategy of the Spirit: J. Philip Hogan and the Growth of the Assemblies of God Worldwide 1960–1990*. Carlisle, UK: Paternoster, 1997.

Wilson, Fiona. "Globalisation from a Grassroots Perspective." In One World or Many? The Impact of Globalization on Mission, edited by Richard Tiplady, 167–88. Pasadena, CA: William Carey Library, 2003.

World Gospel Mission. "The Future of Missions." In "Unsolved Mysteries in Missions" Blog (July 8, 2009). http://unsolvedministries.blogspot.com/2009/07/future-of-missions.html (accessed October 28, 2009).

York, John V. *Missions in the Age of the Spirit*. Springfield, MO: Logion, 2000.

10

Assessment and Interaction

David Reed

THE TITLE OF THE symposium that produced most of these papers, "The Many Faces of Pentecostalism," gives more than a hint of the challenge facing Pentecostals at the beginning of the twenty-first century. The seismic changes that have occurred since Pentecostalism's humble beginnings have become the fodder for today's scholars of Pentecostalism. While many, like Walter Hollenweger, have argued that the seeds of a multi-faced ecumenical Christian movement were embedded in the Azusa Street Revival, it has taken a century to witness the potency of those seeds and the proportions of the harvest. But the success of Pentecostalism's phenomenal global growth has exacted a price in the clash of times, beliefs, practices, and cultures within a movement that is now so diverse that we are left scrambling to find a cohering center of identity.

Contributors to this symposium represent the second generation of scholars exploring global Pentecostalism. In some ways, the first generation belonged to the singular figure of Walter Hollenweger. When he began his research in the 1960s, his vantage point in Europe provided him with a global horizon uncommon for North Americans. He charted the *geographical* Pentecostal landscape of Africa, Asia, and Latin America at a time when North Americans were scarcely aware of sibling movements emerging from these lands. He remapped the *theological* landscape with a cultural lens for rethinking how Pentecostals "do" theology. During his tenure of nearly two decades at the University of Birmingham, he guided the research of doctoral students from every continent.[1]

This Symposium signals a maturing of global Pentecostal research in the number of contributors, the quality of their work, and the range of topics. The presenters work in the fields of Scripture, history, theology, inter-cultural studies, organizational leadership, and the social sciences.

REFLECTIONS, ASSESSMENT, AND QUESTIONS

The papers represent a cumulative piece of work that has produced surprises, presented complexities, and posed more questions. From them I have selected for reflection a few themes that I hope will stimulate ongoing conversation.

Pre-millennial Eschatology—The Engine That Powered Early Pentecostal Mission

Allan Anderson recounts the hardships endured by the earliest Pentecostal missionaries who, within months of the outbreak of the Revival, circled the globe. As he points out, their sacrifices cannot be understood without grasping the urgency of the conviction that they were living literally in the last days before Christ's return, perhaps months at most.

Related to the eschatological urgency was the conviction that this Revival was an endtime "Holy Ghost movement," not just the birth of another denomination. Anderson gives us a rare glimpse into the Revival at a time when it was both nimble and chaotic, akin to the unruliness of the "Wild West." Most scholars studying this period would likely agree that organizational structures and procedures were necessary to advance home and foreign missionary work and permit the leadership to address moral and doctrinal irregularities among its ministers and evangelists.[2]

---

1. His research on Pentecostalism began with the publication of his ten-volume *Handbuch der Pfingstbewegung* (PhD diss., University of Zurich, 1966). The one-volume introduction to global Pentecostalism first appeared in English in 1972. Since that time he has been both an advocate and provocateur of this multi-faced global movement.

2. The Assemblies of God is an excellent case study of this development from its first organizational meeting in 1914 to the decision to expel the "New Issue" from its membership two brief years later in 1916. While there was initially stiff resistance to such organizational expansion, the Assemblies of God was able to accomplish its missionary mandate more effectively with improved organizational coordination.

But some early pioneers like John G. Lake, early missionary to South Africa, perceived such organizational development as a death-dealing blow to the spontaneous work of the Spirit. He made no effort to conceal his disdain in a letter to Charles Parham as early as 1927:

> Gaston the head of The Assemblies of God, is endeavoring to do his best, and is doing a fine work in keeping his institution orderly. True, they have drifted clear away from a true scriptural Pentecostal ideal, and every day are becoming more and more a little bigoted denomination. The spirit of denominationalism in the Assemblies of God is probably narrower than even in the old churches from which Pentecostal people have been escaping for the last thirty years. So that as a power to bless mankind and put an ideal before the world such as the scriptures outline and as our soul is longing for, it does not seem to me they are worth discussing or considering.... One of the things we are all compelled to admit is that so far as real Pentecost from God is concerned, [the Pentecostal faith] is rapidly dying out in the world. I believe in this connection that your own over-emphasis on the question of false manifestation has done much to break down faith in God for all manifestation.[3]

While Lake does not mention the last days specifically, his imminent eschatology was embedded in his conviction of the urgency and uniqueness of the Revival.

But this imminent eschatological expectation was poised on one edge of a very sharp blade in early Pentecostalism. Although they perceived the world to be getting darker as Christ's return drew near, they were not devoid of joy at what they saw God doing in the present. Anderson points out that "premillennialism was not entirely pessimistic. The outpouring of the Spirit in the last days made mission and evangelizing the nations possible." Gerald Sheppard has also reminded us that early Pentecostals were reluctant Dispensationalists and carried a wider vision for God's purpose for this present world.[4] The vigor of the emerging global Prosperity movement—though heavily criticized by many Classical Pentecostals—suggests that there is a potent seed of this-world transformation at the heart of Pentecostalism. Less radical, but perhaps more corrosive, is the shifting of the center of gravity of North American Pentecostals to the cultural and economic middle class. The urgency of

---

3. Lake, "Letter to Charles Parham" (March 24, 1927).
4. Sheppard, "Pentecostals and the Hermeneutics of Dispensationalism," 5–33.

Christ's imminent return, especially in evangelistic preaching (which is where it has always *really* mattered for Pentecostals), has waned dramatically as Pentecostals are making this world their home.

On the other hand, an important challenge facing Pentecostals is whether or not—or if so, how—a true longing for the next world can generate a transformational vision for this world. The stereotypical "either-or" dichotomy is a false one. Neither nostalgia nor desperation will suffice for mapping a missionary strategy in the twenty-first century. Is Pentecostalism then doomed to become "just another denomination" that settles for the good life here? If the Pentecostal movement cannot return *simpliciter* to its roots, is there a seedling in its beginnings that can be retrieved for its second century? Steven Studebaker comments that in some respects, "Pentecostalism may have come full circle from the interracial and ecumenical experience of the Spirit at Azusa Street to a global multicultural and trans-denominational movement of the Spirit." The current demographic suggests that the majority world will be the true inheritors of the Revival, while white North Americans seem to have lost their taste for the life of the world to come. Peter Toon may offer a helpful reminder—Christians are at their transformational best in this life when they long most deeply for the next.[5]

The Secret Pentecostal Weapon of National Missionaries—Non-Western Nationals and Western African-Americans

The momentum in the West to profile and promote missions has often eclipsed the real heroes. Anderson tells us who they were—"national people 'sent by the Spirit,' often without formal training." As he points out, the nationals honed their leadership skills even while the missionaries held the power.

Many Pentecostal missionaries, unlike those in mainline missions, were in fact committed to an indigenous church and leadership. The "Pentecostalization" of nationals appeared in at least two ways. One was the spiritual attitude of early Pentecostal missionaries themselves. It was the conviction that the Holy Spirit, not the missionary, is the Prime Mover. And when the effect of a revival is greater than the effort of the missionary, the conclusion is that the agency is divine. F. S. Ramsey, an early missionary to northern China, reflects this conviction in a report

---

5. Toon, *Longing for the Heavenly Realm*.

of a spontaneous revival in Shansi Province, "It was remarkable to note that there was no missionary of any kind there to superintend this remarkable outpouring. The leader was Jehovah. Hallelujah!"[6]

A second, less obvious example comes from the "charismatic" ministries of the national Korean Bible women in early twentieth century Protestant missionary work. Because the missionaries were non-charismatic, they were unskilled in confronting the spiritual realities that plagued the average Korean. Consequently, local people turned to the Bible women who provided personal and spiritual relief through healing and deliverance. According to one account:

> These women are highly respected and are believed to have the ability to offer up prevailing prayer. If anyone is in trouble of any sort in mind or body, or estate, the Bible woman is sent to pray and sing psalms. When anyone gets tired of trying to propitiate the evil spirit, it is the Bible woman who must come and take down the fetishes and burn them. They are called upon to cast out devils; as well as to offer the fervent effectual prayer for the healing of the sick. *Their faith is often greater that that of their teachers.*[7]

This is an example that, even within Western mainline missions, a kind of "pentecostalization" was taking place on national soil.

The Humpty Dumpty Effect in Pentecostal Doctrine and Pentecostal Experience—Can They Be Put Together Again?

A burning question for Classical Pentecostals is whether or not the *doctrine* of Spirit baptism and the *experience*, which its adherents claim for it, including glossolalia, still walk hand in hand or travel on parallel journeys. The underlying and more urgent question is: does Pentecostal identity rest on the inseparability of the two? Studebaker's paper strikes a raw nerve since a global glance at Pentecostal diversity and the drifting apart of doctrine and experience in North American Pentecostalism reveal a slow-moving breakup of the consensus that the experience is dependent upon the doctrine. Furthermore, recent reflection among

---

6. The report was originally published in Frank J. Ewart's magazine, *Meat in Due Season*, and later excerpted in his book, *The Name and the Book*, 47.

7. Scranton, "Day Schools and Bible Women," 53 (emphasis added), cited in Kim, "Healing the Wounded Heart," 107.

Pentecostal scholars on this issue is increasing, a sign that the calls for retrieval or revision are well underway.

While this watershed moment raises Pentecostal anxiety, the Pentecostals themselves are in the best position to chart a creative way forward, since it may offer a more nuanced alternative to the typical evangelical approach. It is a Protestant, and particularly evangelical, trait to assume that all things good flow directly from right doctrine, or "orthodoxy." And conversely, bad Christian practices issue from "un"-orthodox beliefs.

Pentecostals, like other orthodox-believing Christians, have always held true ("biblical") doctrine to be of highest value. Yet "experience" is quintessential to being Pentecostal. On the doctrinal side, some scholars argue that Classical Pentecostals like the Assemblies of God came under the spell of the confessionalism of Wheaton evangelicals more than a half century ago through their association in the National Association of Evangelicals.[8] This has had the effect of minimizing distinctive Pentecostal experience and theology.

Studebaker's paper sets before us the dilemma. By holding up a mirror to show us the many global faces of the Pentecostal "us," we witness a dizzying array of doctrines and practices that stretches the credibility of what it means to be Pentecostal. Yet the profile is recognizable enough to challenge the narrow parameters with which we conventionally define Pentecostalism in North America. This means that the task before us is at least to consider that doctrine is important but not sufficient to define the scope of the Spirit's work or contain the range of human faces touched by the Spirit's power.[9] To return to John G. Lake's letter to Parham, Lake is willing to consider that a little overemphasis may even have a positive spiritual effect. Referring to the "Jesus Only" or Oneness group that was expelled from the Assemblies of God fellowship in 1916, he observes:

---

8. Russell Spittler traces this shift in the Assemblies of God towards Fundamentalism; see, Spittler, "Pentecostal View," 144–45.

9. The barrier to intra-Pentecostal dialogue and fellowship is not liberalism but exclusivism. Many Pentecostal groups claim such exclusive rights to the truth that they refuse to fellowship with other Pentecostals; e.g., the United Pentecostal Church International, the followers of William Branham's teachings, True Jesus Church (Chinese-founded), and Spirit of Jesus Church (Japan).

> They show more genuine spirituality than any other branch of the movement. The mere fact of their emphasis of Jesus, that the other divisions of the movement regard as extreme, has tended to bless them in that it has brought them into close touch with the Lord's life and Spirit.[10]

In other words, high confessionalism is not sufficient—certainly not a guarantor—for an authentic move of the Spirit. The experience of the Holy Spirit in manifestations recognizable as "Pentecostal" must be at least a factor in making room at the family table. As Studebaker suggests, a robust Pentecostal doctrine of Spirit baptism will "succeed in giving the Holy Spirit a theological expression that corresponds both to the Pentecostal experience of the Spirit and to the reforming nature of that experience."

On the related topic of glossolalia, Randall Holm sounds an alarm: "Tongues-speech is in jeopardy." Here also we witness the Humpty Dumpty effect—Pentecostal experience seems to have journeyed on, leaving tongues to fend for itself as the singular physical evidence of Spirit baptism. The present drifting apart prompts a host of questions. Are we lacking a sound theology of glossolalia? Has the Third Wave been successful in eroding the exclusive claim accorded tongues by Classical Pentecostals, a doctrinal boundary thought by Third Wavers to be too exclusive and unnecessary? Are tongues as evidence a hurdle for a postmodern culture? Is the display of tongues in worship a discomforting detraction for Pentecostal seeker-sensitive churches? Has the cultural landscape changed so drastically that speaking in tongues is no longer a longed-for spiritual commodity?

Holm's exploration of Abraham Heschel's spiritual theology for revisioning the role of tongues for Pentecostals is bold and creative. His theological exploration implies a critique of the conventional Pentecostal doctrine and practice, namely, that tongues-speaking functions as an evidential sign of the inward endowment of the Spirit's power, and subsequently, as companion to the gift of prophecy. The effect of such teaching is twofold: a sign intensely (sometimes desperately) sought, but after receiving, promptly forgotten. This desertion of the gift has not gone unnoticed in some Pentecostal-type circles. A case in point, the independent Chinese-founded True Jesus Church criticizes Western Pentecostals for such neglect. While the TJC, like Western Pentecostals,

---

10. Lake, "Letter to Charles Parham" (March 24, 1927).

teaches that tongues is the initial physical sign of Spirit baptism, it is more intentional in promoting the gift as a means of personal spiritual edification (1 Cor 14). To that end, worshippers are instructed to speak in tongues (as they are able) exclusively during the time of prayer in corporate worship.

The dilemma of "what meaneth this" has inspired a number of scholars to seek a more theologically textured understanding for an experience that appears to be rapidly evaporating from Pentecostal life. Holm highlights various theological approaches to glossolalia, raising the possibility that there may be a variety of valid "theologies" of tongues. To this list could be added a host of approaches from the fields of world religions, anthropology, psychology, and sociology. Holm's paper raises two important issues.

First, Holm is delving deeply in a process of reflecting on the nature and significance of tongues that has been going on since the charismatic movement of the 1960s. The difference is that, until recently, the market belonged to charismatics, non-Pentecostals, and secular scholars. Classical Pentecostals seemed satisfied that the "supernatural" interpretation was sufficient. Their only question was how a Christian (especially a Roman Catholic!) could receive this special gift without leaving the "old church" and the sinful trappings associated with it. To explain the phenomenon, some Pentecostals borrowed shamelessly from their own Fundamentalist nemesis: it must be demonic.

But within the last two decades, the experience of tongues has drifted so far from its original moorings among Classical Pentecostals that Holms suggests it may be on the brink of extinction. Predictions aside, Pentecostals are now engaging in a creative process of finding a theological home for tongues. Already there are theologies—plural—underway.[11] I wonder about two things. One is whether these new theologies will supplement or replace the Classical doctrine of tongues as initial evidence. The other is: what boundaries, if any, will be placed around the new theologies? Will it be enough if they are trinitarian and normed christologically?

My second query is: can a Pentecostal theology of tongues, with its commitment to supernatural origins, embrace a naturalistic view? That

---

11. In my memory, Russell Spittler represents one of the earliest Classical Pentecostals to provide a brief but comprehensive and multi-disciplinary treatment of glossolalia; see Spittler, "Glossolalia," 335–41.

is, what are we to make of James K. A. Smith's "naturalizing glossolalia," a proposal that appears to bear the marks of a Reformed doctrine of common grace?[12] What is lost, if anything, for Pentecostals who believe that tongues-speaking is a charism reserved for followers of Jesus who have received the promised Spirit baptism? If embraced, will it still have the capacity to enrich and empower the spiritual lives of those blessed by the gift? One possible direction is to accept that the linguistic phenomenon itself may originate in natural human capacity, but its spiritual effect is a divinely enabled act of the Holy Spirit.

Globalization on Canadian Soil—Where Can It Be Found?

Michael Wilkinson explores the emerging field of globalization within a social science discipline, and turns to test his insights on Canadian Pentecostalism. My reading of his paper is that Canadian soil is fertile but Pentecostals have yet to till it well. However, there are occasional signs of activity and glimpses of opportunity. My comments follow Wilkinson's three foci: theology of Spirit baptism, multi-faith cooperation, and denominationalism.

First, there has been no significant change in the Pentecostal Assemblies of Canada's (PAOC) position on the classical doctrine of Spirit baptism; worse, Ronald Kydd, PAOC's premiere scholar, whom Wilkinson cites, converted after two decades in the PAOC to the Anglican Church. But that, it seems to me, is not the whole story. There are three factors that may bear some relation to the way Canadian Pentecostals distinctively "live" their doctrine. One is the *demographic reality* that Canada is (1) one-tenth the population of the United States, (2) a nation of regional identities unlike America's "one nation under God, indivisible . . . ," and (3) geographically rural but demographically urban. These Canadian characteristics ultimately affect the way in which denominations understand themselves and relate to one another.

The second feature is a corollary and an outcome: this demographic profile has *shaped Pentecostals' relationship with other Christians, especially Evangelicals*. Comparatively small in number, Pentecostals have needed to cooperate in order to address social and political concerns important to them.

---

12. Smith, "What Hath Cambridge to Do with Azusa Street?"

Two examples come to mind. One is the PAOC's membership in the Evangelical Fellowship of Canada. Being the largest member body in the EFC gives Pentecostals a significant identity and voice within the wider evangelical community that does not likely occur in the American National Association of Evangelicals.

The other example is Pentecostal cooperation with Tyndale University College and Seminary in Toronto. Though this is a non-denominational Evangelical institution, Tyndale's recently retired president is a leading Pentecostal, and the PAOC's Master's Seminary is an institutional partner with Tyndale. The Pentecostal Assemblies of Newfoundland and Tyndale also recently forged a similar partnership for ministerial education.

The third factor points to a theological distinctive of Canadian Pentecostalism: its *Reformed evangelical influence*. While key founders of the PAOC had Holiness roots, the singular figure of J. Eustace Purdie left a Reformed stamp on the PAOC. An evangelical Anglican minister who never abandoned the church of his birth, Purdie was principal of one of the PAOC's leading Bible schools for a quarter century. His strong Reformed theology of grace and justification were evident in his catechism and in the classroom.[13] The Apostolic Church of Pentecost, a smaller Canadian Pentecostal organization, holds the Reformed doctrine of "eternal security."[14]

The theological question is this: will this uniquely Canadian Pentecostal–Evangelical relationship result in the evangelicalizing of Canadian Pentecostals? If so, in what ways? Will our more culturally reserved character contribute to Pentecostalism's attractiveness, or will it be the means of its gradual demise?

Canada's multi-cultural identity brings with it the possibility of encounter with non-Christian faiths. Wilkinson accurately describes the government's multicultural policy of openly encouraging cultural diversity. Yet, there appears to be no significant multi-faith initiatives taken by Pentecostals. While this may be true, there is at least a degree of multi-faith cooperation—admittedly at arm's length—through the

---

13. See Craig, "Out and Out for the Lord."

14. The Apostolic Church of Pentecost was founded by Franklin Small, an original signatory to the Pentecostal Assemblies of Canada who later formed his own organization. ACOP has held to the doctrine of eternal security from its inception in 1921. Its membership is concentrated in the western provinces. The ACOP is the only significant global Pentecostal organization to hold the doctrine of eternal security.

PAOC's participation in the Evangelical Fellowship of Canada. The EFC frequently forms political alliances with Sikhs and other non-Christian groups in order to speak to government policy on such common concerns as freedom of religion and abortion.

Finally, Canadian Pentecostals continue to be intransigent in their denominational loyalties. But again this is not the whole story. As elsewhere, independent charismatic churches continue to sprout up around them on quite parallel tracks.[15] Difference in emphases—emphasizing prosperity and de-emphasizing tongues—perpetuates the hard but thin line between them. And as Wilkinson points out, growth in either of these streams is largely of the immigrant variety. The independent churches appeal to a postdenominational Christian culture, but are likely eroding Classical Pentecostal identity and numbers as well. Toronto is a prime example. Two of the largest churches in the city are less than twenty years old and thoroughly multiethnic. One of them was originally PAOC.

The independent charismatic church movement is not limited to Canada's urban centers. At a time when mainline denominations are engaged in massive closures of small rural churches, independent charismatics are strategically helping to re-church rural Canada. Names like Victory Tabernacle, Gateway Church, Life Tabernacle, and their "box church" architecture are just two small clues that independent charismatics, not only Pentecostals, are now filling the rural churchscape. In other words, this post-denominational shift is affecting Canada's rural territory as well as our urban centers. At this stage in the evolution of Canadian Pentecostal denominations, dwindling numbers have not yet sparked creative alliances.

Leadership Gone Global!

Byron Klaus brings the skills and insight of a practical theologian to the topic of Pentecostal leadership, mission, and globalization. Writing as an insider, he calls the Pentecostal movement to self-critical reflection as it faces the challenge of globalization from without and the temptation of triumphalism from within. He reflects on the driving force that propelled early Pentecostals, and the reality that a century later Pentecostalism is encrusted with the "barnacles" of an aging institution. He applauds the boldness of the early missionaries and confidence in the power of the

---

15. Independent charismatic churches may have an associational affiliation with a larger fellowship, but their church polity is usually local church or congregational.

Spirit to accomplish God's mission. But he worries that, a century later, this very confidence has been corrupted by a toxic blend of naive spirituality and secular success.

Klaus's concern for the future of Pentecostal leadership is captured in his stinging indictment of Jesus' disciples as displaying "a startling level of cluelessness" when confronted with Jesus' challenge, "Not so with you" (Mark 10:35–45). Klaus traces the shift from a counter-cultural spiritual and moral model of leadership to a secular CEO model of leadership borrowed from the capitalist and business world, which is then packaged and marketed around the globe through books and seminars. He poses the question of that perennial temptation of Pentecostal leaders to slide into the troughs and ruts carved out by culture, instead of retaining their spiritual and moral identity, authority, and leadership.

It is possible that this description of the state of Pentecostal leadership is, at least in part, an illustration of the evangelicalization of Pentecostalism. Evangelicals are traditional in their doctrine but have a penchant for borrowing generously from the culture in order to communicate effectively. Pentecostals of an earlier generation relied more heavily upon the Spirit's anointing in preaching and power in healing to accomplish their mission and bring about revival.

There is much here with which to agree. And Klaus must be applauded for sounding a warning. But I wonder if at times he is viewing the past through rose-colored glasses. There has always been an ingrained pragmatism in Pentecostalism. I continue to be amazed at the ability and gravitational pull of Pentecostals to grow large churches, success being due to a unique blend of Pentecostal experience and cultural savvy. The earliest example, and perhaps the first megachurch in America, is Aimee Semple McPherson's 5,300-seat Angelus Temple, built in 1923 only seventeen short years after the Azusa Street Revival. Admittedly, she was less CEO than movie star. But today's thousands of unconventionally large Pentecostal churches dotting the world's landscape convinces me that Pentecostal leaders from the beginning have never been satisfied, as are the historic churches of Christendom, with being merely the official spiritual presence in town. Size for Pentecostals means not just success; it is "Holy-Ghost success."

I am not entirely persuaded by all of Suico's criticisms of the prevailing CEO model of Pentecostal leadership in Asia. It seems that Suico is unhappy with the CEO model because, in part, the leader's authority is validated by the size of the building and numbers rather than "spiritual and moral integrity." But it is not clear if Suico is philosophically opposed to large churches, or just the perceived abuses of authority. Does he believe that large churches, by virtue of their size, require a CEO model of leadership and therefore should be discouraged? If so, his proposal would be a return to a traditional hierarchical model of leadership, with all its deficiencies. One of the enduring marks of Pentecostal leaders is that, while there is an autocratic strain in the tradition, they balance this—at least more than mainline church leaders—with a strong commitment to the ministry of the whole people of God.

It is no surprise that there are weaknesses, possibly even flaws, in large churches. The question is whether or not particular criticisms are well-founded.[16] A case in point is City Harvest Church, the largest megachurch in Singapore. Congregations of this size are routinely criticized for their capitulation to numbers, a spirit of capitalistic competition, and lack of community. But sociologists Donald E. Miller and Tetsunao Yamamori tell another story. While the senior minister has "excessive charisma," the overall ministry of the church is, like many other Pentecostal megachurches, more *organic* than hierarchical. Ministry leadership is spread generously throughout the thirty thousand membership and over one thousand cell groups. The pastor intentionally incorporates a ministry of "affection and care" precisely as an antidote to the highly individualistic and competitive culture of Singapore.[17] Perhaps size matters in Asia, where Christianity is a religious minority with little political influence. A megachurch in Indonesia, even without the traditional church sign, makes its own statement about "presence."[18]

---

16. For instance, see the insightful study of the myths and reality of the American megachurches by Thumma and Travis, *Beyond Megachurch Myths*.

17. Miller and Yamamori, *Global Pentecostalism*, 92–94, 188. In a recent visit to Sunday worship at City Harvest Church (June 2009), I observed that the auditorium filled with eight thousand worshippers was arranged in sections, each seating no more than fifty people. At the end of the service, the section leaders gathered their "tribe" together and led them in intercessory prayer.

18. Examples in Indonesia are the 45,000-seat Bethany Graha Church in Surabaya, and Pastor Niko Njotorahardjo's newly built 12,000-seat convention center on the outskirts of Jakarta.

CONCLUSION

Is Pentecostalism still, in Cox's words, "a religion made to travel"? Is it today a quintessentially missionary movement? Would the answer be different if Cox were referring to fifth-generation North American Pentecostals instead of first- and second-generation indigenous Pentecostal churches in the majority world?

How are we to assess a movement that is united in its experience and doctrine of the charisms of the Holy Spirit but globally one of the most fragmenting movements in the history of the church?[19] Although Pentecostalism is a nightmare for ecumenical unity-seekers, is Anderson correct that this proliferation is an asset for a movement made to travel, "unencumbered by out-of-date ecclesiastical structures and hierarchies?" If so, and given that Christian unity is still a gospel mandate, the church will need new tools and an expanded imagination as it enters a century like no other in the history of the church.

---

19. As David Barrett demonstrates, the proliferation of groups in the global Pentecostal-Charismatic movement continues unabated; see Barrett, "Global Statistics," 284–302.

BIBLIOGRAPHY

Barrett, David B. "Global Statistics." In *New International Dictionary of Pentecostal and Charismatic Movements*, edited by Stanley M. Burgess, 284–302. Rev. ed. Grand Rapids: Zondervan, 2002.

Craig, James. "'Out and Out for the Lord:' James Eustace Purdie, an Early Anglican Pentecostal." MA thesis, University of St. Michael's College, 1995.

Ewart, Frank J. *The Name and the Book*. Chicago: Daniel Ryerson, 1936.

Lake, John G. "A Letter to Charles F. Parham." In *John G. Lake, The Complete Collection of His Life Teachings*, edited by Roberts Liardon, 474–80. New Kensington, PA: Whitaker, 1999.

Kim, Lisa. "Healing the Wounded Heart: Towards an Integrative Healing of Women's Suffering/Han-Experiences from the Perspective of Korean Protestant Spiritualities." ThD diss., University of Toronto, 2006.

Miller, Donald E., and Tetsunao Yamamori. *Global Pentecostalism: The New Face of Christian Social Engagement*. Los Angeles: University of California Press, 2007.

Scranton, Mary F. "Day Schools and Bible Women." *The Korean Mission Field*, March 1907.

Sheppard, Gerald T. "Pentecostals and the Hermeneutics of Dispensationalism: The Anatomy of an Uneasy Relationship." *Pneuma* 6, no. 2 (1984) 5–33.

Smith, James, K. A., "What Hath Cambridge to Do with Azusa Street? Radical Orthodoxy and Pentecostal Theology in Conversation." *Pneuma* 25 (2003) 97–114.

Spittler, Russell. "Glossolalia." In *Dictionary of Pentecostal and Charismatic Movements*, edited by Stanley M. Burgess and Gary B. McGee, 335–41. Grand Rapids: Zondervan, 1988.

———. "The Pentecostal View." In *Christian Spirituality: Five Views of Sanctification*, edited by Donald Alexander, 133–54. Downers Grove, IL: InterVarsity, 1988.

Thumma, Scott, and Dave Travis. *Beyond Megachurch Myths: What We Can Learn from America's Largest Churches*. San Francisco: Jossey-Boss, 2007.

Toon, Peter. *Longing for the Heavenly Realm: The Missing Element in Modern Western Spirituality*. London: Hodder & Stoughton, 1986.

Index of Names

Abrams, Minnie, 41, 44
Adeboye, Enoch A., 56
Adefarasin, Paul, 66n31
Adelaja, Sunday, 60
Allen, Roland, 132, 133, 213
Anderson, Allan, 2n1, 21, 74, 77, 90, 93n8, 94, 102, 222, 223, 224
Anderson, Gordon L., 89n2, 92n7
Anderson, Robert Mapes, 130n11
Anderson, Rufus, 213
Appadurai, Arjun, 72n8
Appleby, Blanche, 47
Araujo, Alex, 200n3
Arnott, John, 98
Asamoah-Gyadu, J. Kwabena, 63
Austin, J. L., 114, 115n14
Awrey, Daniel, 35
Azariah, V. S., 217

Bakker, Jim, 97
Bakker, Tammy Faye, 97
Barratt, T. B., 35
Barrett, David B., 55, 167n42
Barth, Karl, 146
Bell, E. N., 45
Berntsen, Bernt, 40
Bettex, Nellie, 45, 46
Bettex, Paul, 45
Beyer, Peter, 71, 73, 75–76
Boddy, Alexander, 32, 33, 38–39
Boli, John, 4n7, 5
Bosch, David, 51, 175–76, 178n10, 179, 185n32
Boyd, Jenny, 30n3

Bradin, George, 59
Bredesen, Harald, 96
Brezhnev, Leonid, 61
Brouwer, Steve, 56n14
Browne, Rodney Howard, 88
Browning, Don, 10–11
Brumback, Carl, 112n6
Brunner, Emil, 179n13
Buber, Martin, 116, 119–20
Bühlmann, Walbert, 209

Carey, William, 208
Ceausescu, Nicolae, 60
Cerillo, Augustus, 184
Cesar, Waldo, 2n1, 129n6
Chan, Simon, 93
Chandra, Dorothea, 36
Cheung-Judge, L. Mee-Yan, 147n45
Cho, David Yonggi, 58, 91
Chuckerbutty, Shorat, 35, 36
Clark, Matthew S., 91n5
Clark, Stephen, 96
Clifton, Shane, 102n25, 103n27, 106n32
Cole, Anna Deane, 42
Copeland, Kenneth, 97
Cox, Harvey, 2n1, 67, 93n8, 128, 152, 153–54, 234
Creps, Earl, 89n2
Csordas, Thomas J., 82n31

D'Souza, Dinesh, 200n5
Daniels, David, 131n13
Darby, J. N., 130

Dayton, Donald, 100n19, 130n11
Delgado, Sharon, 12–13
Dempster, Murray, 2n1, 136n27, 205–6
Dhinakaran, D. G. S., 57
Di Giacomo, Michael, 77n19
Dieter, Melvin E., 100n19
Dionson, Narciso C., 100n20
Doering, Alma, 40
Droogers, André, 10, 52n5
Duff, Alexander, 133

Elliott, Jean Leonard, 80n23
Ellwood, Wayne, 168n46
Enns, Peter, 121–22
Escobar, Samuel, 168, 205n17

Farrow, Lucy, 34
Faupel, D. William, 40n39, 100n19, 130n9, 130n11
Fedotov, Ivan, 61
Fee, Gordon, 135, 137
Ferguson, James, 186
Fetler, William, 59
Fleras, Augie, 80n23
Flower, J. Roswell, 162
Freston, Paul, 153n8, 159n25, 168n49
Friedman, Thomas, 157
Friere, Paulo, 141

Garr, A. G., 35, 39
Garr, Lillian, 35, 36
Giddens, Anthony, 71n3
Goff, James R., 103ns29–30
González, Justo, 17
Gorbachev, Mikhail, 61
Gordon, A. J., 134
Grandona, Mariano, 143
Greely, Andrew, 81
Griffith, R. Marie, 82n31
Grigg, Viv, 183n25
Groat, Eva, 36
Guder, Darrel, 147n44
Gupta, Akhil, 186

Hagin, Kenneth, 97
Hanciles, Jehu J., 181, 188, 190, 203n12
Hansen, Sophia, 40
Harrison, Lawrence, 143
Harrow, J. M. L., 46
Hartman, David, 191
Hastings, Adrian, 17
Held, David, 4n7
Herron, C. B., 42n47
Heschel, Abraham, 116–18, 227
Heuser, Roger, 145n41
Hiebert, Paul, 157n14, 158n21, 183n26, 212n38
Hill, Agnes, 36
Hobsbawn, E. J., 3n4
Hodges, Melvin, 133, 162, 178, 213
Hofstede, Geert, 142
Hogan, J. Philip, 151, 152, 155–56, 160–64, 165, 171, 211n37
Hollenweger, Walter J., 2n1, 21, 52, 93n8, 104n30, 131n13, 136, 221, 222n1
Holm, Randall, 227–28
Hoover, Willis, 94
Huntington, Samuel, 143, 157n15
Hylson-Smith, Kenneth, 8–9

Inda, Jonathan, 157, 165, 186

Jacobsen, Douglas, 95, 100–102
Jenkins, Philip, 9, 129, 141, 167
Johnson, Alan, 135, 177n8
Juergensmeyer, Mark, 191n50
Junk, Thomas, 40, 43

Kay, William K., 89n2
Keller, Timothy, 183
Kelley, Robert, 145n41
Kenichi, Ohmae, 166n40, 187–88
Keyes, Lawrence E., 167, 212n38
Kilpatrick, John, 98
Kipling, Rudyard, 212n29
Klaus, Byron D., 2n1, 145n41, 159, 231–32

Index of Names

Knight, John A., 100n19
Koch, Kurt, 92n7
Kruschev, Nikita, 61
Kuhn, Thomas, 51
Kuzmic, Peter, 160
Kydd, Ronald, 79, 229

Laing, Mark, 167n42, 211, 212n38
Lake, John G., 43, 223, 226
Land, Steven J., 93n8
Latourette, Kenneth Scott, 209
Law, May, 42
Leatherman, Lucy, 34, 38
Lechner, Frank J., 4n7, 5
Lederle, Henry I., 96
Lindbeck, George, 102n25
Luce, Alice, 36, 132
Luhmann, Niklas, 73
Lundy, David, 189n44–45
Lyon, David, 72n8

Macchia, Frank, 74–75, 78–79, 105, 113
Markoff, John, 203n13
Martin, David, 2n1, 58, 129, 153n8
Martin, Ralph, 96
McCarty, D. L., 46
McConnell, Douglas, 199n2, 203n11, 213n40, 214n42
McGee, Gary B., 33n13, 133
McGuire, Meredith B., 82n31
McIntosh, T. J., 39
McPherson, Aimee Semple, 232
Menzies, Robert P., 87n1
Miller, Donald E., 2n1, 206–7, 233
Miller, Mark, 141
Miller, Thomas, 77n19
Mok Lai Chi, 32
Montague, George, 79
Montgomery, Carrie Judd, 34, 35
Moorhead, Max Wood, 32
Morrison, Grant, 118n24

Nachtigall, Patrick, 12–13

Neill, Stephen, 179
Nèmeth, Sàndor, 61
Netland, Harold, 189n44
Nevius, John, 133, 213
Newbigin, Lesslie, 138, 176ns3–4, 211
Niebuhr, H. Richard, 81, 136
Noll, Mark, 210

O'Dea, Thomas, 143–44
Oden, Thomas, 145
Osmer, Richard, 156n11, 158n21
Oyedepo, David, 56

Padilla, C. Rene, 176n5
Parham, Charles Fox, 38, 41, 95, 103ns29–30, 223, 226
Pate, Larry D., 167, 212n38
Patrick, Eleanor, 59
Paul (Apostle), 192
Pelikan, Jaroslav, 185
Perkin, Noel, 162
Petersen, Douglas, 2n1, 130n10
Pierard, R. V., 153n8
Pinnock, Clark, 79
Pocock, Michael, 199n2, 203n11, 213n40, 214n42
Poewe, Karla, 82n31
Polhill, Cecil, 36
Poloma, Margaret M., 82n30, 89n2
Pomerville, Paul, 133
Postman, Neil, 202n8
Powar, Soonderbai, 35
Purdie, J. Eustace, 230

Ramabai, Pandita, 32, 34, 35, 36, 41, 94
Ramsey, F. S., 224
Raschke, 128n3
Reasoner, Victor P., 100n19
Robbins, Joel, 159n25
Robeck, Cecil M., 32, 40n39, 94n10, 103
Robert, Dana L., 169n50

Roberts, Oral, 97
Robertson, Pat, 97
Robertson, Roland, 71–72, 77, 158
Rosaldo, Renato, 157, 165, 186
Rowell, John, 216n45
Ryan, Alan, 54n12
Ryan, M. L., 32, 43

Saayman, Willem A., 32, 65n29
Samarin, William, 113
Sánchez Walsh, Arlene M., 2n1
Sanneh, Lamin, 138, 159, 167
Satyavrata, Ivan, 127–28
Scholte, Jan Aart, 3, 7–8, 18
Scranton, Mary F., 225n7
Searle, John, 114
Seel, John, 177n8
Sexton, Elisabeth, 32, 33, 46
Seymour, William J., 38, 95, 104n30
Shakarian, Demos, 96
Shaull, Richard, 2n1, 129n6
Shaw, Marty, 215
Shenk, Wilbert R., 16, 17, 188–89, 194n54
Sheppard, Gerald, 223
Simpson, A. B., 38, 134
Sisson, Elisabeth, 48
Small, Franklin, 230n14
Smith, James K. A., 114–15, 121, 229
Spittler, Russell, 226n8, 228n11
Stackhouse, Max L., 166, 190, 200
Stearns, Peter N., 181n15
Steger, Manfred B., 166n40
Stoll, David, 56, 129
Stott, John, 176n3, 205n17, 207n23
Stronstad, Roger, 75n15
Studebaker, Steven M., 79, 224, 225–27
Suenens, Léon-Joseph, 96
Suico, Joseph, 139, 232–33
Swaggart, Jimmy, 97
Taylor, James Hudson, 31
Teraudkalns, Valdis, 59n21, 61
Thumma, Scott, 233n16
Tiplady, Richard, 201
Tomlinson, John, 6–7, 19, 20

Toon, Peter, 224
Torrey, R. A., 100n19
Travis, Dave, 233n16

Ukpong, Justin, 14–15, 18, 21

Valerio, Ruth, 168n47
Van Rheenan, Gailyn, 190, 191n52, 199n2, 203n11, 213n40, 214n42
Venn, Henry, 133, 213
Villafañe, Eldin, 137
Voronaev, Ivan, 60–61

Wacker, Grant, 35, 131n12
Wagner, C. Peter, 97, 152n3
Waldvogel (née Blumhofer), Edith L., 100n19
Wallerstein, Immanuel, 3n4
Walls, Andrew, 16, 17, 52, 159, 161, 163, 167, 194, 209–11, 212
Warner, R. Stephen, 82n29
Watt, Charles Peter, 89n2, 97n17, 98
Watts, Isaac, 185
Webber, Robert, 134
Weber, Max, 144, 153n7
Welker, Michael, 122–23
Wessels, Roland, 100n19
Wilkinson, Michael, 229, 230–31
Williams, Morris O., 216n46
Williams, Rodman, 79
Wilson, Everett, 155n10
Wilson, Fiona, 200n3
Wimber, John, 97
Winter, Ralph, 134
Wittgenstein, Ludwig, 50
Woodworth-Etter, Maria, 34
Wright, Chris, 177
Wuthnow, Robert, 82

Yamamori, Tetsunao, 2n1, 206–7, 233
Yong, Amos, 22, 74, 75–76, 79, 80, 105, 138
York, John, 216–17

Index of Subjects

Africa, 54, 56–57
apostolicity, 135
Assemblies of God, 44, 47, 48, 95, 104, 146, 155, 163, 223, 226
Azusa Street mission, 31, 35, 37, 38, 91, 103, 104

Canada, 80, 229–31
Catholicism
    and the Charismatic movement, 96
    and Latin America, 56
Charismatic movement, 53, 92, 96–98, 103, 104
China, 40, 57
Christ, 121–22, 130, 131, 214
    and leadership, 140, 146
    and missions, 176
Christianity
    as a global religion, 8–10, 18–19, 53, 167, 209–11
    and inculturation, 159, 161
    and leadership, 142–43
    and pluralism, 191–92
church history, 16–18
community, 66, 137
consumerism, 142

denominationalism, 78, 81–82

ecclesiology, 65–66, 138, 178, 179–80
    and organization, 143–44
ecumenism, 75

eschatology, 30–31, 130, 131, 132, 134, 136, 193–94, 222–24
Europe, 54, 58–59, 62
Evangelical Fellowship of Canada, 230
evangelicalism, 98, 205, 226, 230
evangelism, 131, 134, 135, 162, 205

globalization
    and Christianity, 8–11, 18–19
    and communication, 170
    and culture, 5, 141–42, 165–66, 169, 186–87
    definition of, 3–6, 127–28, 156–58
    economic, 12–14, 15, 187–88
    and proximity, 6–7
    and respatialization, 7–8
    theological assessment of, 12–14, 199–202
    theories of, 6–8, 71–72, 158
glossolalia, 61, 78, 79, 88, 89, 95, 97–98, 100, 102, 110–15, 117–22, 227–29
    and missions, 37–41

hermeneutics, 14–15
Hungary, 61

imperialism, 185
India, 31, 35–36, 57

kingdom of God, 135, 176–78, 180, 205–6

Index of Subjects

leadership, 65, 139–40, 144–45, 146–47, 232–33
Liberia, 31, 43

migration, 181–82
missions, 64, 131, 132–37, 155–56, 160–64, 167, 168–69, 170–71, 174–75, 194–95, 214–17, 224
  and culture, 185–86, 188–89
  definition of, 175–80
  and funding, 43–47
  and global Christianity, 211–12
  and hardships, 42–48
  and imperialism, 30
  and indigenous leadership, 32, 35–36, 162, 213
  and paternalism, 212–13
  and premillennialism, 30
  and restricted access countries, 207–9
  and Spirit baptism, 31, 33, 38, 40–41
  and spiritual gifts, 41
  and technology, 202–4
  and urbanization, 183–84
  and women, 34–37
modernity, 111, 122
Mukti Mission, 35
multiculturalism, 80, 131, 189–90

nation state, 4, 187

Pentecost, 20, 33, 137, 146, 178
Pentecostal Assemblies of Canada, 78, 79, 80, 104, 229
Pentecostalism
  and culture, 136
  Classical, 20, 21, 75, 78, 87, 88, 89, 90, 92, 95, 96–100, 103–5, 115, 123–24, 226, 227, 228
  and communism, 59, 60, 61–62
  description of, 50–51, 53, 67, 77
  and doctrine, 105, 226
  and Eastern Europe, 54, 62
  and experience, 93, 101–2, 225–27
  as a global movement, 20–21, 55–56, 63, 91, 92–93, 94, 105, 128–29, 138, 152–53, 159–60, 163
  and globalization, 19–21, 54, 67, 72, 73
  historical aspects of, 94–95
  and historical theology, 99–100, 101–4, 130–31
  and indigenous leadership, 224–25
  and Latin America, 56
  and periodicals, 32–33, 45
  and the poor, 58, 205
  and prosperity, 65
  and the Russian Orthodox Church, 62
  and scholarship, 154–55, 221–22
  and social concern, 206–7
  as a social movement, 77, 82
  study of, 51–53
  and women, 35, 37
  and world religions, 76, 80
pluralism, 80, 166, 191
pneumatology. *See* Spirit
post-millennialism, 133
post-modernity, 111, 122–23, 128
poverty, 168–69, 182–83
prayer, 116–17
premillennialism, 30, 130, 223

religion, 73, 76, 82, 190–91
religious fundamentalism, 169, 190, 191
Romania, 59–60
Russia, 60–61

soteriology, 65
South Korea, 57–58
Soviet Union, 59, 60–61
speech-act theory, 114–15
Spirit baptism, 74–75, 78–79, 87, 88, 89, 90, 91–93, 95, 96–100,

Spirit baptism (cont.)
101–6, 111, 112, 118, 130,
131, 137, 225, 227, 229
Spirit, 53, 63–64, 65, 79, 92, 93,
97–98, 100–101, 106, 120,
121–22, 123–24, 130, 131,
146, 227
  and globalization, 20, 21
  and missions, 33, 37–38, 41, 42,
48, 64, 133, 134, 137, 160, 178
  and world religions, 76

technology, 202–4
Third Wave, 81, 88, 89, 92, 96–98,
104, 227, 231
tongues. *See glossolalia*
Trinity, 79

Ukraine, 60
urbanization, 165, 182–84

Wesleyan-Holiness movement, 101,
102, 130
worship, 63

www.ingramcontent.com/pod-product-compliance
Lightning Source LLC
Chambersburg PA
CBHW050850230426
43667CB00012B/2221